ID# : 192692

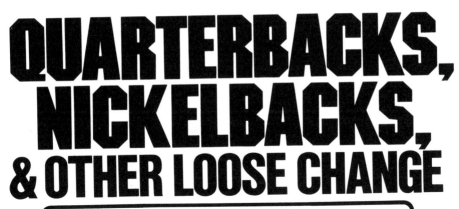

QUARTERBACKS, NICKELBACKS, & OTHER LOOSE CHANGE

A FAN'S GUIDE TO THE CHANGING GAME OF PRO FOOTBALL

KEVIN LAMB

Contemporary Books, Inc.
Chicago

Library of Congress Cataloging in Publication Data

Lamb, Kevin.
   Quarterbacks, nickelbacks, and other loose change.

   Includes index.
   1. Football.   I. Title
GV951.15.L36   1984   796.332'2   84-11414
ISBN 0-8092-5399-2

Published by Contemporary Books, Inc.
180 North Michigan Avenue, Chicago, Illinois 60601
Manufactured in the United States of America
Library of Congress Catalog Card Number: 84-11414
International Standard Book Number: 0-8092-5399-2

Published simultaneously in Canada by Beaverbooks, Ltd.
195 Allstate Parkway, Valleywood Business Park
Markham, Ontario L3R 4T8 Canada

CONTENTS

LOOSE CHANGE

Acknowledgments

It would have been hard to imagine writing this book without the valuable guidance and competition I've had through the years in covering pro football. My gratitude goes out, then, to Ray Sons, Marty Kaiser, and Ken Paxson of the Chicago *Sun-Times;* John Wiebusch of *Pro!* magazine; Peter Griffin of *Sport;* and Don Pierson and Terry Bannon of the other Chicago newspapers, all for helping me keep my wheels turning. Also to the NFL, its teams, *Pro Football Weekly, The Sporting News,* and countless other writers for the reams of reference material weighing down my file cabinets. And to Dan Pompei and Ted Plumb for their specific assistance in assembling all these words, and Shari Lesser, whose faith and enthusiasm made it all possible. Mostly, though, I'm grateful and appreciative beyond words to Carol, for her support, patience, and skillful copyediting, and to Ryan and Courtney for accepting all those nights when Daddy couldn't come out and play. This is their book, too.

Nothing to Fear
but the Forearm Shiver
... It doesn't take a nuclear physicist
to split a zone defense

Pro football looked complicated enough even before its trends and tactics started changing as fast as interest rates.

Twenty-two people in motion can make for a chaotic sight, especially when they are big and fast and their motion appears helter-skelter. The thought that their steps have been intricately planned, that they actually know where they're going, can be downright intimidating.

What they're doing is complicated, all right. It's just about as complicated as driving a car.

Think about it. The most complicated mental exercise in pro football, the one that makes a fan feel most like a mental dwarf, is the reading of defenses.

Look at the quarterback. In the heartbeat or two it takes for a quarterback to backpedal for a pass, he must determine whether the defense is rotating into a strong-side zone, or covering his receivers man-to-man with a trailing technique, or zoning the outside receivers with man coverage inside, or using any of dozens of more fancy-sounding pass-coverage schemes.

Now look at the driver. He's moving faster than football players possibly can move, among objects larger than the largest football players. And the driver, in that same heartbeat or two, must determine whether the cars ahead of him are stopping, changing lanes, slowing down, or turning into his path, to say nothing of what might be going on in his rear-view mirror.

1

The quarterback must react to his reading, must decide immediately which receiver in his team's pass pattern is the best target within the defense's coverage. He also must keep in mind that the receivers may have changed the locations of their targets, because they are reading the defense, too, and adjusting to it. But the driver makes similar split-second decisions—whether to turn, to slow down, to speed up, to brake, to swerve. And if the driver makes an incomplete pass, there is nobody in a striped shirt to pick up his car and put it back where he started. Both require countless split-second decisions.

Driving just seems simple because after doing it a while, the whole process of driving is almost instinctive. That is because the veteran driver knows what to look for, knows which information will expedite decision-making.

Driving would be confusing, too, if the driver tried to base decisions on the color of the fence on the corner, or the license number of the car ahead. But drivers learn to dismiss those things and pay attention instead to the stop sign on the corner and the brake lights on the car ahead. Just as Joe Theismann's experience at quarterback has taught him that the location of a particular opponent's left linebacker tells him nothing about that team's pass coverage, while the positioning of the free safety tells him all he needs to know. *He knows what to look for.*

"The game has changed so much. You've got a first-and-10 team, and then you've got a different second-and-long team, and then you've got a different third-and-short team. On offense and defense. You've got your best players in the game all the time.

"And the coaches are doing so many more things from so many formations. Years ago, it used to give you an edge if you worked in the off-season. So many of them just left it and went to their boats and their golf courses. Now you have to work all year just to keep up.

"I wish we had that kind of game back then. It would have been a hell of a lot more fun."—**Sid Gillman**, Hall of Famer whose 1955–84 pro football career includes 17 years as head coach, eight as assistant coach or consultant.

Pro football has gotten more complicated in recent years. A player has more options, and they're more intricate. He no longer simply follows one set of instructions, choreographed like a Busby Berkeley production number. He has to *think*. A defensive player's instructions change according to where his offensive opponent goes. And the offensive opponent adjusts his maneuverings according to how the defensive player adjusted his. And so on. All in the time it takes to dial a phone number.

But the player still has instructions. There may be more of them, based on more different contingencies, but they're all rehearsed. The quarterback and the receiver and the linebacker and the cornerback still react to what they see. They're still told what to look for.

All it takes to understand what they're doing, and how they do it and why, is learning what to look for.

X X X X X
O O O O

A fan can't learn as much as a quarterback knows. But there's no reason a fan can't learn enough to appreciate what's happening on the field and why. So, what more does a fan need to know?

The problem, as pro football is played in the eighties, is that there are different things to look for all the time. Teams are *doing* different things all the time. It is so easy now to lose track of substitutions, lose count of formations, lose hope of ever coming to grips with terms like sight adjustments, hot receivers, and combo zones.

What's passable as Monday-morning office banter in September might be passé by December. Could anything have been more embarrassing than finally deciding to tell the carpool gang the one-back offense is unbeatable on the Friday before the Raiders dismantled the Redskins and their single back in the single most lopsided Super Bowl ever? Maybe it was worse that time the blonde cheerleader suddenly turned deaf at your nervous request for her autograph on a high school yearbook. But at least back then, every NFL team used the same basic formations.

"When we defensed Lombardi's great teams, they'd line up in a formation and pretty much stay with it," says George Allen, who was Chicago's defensive coordinator before moving up to head coach with the Rams, the Redskins, the USFL's Chicago Blitz, and eventually the Arizona Wranglers. "They'd run a play and we had to stop them. That was it. Now everybody's got multiple sets, shifting, changing formations, sprinting out. They're doing all kinds of things."

They have created new positions. Greg Townsend, a rookie with the Los Angeles Raiders in 1983, was compared favorably with the San Francisco 49ers' Fred Dean. On the 49ers' roster, Dean was designated as a defensive end, but that was not his position. His position was pass rusher. Like Dean, Townsend usually lined up on the end of the defensive line, and he almost always stayed on the bench if the offense was expected to run. "He's small," teammate Howie Long said of Townsend. "He's not an every-play player. He's a player of the eighties, a situation player."

Eighties football is a different game, tailored more sleekly for the likes of Townsend and Dean. "Basketball on turf," is what Atlanta general manager Tom Braatz calls it. "The game is played farther downfield," says Jim Finks, Chicago's former general manager. Where the important action used to confine itself near the congested line of scrimmage, now it's often in open spaces, one-on-one. More and more, speed and guile are beating size and strength.

NFL coaches always have been fond of saying their game goes in cycles, one trend lasting only until the next trend beats it. But the cycles have usually evolved in the slow manner of geological cycles, except that a pro football era lasts 5 to 10 years instead of 50 million to 100 million. Not until the late seventies did pro football's cycles start spinning like a top. By 1983, offenses and defenses were countering each other with innovations so fast that it was hard to remain a trendsetter for any longer than it took to develop a reel of game film. Even game film was changing. It was becoming videotape.

"I think it's changing times in the NFL," Washington coach Joe Gibbs said before the 1982 season. "The things that used to be done for years—people are changing their minds about them. Whether it's offensive or defensive personnel or how to use them, everything's rapidly changing. Football has become much more progressive. There's been a change in people's thought processes."

Lineups change from play to play. Scores change from possession to possession. Champions change from year to year. So do stars. Formations change three or four times from huddle to snap. And don't forget rules. The rules changed before the 1978 season, making life easier for pass blockers and harder for pass defenders, and it was those two rule changes that started pro footfall's cycles spinning, to say nothing of the fans' heads.

One thing remains the same, though. Before the Raiders-Redskins Super Bowl in 1984, Raider linebacker Matt Millen shared this comforting observation:

"I was watching film the other day," Millen said, "and it was one guy carrying the football and 11 guys trying to knock him down."

That's all football is. Or, to put it another way: There are two teams, and each team tries to move the ball in the opposite direction. Period.

Each team also tries to control the ball, but only because controlling the ball makes it easier to move in the right direction. And each team's ultimate goal is to score. But that is a natural result of moving the ball in the right direction.

Every innovation, every new formation or play or defensive

scheme, is no more than an attempt to move the ball in the right direction.

So really, there is no reason anyone needs to be intimidated by pro football, not unless a player is running toward him with his forearm up. Yes, the game is complicated. More than it was five years ago. But they're not splitting atoms out there, just zones and gaps and uprights.

X X X X X
0 0 0 0

Nothing is entirely new in pro football. The late George Halas, the legendary coach and owner of the Chicago Bears, used to bristle at the suggestion he had introduced the T-formation to football with men in motion in the early forties. "We weren't doing anything then that we hadn't done in the twenties," Halas would say.

Likewise, two tight ends and one back. Theismann says his Redskins can operate from about 500 different formations with a single back. But no matter how many formations they use, all can be grouped into two basic formations. Either the second tight end is next to a tackle on the line, or he's not.

If he is, the formation is a natural offspring of the old straight T. The only difference is the halfbacks have moved outside to become wide receivers because the passing game is so much more important than when the T was in vogue.

If the second tight end is away from the tackle, you have a variation of the I-formation. The only difference is that the blocking back has moved from behind the quarterback to where he is more of a pass-catching threat. And going back farther, the I was a variation of the single-wing.

As the diagrams on pages 6–8 show, the shotgun or spread formation is even closer to the single-wing. The similarity escaped most rival coaches when San Francisco's Red Hickey made the shotgun his team's basic formation in 1961. The 49ers won four of their first five games by scores of 30–3, 49–0, 35–0, and 38–24. Then they played Halas' Bears. Halas not only noticed the similarity, he dusted off his old defenses for the single-wing. Halas moved middle linebacker Bill George up to the line, nose to nose with the vulnerable center, and the Bears won 31–0.

In doing so, Halas made the prevailing 4–3 defense of that time look much like the 3–4 most teams use today. But that was no innovation, either. Today's 3–4 is merely an offspring of the 5–2 defense popularized more than 30 years ago by Oklahoma in college ball and Philadelphia in the NFL. The only difference is the ends of yesteryear are standing up as linebackers so they can cover passes.

One of the basic formations with two tight ends and one back is a balanced line with the tight ends lined up next to the tackles. Notice how the wide receivers . . .

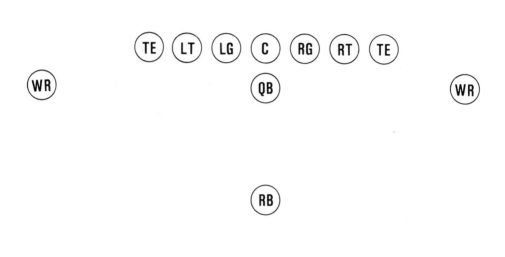

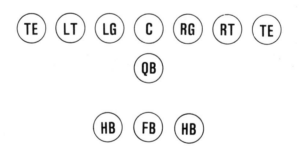

. . . are just very widely split halfbacks from the old full-house T-formation.

In the other basic, one-back formation, the second tight end (shaded) plays off the line of scrimmage. For running plays, he is a blocking back . . .

BB	blocking back	RG	right guard
C	center	RT	right tackle
FB	fullback	TB	tailback
HB	halfback	TE	tight end
LG	left guard	T2	second tight end
LT	left tackle	WB	wingback
QB	quarterback	WR	wide receiver
RB	running back		

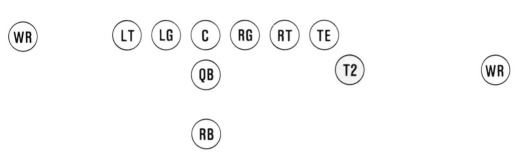

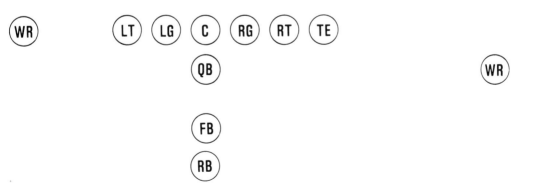

. . and the blocking back's new location is the only difference from the I-formation.

After going in motion, the blocking back often winds up right where the blocking back played in the old single-wing. The running back is where the single-wing tailback used to be, except he no longer takes the center's snap directly. The only other difference is that the single-wing's halfback and wingback have become wide receivers.

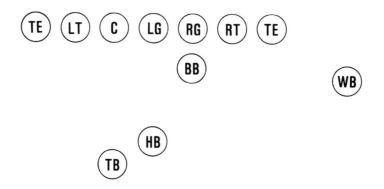

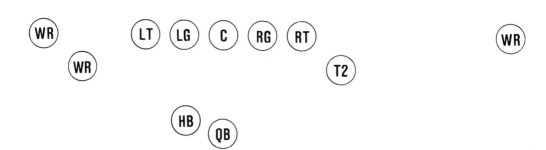

Even more similar to the single-wing is the modern shotgun formation, where the man in the tailback's old spot (the quarterback) still takes a long snap from center. Some shotgun sets even leave the halfback and blocking back (now a wingback) pretty much where the single-wing had them.

From the fifties through the seventies, the prevailing defensive alignment in the NFL was the 4–3 (with linebackers shaded).

C	center	RE	right end
LE	left end	RG	right guard
LG	left guard	RT	right tackle
LT	left tackle	SO	strong-side outside linebacker
MB	middle linebacker	TE	tight end
NT	nose tackle	WO	weak-side outside linebacker

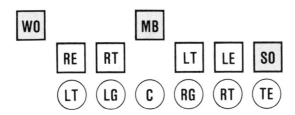

But to put pressure on the center, especially if he had to make a longer snap in the shotgun, the middle linebacker occasionally moved up to the line, or a defensive tackle slid over from the guard to the center, creating the 5–2 or "Oklahoma" defense made popular by Bud Wilkinson in the late forties.

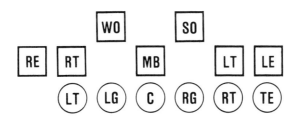

As passing became more common, teams turned more and more to the Oklahoma defense, with the ends standing up so they could cover receivers. So the 5–2 evolved into the prevailing defense of the eighties, the 3–4.

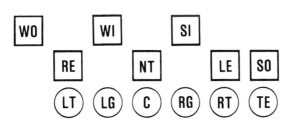

A pro football innovation, then, is actually selective imitation. A coach deals with a problem by borrowing something from the past and adapting it to his current needs. In the case of Washington, the first current team to play exclusively out of one-back formations (except on short-yardage downs), coach Joe Gibbs's need was to slow down the growing stampede of blitzing outside linebackers from 3–4 defenses, of which the New York Giants' Lawrence Taylor was the prototype.

Taylor ordinarily lines up on the weak side, the side opposite a single tight end. Few backs can block him. So Gibbs replaced his blocking back with a second tight end, who was bigger and more accustomed to blocking big men on the line. Gibbs not only had someone to block Lawrence Taylor and his imitators, he had another potential pass receiver on the line of scrimmage.

He did not have a copyright, though. The season after Washington won the Super Bowl in January 1983, more than half the league was using single-back formations. But none of the imitators had Washington's success, just as Green Bay's power sweep did not necessarily make champions of the teams that imitated it in the sixties.

"By the time other teams catch on to something new, a lot of times defenses have already adjusted to it," says Bud Grant, who was often at the forefront of trends as Minnesota's coach. "It's like Chuck Noll says: 'Don't get in on the bottom end of trends. Be the innovator.'"

Clever formations aren't the only reason teams win games. Good players help, too. That was why Washington, with its state-of-the-art offense, was unable to beat the Raiders in the latest Super Bowl. The Raiders' victory did not mean their formations and plays, largely unchanged in 20 years, were better than Washington's. It did not expose the one-back offense as a thing whose time had passed. It meant simply that the Raiders had better players, players so good that the Raiders did not need to bother with confusing their opponents, as most teams try to do.

Good players have always made good formations look better. The Bears ushered in the modern T-formation era in 1940, when they beat Washington 73–0 in the NFL championship game. That is widely known. Often overlooked is that the 1940 Bears had six players who are in the Hall of Fame.

X X X X X
0 0 0 0

The typical NFL game in 1983 had 154 plays, 22 of them kicking plays. A very small number of them were significant. They tilted the game's outcome toward one of the teams, the team that either moved the ball a long way in the right direction or suddenly took control of the ball. So another thing that has not changed about pro football is this:

There are very few big plays in any game. The team that makes the most or the biggest of them will win.

Or, as Lionel Antoine, a former offensive tackle for the Bears, put it: "You beat up on each other 60 or 70 times every week because you know one of those times is going to win or lose the game for you."

"And you never know when it's going to be," said Alan Page, who made more than his share of big plays at defensive tackle for Minnesota and Chicago. "There's no knob to turn. You just have to go out and do it."

In that 73–0 championship game, for example, Bill Osmanski ran 68 yards for a Chicago touchdown on the first play from scrimmage. And the rout, as they say, was on.

The Raiders' 38–9 Super Bowl victory against Washington turned on two of its least likely plays. One of them was the game's first punt, which Derrick Jensen blocked and recovered for a touchdown while millions of spectators looked elsewhere. The other one began 12 seconds before halftime, when the Redskins presumably planned to run out the clock but instead threw a touchdown pass to the wrong team—to the Raiders' Jack Squirek. The Raiders did not have the ball at the beginning of either play, but they moved it in the right direction and across the goal line both times.

Big plays look bigger, naturally, in games that are decided by less lopsided scores. That is when fans remember the forced fumble, the blocked kick, the diving catch, the broken tackle, the pass on the run. Page once enabled Minnesota to beat San Francisco 28–27 by taking the ball from a 49er who already had made a first down that would allow his team to run out the clock with a 27–21 lead. Coaches can direct players toward the proper spots for making that kind of play, but the players are the ones who must make the plays.

"You should be looking for a turnover on every play," Page said later. "A lot of people see chances time after time, but they don't go for the ball. If you're not born with that sense, I don't know if it's possible to develop it."

Breaking the Code

. . . The password is "playbook"

It does not alarm many NFL players and coaches that their game is so often seen as hopelessly complicated. That perception only makes them more admired, which generates interest, which breeds more admiration. And so on, until pretty soon, if we don't catch ourselves, we start wondering why the Nobel Prize committee has overlooked Tom Landry, Don Shula, and Terry Bradshaw all these years.

Fan confusion places a maze between the public and the player or coach who deserves blame for a bad play, or a bad game, or a bad season. Ask a coach what went wrong on that play when two open receivers bumped into each other, and he can always answer in terms of orange formations and slice techniques and scoop blocks, which discourages further conversation. Coaches and players do not like to encourage second-guessing, which is understandable since the public has a full week to evaluate decisions that had to be made in half a second.

But football people are hardly the only professionals who talk in tongues when asked to explain their trade. Lawyers, too, don't want people breaking their code of torts and motions and writs, lest their job might appear simple enough for anyone to do. Plumbers have their valves and pipe numbers. Printers have their fonts and veloxes. Insurance salesmen have their indemnities and actuarial extrapolations.

Whether a football coach or an insurance salesman speaks in

the code of his trade, his message is this: "Trust me. I know what these words mean. You don't need to."

In most cases, the public doesn't *care* to break the code. Actuarial extrapolations are boring. The only reason combo zones are fascinating instead of boring is that football is entertainment.

The line between fascination and boredom is a fine one. For someone who does not find football entertaining, combo zones are boring. On the other hand, if combo zones were shown to be fascinating on their own, that could make football more entertaining to the person who finds it only mildly entertaining. The more a fan understands the game, the more he appreciates it.

The more he appreciates it, the more likely he is to stick with it through strikes, drug scandals, and contract litigations. That's why football people would be wise to enlighten fans about the game's intricacies, rather than use the intricacies as an intimidating shield from criticism. When was the last time you heard someone in the stands start to boo and then interrupt himself and explain, "I can't boo that play. I don't understand it."

You'd think NFL teams with dwindling attendance, and especially USFL teams, would be falling over themselves to teach fans what to look for. In the long run, better that than a Hip Pad Day.

X X X X X
O O O O

Football owes its popularity to the two levels on which it can be watched. Practically everybody can grasp the simplest level. Each team tries to move the ball in the opposite direction.

Football's action is entirely linear, and it comes in short enough spurts that it does not require prolonged concentration. At its simplest, football is the simplest of popular sports.

For the fan, football's simplest level offers primitive enchantment without primitive realities. It is violence without blood or agonized shrieking. The fan is far enough from the action to miss the snapping of bones and ligaments and cartilage, the twisted expressions of young men using aching or bruised or stretched muscles, the grunting and growling and groaning. From the spectator's vantage point, the people involved in all that mayhem look no more vulnerable than bumper cars. It is easy to forget they're human beings enduring pain in order to play a game they enjoy.

Football's simplest level is so basic, the sport has the most fans in the United States. But fans are not necessarily devotees. A serious fan wants more. A serious fan wants to play the game along with the participants, to speak its language fluently and understand its strategic maneuverings.

A serious fan wants to appreciate football on its second level. That should be no problem. Football is the sport with the most strategic possibilities, if only because its games are a week apart and most of its action can be rehearsed.

But football people are generally loath to shine light on the whys and the wherefores of their decisions. They have paved over their fertile second level, short-sightedly patronizing and frustrating the same analytical devotees that baseball embraces.

Where a baseball fan doesn't see managers as any more sophisticated than himself, a football fan is presented with a lofty image of The Coach, suitable for saluting or worshipping but not for questioning. Where baseball encourages its fans to believe they know as much as any manager about when to hit-and-run or when to pull the pitcher, football encourages its fans to know nothing more than where to send checks for season tickets. Where baseball charms its fans, in the manner of a train ride through the countryside, football fascinates them at arm's length, like live photographs from the moon.

It doesn't have to be that way. In a high-tech society, football is a high-tech game. Football's second level of interest could be as compelling as its first if the sport were more generous about letting its fans inside the game and its thought processes. Coaches might find themselves second-guessed more often, but maybe safeties would be booed less often for following a pass-catcher into the end zone after a cornerback blew his coverage.

Maybe the Cleveland Browns would not have been ridiculed so much for the way they lost their playoff game to the Raiders in 1980. It was a cold-weather classic. The Raiders took a 14–12 lead in the fourth quarter, the Browns fought back with a 73-yard drive to the Raiders' 13-yard line, and the Raiders clinched the victory when Brian Sipe threw an interception to Mike Davis with 41 seconds remaining. Browns fans—and sportswriters, too—wondered what Sipe and coach Sam Rutigliano could have been thinking to throw a pass from field goal territory. They wondered because they had never been told of the risks in snapping, placing, and kicking a field goal when the players are too cold to feel their fingers and the field has no more give than a parking lot. They wondered because they did not understand Sipe's explanation that he was "a victim of my own programming."

Sipe did his job almost perfectly on that costly play. He read the defense properly. He passed toward the receiver most likely to be open. Davis simply made a great play. That happens. It's too bad Davis's play wasn't more appreciated because few people aside from the players and coaches knew what to look for.

X X X X X
0 0 0 0

Coaches like to create the illusion they have innumerable secrets. Raiders coach Tom Flores, during his week of preparation for the 1984 Super Bowl, jokingly announced, "We only had to shoot down two helicopters that came over our practice field." But their biggest secret of all is that they have no secrets.

"The one constant trend in pro football," says Ted Plumb, the Bears' receivers coach, "is that people will follow the next trend."

Everything is on film, and everyone sees everyone else's film. Pro football teams all fish the same celluloid pool of creative thought. So the repertoires of offensive and defensive plays do not vary greatly from one team to another.

What varies is the terminology. One team's "Sarah" might be another team's "Sally." You might know her as the strong safety. What do players always say after they've joined a new team, or after their team has changed coaches? They say, "I'll be fine once I get the terminology down."

Learning new terminology is not as hard as learning a foreign language. It's more along the lines of, "We called it 'soda' back in New York, and they say 'pop' here in Kansas City." The problem is that two or three words might represent the assignments for 11 players. And a player must translate those two or three words in considerably less time than he would have, say, for ordering eggs over easy in a Paris coffee house.

"The one constant trend in pro football," says Ted Plumb, the Bears' receivers coach, "is that people will follow the next trend."

Terminology should not be confused with lingo. To define our terms, here, let's think of lingo as a term that is constant throughout football. Blocking down, for example, means blocking toward the center on any team. Cut block means a block below the knees. Post means a pass route that angles toward the center of the field. Combo zone means a zone pass coverage that also includes man-to-man or a different type of zone on certain parts of the field. This is universal football lingo.

Terminology is peculiar to one team, although a team that hires a head coach from Dallas's staff is likely to use Dallas's terminology, too. Football terminology, like code words in any profession, is primarily a convenience. It enables team members to say "Mac" instead of "strong-side inside linebacker," or "Combo-5" instead of "that pass coverage where the cornerbacks play short sideline zones, the safeties play deep sideline zones, and the linebackers cover the inside receivers man-to-man."

Offensive terminology includes numbers for the running lanes, usually with the even-numbered holes on the left because George Halas once numbered his plays that way. The running backs have numbers, too, so play 22 might mean "halfback runs between left guard and left tackle." There was a time when Halas's numbering system was less common, so a newly acquired player's instincts often took him wrongly to the right for an even-numbered play. That can be dangerous if the new player is a guard and his assignment is to pull on an end run, leading the ball carrier around the corner. Guards who pull toward opposite sidelines can have a nasty collision somewhere behind the center.

Some teams also number their basic pass routes, usually along the lines of the diagram on page 17. Receivers generally are assigned letters: X for the split end, Y for the tight end, and Z for the flanker, who is the wide receiver on the tight end's side. So play 189 might have the split end running a short route to the sideline (1), the tight end a deep post (8), and the flanker deep along his sideline (9). (Three pass routes together, plus any routes the backs run, are called the *pass pattern*. And one more thing: *routes* are called "routs." Football people never pronounce it like "roots.")

Learning all this is not a chore for someone who has played a lot of football. It is not unusual for a player to speak fluent terminology and speed-read defenses even if he cannot read a telephone book without moving his lips.

X X X X X
O O O O

The playbook is the player's dictionary. It has other functions, but mainly, it defines the team's terminology.

One of pro football's most popular mystiques concerns the danger of letting one's playbook fall into the wrong hands. Suppose it did. Suppose the Oilers' coaches found a Bengals' offensive playbook. What could they learn?

They could learn how the Bengals name their plays differently from the Oilers. They already know the Bengals' plays and formations and blocking schemes, though. They've seen them on film. They might find some gimmick plays, like halfback passes and double reverses, that they hadn't seen on film. But gimmick plays are fairly standard, too. They can be surprising, but it would be a waste of the Oilers' practice time to work on plays the Bengals are unlikely to use. Any playbook will have plenty of seldom-used plays.

The Oilers also would learn the Bengals' fine schedule—how much it costs a player to be late for a meeting or a practice or a team bus. That sure would come in handy on third-and-two.

Many pro teams number their basic pass routes by climbing up the branches of an oddly shaped tree, which results from diagramming all the basic routes at once. This diagram is for the wide receiver nearest the right sideline.

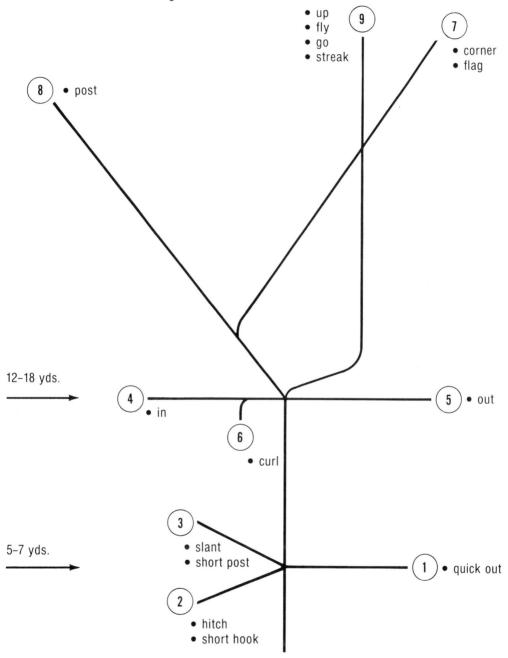

Variations can be run off these routes. For example, a receiver could turn a fly into a comeback by pulling up short and coming back toward the quarterback, either inside or out. Receivers also run combination routes, such as out and up or hitch and go. The depths for the short and intermediate routes vary from team to team but are precise for any specific route on a particular team.

Besides being a dictionary, a playbook is an employee's manual. It gives instructions for insurance claims, team policy regarding press and fan relations, how to use exercise equipment, rules for dress or curfew, how to line up in a huddle, where to sit on the bench. When Carl Eller, a defensive end with part-time military experience, was with the Vikings, he presided over the National Anthem Drill each year before the first exhibition game.

There are techniques that vary from team to team. Where one team might zone-block a particular running play by assigning blockers to certain areas, another might cross-block it, sending blockers in an X pattern at the point of attack. Or one team might prefer having its cornerbacks bump the receiver at the line of scrimmage while another wants them to play off the line. Those things, too, become apparent on film.

The most useful intelligence a team could learn about its opponent is the code words it uses for audibles, when it changes plays at the line of scrimmage. But those, like baseball signs, change periodically and are more likely to be in the weekly abridgment of the playbook, the game plan.

A substantial fine for losing a playbook has more to do with carelessness than espionage. If a player can't keep track of his playbook, he might also lose track of the snap count.

Some playbooks even are printed without the plays diagrammed. Coaches figure the players learn more by diagramming plays for themselves. So the playbook simply gives the play's terminology, the formations it can be run from, the down-and-distance situations when it's most likely to be used, and its frequency and success rate the previous season.

Any pretense of a playbook's sophistication is lost with its binding. It usually comes in a spiral notebook, although some players purchase expensive-looking attache cases for carrying them. That way, they look more like businessmen than students.

One of pro football's oldest playbook clichés is even slipping away. It used to be that a player always knew he was about to be cut when a team official told him, "Coach wants to see you. And bring your playbook." Now there are teams that don't bother with the playbook until they collect the other equipment.

Plays, like formations, are no more than starting points. They can help a team win, but only to the extent that its players can run, catch, block, and tackle. As the firing-squad captain said after the condemned man was still standing, "We just didn't execute."

Two Little Rules
... And defenses came tumbling down

The NFL always has tinkered with its rulebook the way a cook experiments with recipes. The owners have added a pinch here and a dash there often enough to make their rulebook the largest in sports, 127 pages.

Most games do not have such latitude. What if Parker Brothers kept changing the number of utilities and the value of Marvin Gardens every time it issued a Monopoly game? Imagine the uproar if the powers that be in chess suddenly changed their minds about how a bishop is allowed to move. But football is different from most games in two ways. First, the game is essentially a form of controlled mayhem, so there is always room for debate over how best to control the activities of 22 people trying to knock each other down. Second, football is a purely linear game, with each team trying to move the ball toward a goal that extends the width of the field.

Even though the team without the ball tries just as hard to move it as the team with the ball, the preferred condition is for the team with the ball—the offense—to make most of the headway. After the 1977 season, the NFL's team owners decided the ball was moving entirely too much in favor of teams *that did not have the ball.*

That is usually the case when NFL rules are changed significantly. It was true in 1932, when the Chicago Bears won the first

19

NFL championship game 9–0 after assembling a 7–1–6 record that included three scoreless ties, five shutout victories, and a 2–0 defeat. So the league added hash marks in 1933 to let offenses spread out in both directions. That didn't help much. Four 1933 games had more than 28 punts. So the NFL allowed the forward pass from anywhere behind the line of scrimmage (instead of at least five yards behind the line). That did the trick.

Defenses did not have as tight a stranglehold on the game in 1977, but the stakes were higher than they had been 45 years earlier. Television was a partner. There were millions of teledollars to be lost if too many fans decided watching leaves flutter to the ground was more entertaining than watching punts flutter to the ground.

What they saw in 1977 NFL games was:

★ In more than one-third of the games, neither team scored more than 17 points.

★ Twenty-four games, nearly one in every eight, were shutouts.

★ Only 45 winners, less than one in four, scored as many as 30 points.

★ The Atlanta Falcons allowed just 129 points, a record for a 14-game season.

★ The leading pass receiver in the NFC, Minnesota's Ahmad Rashad, caught just 51 balls.

★ League rushing yardage actually exceeded league passing yardage.

In a fairly typical game, Chicago's Walter Payton set an NFL record with 275 yards rushing against Minnesota. The final score, despite all those yards, was 10–7, Bears. The two touchdowns were scored on a blocked punt and a 23-yard drive set up by a fumble on a punt return.

This, then, was the way to win an NFL game in 1977:

1. When you have the ball, the most important thing is keeping it long enough to punt it.

2. Move the ball forward by punting it. This is your most reliable offensive play.

3. Have your defense continue moving the ball forward when the other poor saps have to use their offense.

4. Wait until either your defense, punting unit, or punt return unit makes a big play. That will either move the ball across your opponent's goal line or move it so close to the goal line that even your offense can move it across.

X X X X X
O O O O

Offenses were simply helpless. In 1976, the Pittsburgh Steelers shut out five of their last eight opponents and held two of the other three to three points. And, leaguewide, 1977 was worse.

When the team owners assembled in early 1978 to revive their suntans, empty their cocktail glasses, and plot the course of their league, they perceived NFL defenses as being intent on devouring their game. (Owners tend not to be men of understatement.) Several factors were responsible.

The field had become narrower. Defensive players had become so big and so fast that they could cover the 160 feet from sideline to sideline with frightening ease. And they rarely had to cover the full 160 feet because the wide side of the field literally had shrunk by more than 10 percent in 1972.

That was when the hash marks were lined up with the goal-post uprights. They became 70 feet, 9 inches, from the sideline instead of 60 feet, and since most plays start from a hash mark, the wide side of the field was now 89 feet, 3 inches, instead of 100 feet. The sideline was quick to intrude on any running play around the end.

More significantly, a defense was now able to disguise its pass coverage until after the ball was snapped. With the previous hash marks, the defense had to commit itself toward the 100-foot side of the field when it lined up. A quarterback could read the defense before he even had the ball.

"Obviously, professional football has to be interesting. We felt that with the athletes getting bigger and stronger, with better techniques, the way the rules were written there was a definite decline in teams' ability to move the ball. There was not enough premium on moving the ball. To make the game more entertaining, we made some changes to create more of an incentive to move the ball."—**Tex Schramm**, Dallas general manager and chairman of the NFL's Competition Committee.

"Probably the biggest breakthrough offensively is the rules."—**Bill Walsh**, San Francisco coach, in 1980.

"The great athletes were winding up on defense," Joe Gibbs said of the early and middle seventies. "Especially on the line." Those great defensive linemen were winding up on top of quarterbacks. In 1976 and 1977, for every 10 passes that were thrown, there was one quarterback sack.

The effect snowballed. Every coach was eager to get one of those pass-rushing defensive linemen for his own team. So there were more sacks. So there were fewer passes attempted. So there were lower scores. So it became even more important for a coach to rely on his defense to win games, to put his best players there.

The man who gave the snowball a shove, probably the most significant player in the decade before 1978, was Alan Page, the Minnesota defensive tackle who remains the only defensive player ever to win a league MVP award. Before Page, the typical NFL defensive tackle was a big galoot. His job was to overpower his blocker and plow straight ahead. But Page was more quick than strong. He didn't even wear pads on his arms. "I frankly never planned on using my arms to hit anybody," he said.

Page used his legs. He pulled down ball carriers on either sideline, and he sprung into the passing pocket before his blocker was out of his stance. Pretty soon, defenses all over the league had quick defensive tackles. They were closer to the quarterback than defensive ends, and they were beating offensive guards who had tailored their blocking styles more for arm wrestling than hide-and-seek.

The game's recent strategic innovations were on defense. They were the 3–4 configuration with three linemen and four linebackers, and the nickel defense with five defensive backs in passing situations. Basic offense had changed little since the use of two wide receivers and one tight end became commonplace in the early sixties.

Offensive coaches are less inclined toward risks by nature. They have the ball; why risk losing it? And the offense knows where a particular play is going. It is the defense that has to guess, to take chances.

Besides, the offense is generally directed by the head coach. He has more to lose than his assistant coach directing the defense. His primary goal often is to delay his inevitable firing. So too many offensive coaches labor under the misconception that it is safer to fail with standard procedures than to try something off the wall. If a coach's off-the-wall brainstorm doesn't work, he can't explain it by saying, "But everybody's doing it."

Some offensive trends were budding in 1977. The use of backs as frequent pass receivers. The shotgun formation, with the quarterback already in position to pass the ball when he took the snap. Multiple formations and multiple men in motion. Three wide receivers at a time. But only a few teams were doing many of those things, most obviously Dallas, Minnesota, Baltimore, and St. Louis. When the owners met in 1978, they knew these trends needed a shove from the rulebook.

X X X X X
0 0 0 0

Rule changes are in the bailiwick of the NFL's Competition Committee, dominated then and now by Dallas general manager Tex Schramm, Cincinnati general manager Paul Brown, and

Miami coach Don Shula. They are the NFL's chefs, the men who decide how much paprika is necessary for spicing up the game. In 1978, the Competition Committee's mandate was to propose rules that would make passing more attractive. Scores weren't going to climb until coaches stopped thinking of the pass as a risky adventure.

A successful pass requires delicate timing. The timing varies with the type of pass, but ordinarily, a quarterback can't throw in less than two seconds. The receiver needs at least that long to run his route. And if the quarterback takes more than about 3½ seconds to throw the ball, he probably isn't going to throw it. He probably is going to be on the ground with a defensive player on top of him. Considering the penchant football people have for military terms, it is amazing that the 1½-second window of time when a quarterbck can throw the ball has not been called the defense's window of vulnerability. In 1977, that window was barely a peephole. Pass rushers had pulled down maximum time. On the minimum end, bump-and-run defenses kept receivers from running their routes at all, let alone in two seconds.

The vogue pass defense at the time was the double zone, also called the "Pittsburgh zone" because the Steelers played it so well. As the diagram on page 24 shows, the double zone had the safeties playing the deep zones and the cornerbacks playing the widest of the five short zones. So sideline pass routes, the most effective ones for a wide receiver, were double zoned by the corners and the safeties.

In a classic double zone, each corner would roll up, positioning himself nearly nose-to-nose with his wide receiver. The corner would start beating up on the wide receiver as soon as the play began. Sometimes he knocked the receiver off his feet. Often, he kept the receiver from going anywhere close to where the quarterback would look for him. There were times when the cornerback would fall down or lose his balance, and the wide receiver would escape him cleanly, but so what? The corner knew there was a safety behind him, ready to pick up the receiver.

"I personally didn't think that was defense," says Bart Starr, the former quarterback who coached Green Bay from 1975 through 1983. "It's one thing to be able to pressure the receiver, to bump and run with him and keep buffeting him while you're staying with him. That's a marvelous, unique skill. But it's another thing to be able to bump and nudge and intimidate him without any fear of being beaten deep. The cornerbacks were bludgeoning receivers with complete immunity. There was no risk to it."

"We all tried to do it," Viking coach Bud Grant says of the double zone. "The Steelers did it best. That's why Paul Brown spearheaded the rule change. He was in their division."

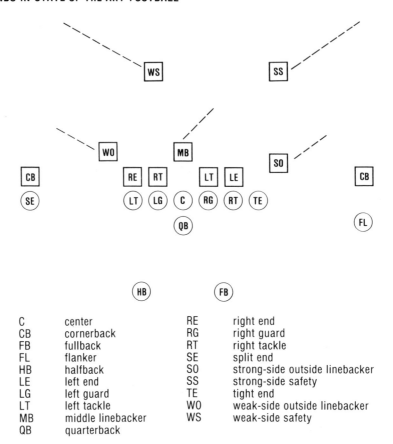

C	center	RE	right end
CB	cornerback	RG	right guard
FB	fullback	RT	right tackle
FL	flanker	SE	split end
HB	halfback	SO	strong-side outside linebacker
LE	left end	SS	strong-side safety
LG	left guard	TE	tight end
LT	left tackle	WO	weak-side outside linebacker
MB	middle linebacker	WS	weak-side safety
QB	quarterback		

In the double zone defense, popularized as the "Pittsburgh zone" in the mid-seventies, the pass coverage has five short zones and two deep zones. The cornerbacks and safeties double-zone each sideline, with the linebackers taking the short middle zones. The cornerbacks roll up to the line of scrimmage, bump the wide receivers after the snap, and, before the rules limited contact, could keep bumping the receivers until they got away, when the safeties picked them up. The weakness in this coverage was its lack of protection in the deep middle of the field, making it especially vulnerable to a team with a fast tight end, which can send three receivers deep.

The Competition Committee addressed itself to prying open that passing window. Whatever it did, the rule change had to appear subtle. Allowing the offense 12 players was out. So was requiring defensive backs to wear handcuffs.

The rules the committee proposed were almost as effective. The owners agreed to both of them:

1. Pass blockers were allowed, for the first time, to extend their arms and open their hands. That was to slow down the pass rush and open that window for 3½ seconds, if not more.

2. Pass defenders were prohibited from bumping receivers farther than five yards downfield. (They could maintain contact beyond five yards if they already had established it, but try doing that sometime. Get somebody to run, trying to avoid you,

	1977	1981		1977	1981	1983
Winner scored 17 or less	69 games (35.2%)	35 games (15.6%)	**Winner scored 30 or more**	45 games (23.0%)	81 games (36.2%)	88 games (39.3%)
Winner scored 14 or less	39 games (19.9%)	15 games (6.7%)	**Loser scored 30 or more**	4 games (2.0%)	10 games (4.5%)	15 games (6.7%)
Loser scored 7 or less	74 games (37.8%)	39 games (17.4%)				
Shutouts	24 games (12.2%)	9 games (4.0%)				

*Teams played 14 games in 1977, 16 in other years.

Just four years after the NFL encouraged passing with its pre-1978 rule changes, there were considerably fewer low-scoring games and more high-scoring games, a trend which continued through 1983.

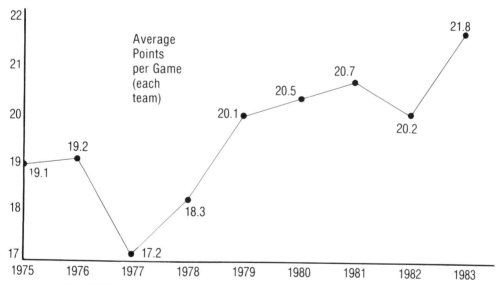

Leaguewide, the NFL's average score per game steadily increased after falling to its lowest level in 1977. The only exception was 1982, when offensive production tailed off because of the eight-week strike.

and try to maintain unbroken contact with him for more than two steps.) That rule, and the illegal chuck penalties it sanctioned, held the bottom of the window down at 2.0 seconds, a figure coaches have since contrived to bring down even more.

Just two years later, the results were dramatic. Scoring was up 16.8 percent, averaging 20 points a game for each team. Touchdowns were up 18.3 percent, touchdown passes 21.4 percent.

After the 1978 rule change, touchdowns rose sharply . . .

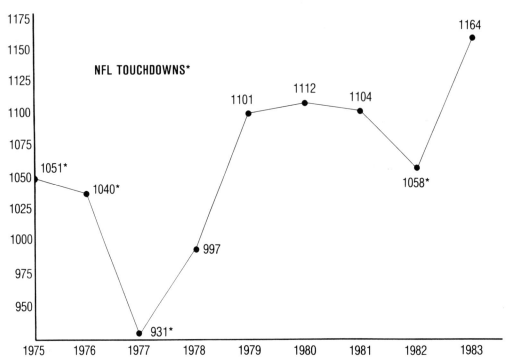

*Actual figures for 1975 (920), 1976 (910), 1977 (815), and 1982 (595) are adjusted to 16-game seasons. Each team played only 14 games in 1975, 1976, and 1977; 9 in 1982.

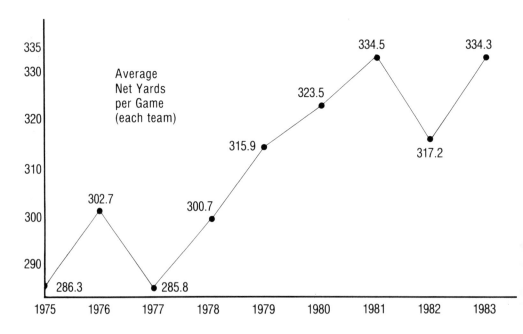

Teams also gained more yards . . .

. . . and the increase in touchdown passes was even more dramatic.

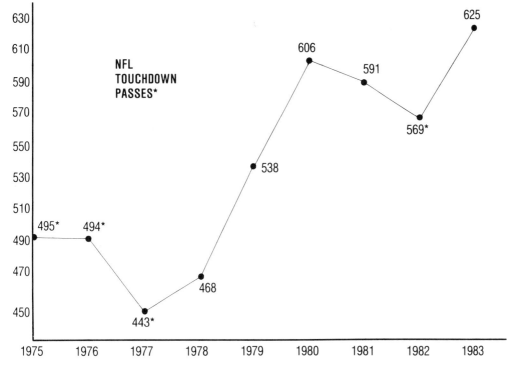

NFL TOUCHDOWN PASSES*

*Actual figures for 1975 (433), 1976 (432), 1977 (388), and 1982 (320) are adjusted to 16-game seasons. Each team played only 14 games in 1975, 1976, and 1977; 9 in 1982.

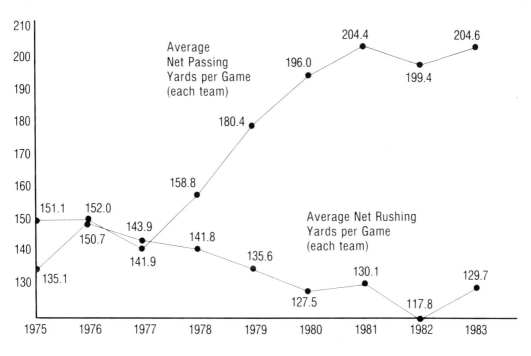

Average Net Passing Yards per Game (each team)

Average Net Rushing Yards per Game (each team)

. . . and that increase was almost entirely the result of improved passing yardage.

Total yardage gained modestly, 10.6 percent, but passing yardage was up 27.1 percent to 180 yards a game. And quarterbacks threw for 300 yards 44 times in 1979, compared to just five in 1977.

"We've got it where we want it," Schramm said after the 1979 season. "Now it's just a matter of monitoring it."

Scoring, yardage, and passing continued to increase, as the charts on pages 25–27 show. Seventeen points was enough to win just half as often in 1981 as it was in 1977. And a team with 30 points was three times more likely to lose in 1983 as it was in 1977. In fact, three teams lost 1983 games when they scored more than 40 points.

"Forty-eight to 47!" St. Louis defensive end Al Baker said after Green Bay beat Washington by that score to set a record for points in a Monday night game. "There didn't used to be enough *time* to score that many points."

Ah, but when teams can pass, there is time for anything. The Steelers forgot that in their 1983 playoff game against the Los Angeles Raiders. When the Raiders got the ball on their own 30 with 1:02 left in the first half, the Steelers went into one of those quaint old prevent defenses with eight men deep, the way everyone used to play whenever there wasn't time for the offense to score before halftime. That simply isn't done anymore, as the Raiders demonstrated by scoring a field goal.

You give a quarterback time to throw, and you give his team time to score. The rulemakers knew that. That was why they took the hands away from defensive backs and gave them to offensive linemen.

They Did All That?

... The rule changes opened coaches' minds and opened up the game

Tom Landry is a master of ironic understatement, which comes as a surprise to people who see the Dallas coach only on a sideline, where he shows all the emotion of a parking meter. As a hypothetical example, if someone preparing to go on a picnic announced he had packed everything but the food, Landry might observe, in a half-chuckling voice, "That's a pretty important thing for a picnic." That was the tone Landry used when he said of the illegal-chuck rule:

"This is a pretty important rule for the passing game."

"Now we're able to have access to the field," San Francisco coach Bill Walsh said not long after the rule change. "You can get receivers across the field, to the far side of the field, and you can *count* on doing that. Where at one time, they'd just never get there."

The passing game always will have moving targets, which makes it difficult enough. There always will be obstacles between the passer and his target. Before the illegal-chuck rule, the targets were not only moving and shielded, but they intermittently disappeared. "The quarterback would be getting ready to throw the ball," said Brian Sipe, who quarterbacked at Cleveland for 10 years before moving to New Jersey in the USFL, "and the receiver would be just starting his route, just getting past the cornerback."

Besides making the quarterback's targets more reliable, the

illegal-chuck rule limited the way defenses could shield them. As Sipe explained:

"There are a variety of coverages, but they all fall into three categories: two deep zones, three deep zones, and man-to-man.

"By allowing the receivers more freedom at the line of scrimmage, they were able to attack the deep zones more effectively. Teams that had tried to cover the deep zones with only two players had relied heavily on contact at the line of scrimmage. They kept you from getting three receivers deep. But if you can get three receivers deep and they're trying to cover them with two deep zones, there are going to be a lot of points scored."

So the double zone, in its pure form, became a dinosaur. Teams continued playing variations of it, mixing in man-to-man coverage. And as we'll see later, their variations in the eighties complicated the quarterback's picture more than before. But in the first two or three years after the rule change, the two-deep variations behaved more like man-to-man or three-deep. Which had two effects.

First, said Sipe, "Every defense has a weakness. If the quarterback can anticipate the defense's coverage, he can call plays that will take advantage of its weakness. And if a defense is using only two basic coverages instead of three, it's that much easier to anticipate."

Besides that, two deep zones and five short zones were cluttering up the area that would otherwise be the most fertile for completions. "Once you drive them out of their short zones," Sipe said, "you see a higher completion percentage. It's easier to sustain drives by passing."

Nice as it was for the receivers to be staying upright, that would have been little help if quarterbacks hadn't also been given a better chance to stay on their feet. The illegal-chuck rule was merely a partner of the pass-blocking rule, which made all pass blockers bigger.

"The first thing a pass blocker does is stick his arms out," Chicago defensive coordinator Buddy Ryan says. "A big guy who's a yard wide, that makes him three yards wide."

It slowed the pass rush. That not only made the quarterback less apt to be sacked, it made him less apt to be blinded or hurried by a pass rusher's nearby arm, which made him less apt to throw an interception or an incompletion.

Once a blocker was allowed to open his hands legally, it was a simple matter for him to close them again and hold a pass rusher. That was illegal, but pass blockers had been holding pass rushers for as long as footballs have had laces. Now their temptation was greater than ever.

A holding penalty would move the ball back 10 yards without a loss of down. An average sack, in 1977, would move it back more than eight yards. Why not hold? First-and-20 is better than second-and-18, and besides, holding calls do not injure quarterbacks.

To many defensive coaches, the blocking rule did not mean their pass rush would be limited. It meant they would have to send more people after the quarterback. They would have to blitz a linebacker or a defensive back or a few of each. (Some coaches call it dogging when they send a linebacker, as in the old term, red dogging. But the younger ones, and most players, call it blitzing any time more than four people rush the passer.)

The principle of an all-out blitz is simple. Three defenders stay back to cover three receivers. The quarterback can't block, so the offense has seven blockers. The defense has eight men rushing. Eight minus seven is the one pass rusher who will sack the quarterback unless he unloads the ball in a hurry.

"They force you to hit something big," Gibbs says of the blitzers, "or you may not get a thing." Which was just what the rulemakers had in mind.

X X X X X
O O O O

Eventually, offensive coaches probably would have found a way to get their game off the ground all by themselves. Landry, for one, would have preferred that. He likes to see coaches figure out their own innovations for beating defenses. Which they did, soon enough. It just took the rule changes to point them in the right direction.

As much as the new rules did to open up the field, they did even more to open up coaches' minds.

"I don't think offenses were having trouble," Seattle wide receiver Steve Largent said of the era that ended in 1977. "They were just set in their ways. There used to be a sort of mindset as to what was proper on offense. Now they're more flexible."

Offensive coaches knew they had been handed a gift in 1978. They just weren't quite sure how to use it. They had to break some habits, like factoring in time for the receiver to fall down twice in running a pass route. Many of them had to refamiliarize themselves with the passing game itself, having pickled and canned and shelved it for use only on those rainy days when they trailed 21–3 at the half. So it took two or three years for the rules to have their full impact.

The rules' immediate impact was that of a memo from the boss. (Dear coach: We have gone to great trouble to make it easier for you to make more liberal use of the forward pass. Please humor an old geezer who signs your paychecks and see that our efforts were not wasted.) Then the rules themselves kicked in and, lo and behold, it *was* easier to pass.

Those coaches who remained skittish at that point were dragged along by the stampede. With everyone else passing, it was dangerous for anyone to buck the trend. Innovation wasn't so risky anymore. The risk was in playing conservatively. "You better not try unless you have a super defense," Sipe says. And who has one of those? Super defenses have been legislated into yellowing scrapbooks and dusty trophy cases, right there with leather helmets.

So the more teams passed, the more they *had* to pass to keep up with each other. This suited most of them just fine because the more they passed, the more they *wanted* to pass.

A good passing game thrives on repeated practice more than a good running game, if only because its timing is more intricate. That was one of the reasons teams had shied away from the pass in the first place. It took too long to get it right. As San Diego quarterback Dan Fouts said, "Most coaches like to be more concise in practice, and our practices take 2½ hours."

The Chargers still would have practiced for 2½ hours and they still would have featured the pass even if the rules hadn't changed. Coach Don Coryell, with Joe Gibbs as his offensive coordinator, had done that in St. Louis, and they continued doing it in San Diego. The Chargers already knew what other teams found out after the rules encouraged them to take that extra time with the passing game. The more they passed, the better they got at passing.

So teams committed themselves to improving their passing games. It showed in the players' workdays, which expanded from 10:30–3:30 to 9–5 and longer. It showed in teams' personnel decisions. One of the significant early shots fired in the passing revolution was the New York Jets' 1980 trade of two first-round draft choices for the second pick in the draft, and their selection of Johnny (Lam) Jones, a wide receiver with world-class speed. The Jets already had Wesley Walker. At that time, two burners seemed excessive. But when jaws dropped and eyebrows leaped at the Jets' selection, it wasn't just because they had spent the second pick in the whole draft on something they already had. It was also because the same question occurred to 27 coaches at the same time:

"How are we going to cover both of them?"

This was the irony about wide receivers: the rules made their position easier, and the rules also made their position more important. The same happened with quarterbacks, not that quarterbacks ever had been merely spear carriers. Now they were more than stars, though. They were investments. Teams gave quarterbacks their own assistant coaches who did little else but share all those fascinating new paths toward the end zone that were being discovered in the film room.

In fact, quarterbacks were so highly regarded that the owners passed one more rule in 1979 that severely limited the ways in which a quarterback could be cuffed around. He didn't even have to hit the ground to be sacked.

"That was important," Walsh says. "Now more teams will have their quarterbacks staying healthy throughout the season rather than losing one in the third or fifth week."

This, then, was the irony about the quarterback: it was easier to find one, by previous standards (27 different quarterbacks had 300-yard passing games in 1983), but harder to replace one. The best ones were better than ever. Fouts led the league in passing from 1979 through 1982 and actually *averaged* 300 yards a game in 1981.

The more coaches explored the passing game, the more quarterbacks had to learn about it. New strategies abounded. Landry had the evolutionary cycle he wanted, with offenses figuring out how to flatten the latest defensive wrinkle and defenses figuring out how to beat the new offensive adjustment, and offenses figuring out how to beat that and so on. Like everything else in pro football, though, the cycle was moving faster. Where it had once proceeded deliberately, like a pendulum, it now was a Ping-Pong game.

Getting a Toehold on Midair

*. . . How the NFL teams took
the white knuckles out of the passing game*

When the San Francisco 49ers leapfrogged more than half the NFL to reach the Super Bowl after the 1981 season, one of their reserve wide receivers was Mike Shumann. He had been cut by Tampa Bay, a fifth-place team the previous year. "They called him a sandlot player," said Dwight Clark, the 49ers' all-pro wide receiver. Shumann's transgression was bending his pass routes toward open areas instead of following them like a figure skater's compulsory figures. That, said Clark, did not go over well in Tampa.

It was a hit in San Francisco. Bill Walsh, the 49ers coach, *required* that kind of resourcefulness from his receivers. "It's different from any offense in the league," Shumann said. "You don't just run your route right into a defender. You go to an area and you get open."

"It seems to be catching on," Clark said after that 1981 season. By 1983, most teams had their receivers adjusting their pass routes to defenses.

The 49ers weren't the only team running option pass routes in 1981. Even Vince Lombardi's great Packer teams had done it occasionally. The teams that didn't need new rules to remind them of the passing game's merit had done it for years. And it has been common all along for a team to adjust automatically to quicker pass routes if it sees a blitz.

But before the late seventies most pass patterns sent each receiver on a strict route. "With only three basic coverages," says Brian Sipe, "you just designed your plays so somebody in the pass pattern would take advantage of at least one of those three coverages. But now they have such a variety of coverages."

Now it's not so easy to flood a zone with two receivers, for example, because the defense will adjust and send an extra player into the zone, too. Now a team risks wasting a play if its receivers all run mindlessly into covered areas. So a receiver adjusts his route to the adjustments he sees in the defense. That's why it's called a sight adjustment.

Sight adjustments aren't just for avoiding wasted plays. Some of them are more aggressive. They enable an offense to look for a big play on every passing down.

Late in San Diego's memorable 1981 playoff game at Miami, Charger wide receiver Charlie Joiner's assignment was to run a short curl route, turning back toward the quarterback. But if the safeties spread into two deep zones, emptying the deep middle of the field, Joiner was to go there. He saw the safeties spreading even before the snap. He changed his route and caught the long pass that set up San Diego's winning field goal. "If I hadn't seen that," he said, "I would have been curling for 10 yards instead of going for a 40-some-yard gain."

These adjustments still don't bring back playground football. A receiver can't be running hither and yon when the quarterback has a second-and-a-half to find him and get him the ball. "That doesn't leave much time for complications," says Ted Marchibroda, the former Baltimore coach who became Philadelphia offensive coordinator in 1984. "You have to keep it simple." For some teams, that means no more than one receiver adjusting on any play. For all teams, it means the adjustment is just as mandatory as the old unadjustable routes.

The quarterback and the receiver look at the same defensive player, their *key*. If that player does what the quarterback and receiver are looking for, they make the same adjustment. Any more intricate than that, and games would be full of sideline passes to receivers slanting across the middle.

Clark says one of his most common adjustments is to cancel his assigned curl route if the defender is shading him to the inside. "That's when I slide across to the sideline," he says. Which he did on a third-and-three play from the Cowboys' 6-yard line in the 49ers' 1981 NFC Championship game against Dallas. The primary receiver was covered, and Clark was not running the pass route prescribed in the huddle, but Joe Montana knew where to look for him. The result was what San Franciscans call, simply, "The

Catch." It was the winning touchdown, the play that put the 49ers in the Super Bowl.

X X X X X
0 0 0 0

Regular sight adjustments are just one of many results of the increased scrutiny coaches have given their passing games. More obvious is the use of more pass-receiving specialists, either backs or wide receivers, and of formations better designed for springing them downfield. And more short passes, no riskier than a pitchout, to roll an open field out in front of good open-field runners. And more passes on first down. And more deceptive plays, like the halfback's shovel pass back to the quarterback after a halfback takes a handoff and heads toward the line.

Before the 1978 rule changes, passing was considered not only dangerous, but somehow cheap. Pro football always has been a bastion of the work ethic, and it just didn't seem right to be able to move the ball 60 yards on one play without carrying it or breaking tackles or blocking people downfield. It was like running laps around the field by cutting across the 50-yard line. There had to be a catch.

There was, of course. The interception, the sack, the incomplete pass, the holding penalty. All those were catches. But the pass-blocking and illegal-chuck rules lessened those risks. And the coach who had only dabbled in the passing game before the rule changes learned one important thing: he could watch his quarterbacks grip the ball and cock their arms without his knuckles turning white.

Hey, the darn thing worked. It wasn't so reckless after all.

"I think a lot of coaches were leery of passing because their experience from when they were playing was the running game," says Chicago safety Gary Fencik. That's where they felt comfortable. More than that, when they allowed their attention to be diverted toward the passing game, they treated it the same way as the running game. With more power than finesse—as in the pass patterns of Tampa Bay (and many other teams) that stubbornly took receivers into the defensive players covering them.

In older times—say, a decade ago—real football teams established the run. If they couldn't do that, they didn't deserve to win. They tried, of course, but they knew this: after establishing that they *couldn't* run, putting the ball in the air was tantamount to waving a white flag.

Players responded by dreading the pass, too. It often went wrong because they used it only when they had to, which was when the rush was heaviest and the coverage was tightest. It wasn't fun. It wasn't something players believed in, either.

Walsh's first triumph, then, was to sell his players on the

usefulness of the pass. He showed them it was no cause for shortness of breath and a tightening stomach (as did several other coaches in the early eighties, including Coryell, Landry, Grant, Gibbs, Cleveland's Sam Rutigliano, and offensive coordinators Joe Walton of the Jets and Lindy Infante of Cincinnati). What can be simpler than running to an open space and playing catch? "The field is 53-1/3 yards wide," says Sid Gillman, a longtime offensive innovator. "If you use the whole thing, they can't possibly cover everybody."

"Bill's the kind of coach," Clark says of Walsh, "you'll be in a meeting and he'll come flying in and say, 'We've got to put this play in.' He'll be real excited when he finds a play he's sure will work. That gets us excited. We know if we can catch a pass, maybe we can get a touchdown. Because we know he has that knack for finding openings. We'll be in practice and he'll say, 'If you run this route just like I tell you, you'll be wide open.' "

Passing breeds general confidence, too. The team that knows it can run will believe in its ability to beat the other team up, but the team that knows it can pass will believe in its ability to beat the other team, period. "There's never a point where we don't feel we can catch up," said Walt Downing, another 49er in 1981. And Downing was an offensive lineman. Linemen characteristically prefer the run. They would rather drive into the defensive lineman than stand back and absorb his attack.

X X X X X
O O O O

In the three years before the 49ers' Super Bowl season, they won 10 games and lost 38. Their record for 1978–80 was the NFL's worst. The second-worst record belonged to Cincinnati, the team the 49ers beat in the Super Bowl, which had gone 14–44. Both teams were 6–10 the year before they reached the Super Bowl.

It was radical enough for two 6–10 teams to turn into Super Bowl teams in one season. But Conventional Wisdom took an even harder blow from the preposterous way San Francisco and Cincinnati did it. They featured the pass.

Passing had been considered a foolhardy way to revive a losing team. First things first. You started with basics, using the running game to go from bad to good. *Then* came the passing game, because that was what separated the champions from the other good teams.

Seattle's Chuck Knox best illustrates that two-step principle of rebuilding. Knox, perhaps the NFL's best coach of the running game, has built three playoff teams, taking all three from bad to good. But he has not been in a Super Bowl, has yet to take a team from good to great.

From 1974 through 1980, six of the seven Super Bowls were won by the Steelers and the Raiders. Both of them had overpowering defenses and relentless running games for controlling the ball, and both of them had explosive passing games for scoring points in bundles, if necessary.

The 49ers, and to a lesser extent the Bengals, did not have overpowering defenses or relentless running games. So instead of following the Steelers-Raiders formula without the Steelers-Raiders ingredients, they made their own formula. They stumbled upon a formula for going from bad to great in one step:

Passing.

They did with the pass what other teams had done with the run. They controlled the ball. Walsh would have preferred to turn that responsibility over to a great running back, but he didn't have one. A running back is either great or he isn't. There is little a coach can do about it.

But unlike a running game, Walsh said, "a passing game can be more than the sum of its parts." An average receiver can play better than a gifted one because he can be taught to maneuver better into open spaces. An average quarterback can play better than a gifted one because he can be taught better ways of finding those open spaces and delivering the ball to them. Where running backs must operate instinctively, passers and receivers can be taught what to look for.

Steve DeBerg, the quarterback Walsh inherited at San Francisco in 1979, improved his completion percentage from 45.4 to 60.0 in one year. He went from 28th and last in NFL passer ratings to 14th. The 49ers' team ranking shot up from 25th to third in passing yards, 27th to third in completion percentage.

And from 19th to fourth in possession time. Even though the 49ers threw the most passes in the NFL in 1979, only three teams controlled the ball more than San Francisco, which didn't have the relentless running game people had assumed was a prerequisite for ball control.

Walsh and DeBerg had worked hour after hour on DeBerg's drop, the simple process of backpedaling from the center to the passing pocket. In time, DeBerg learned to arrive at the pocket faster, so he had more time to read the defense, and with his hand higher, so he needed less time to throw the ball. He learned to keep his feet moving in the pocket, so he would be a more mobile target for pass rushers. And he learned what to look for.

"All you have to do is get a quarterback who can read and give him a simple system of reads," Gillman says. "The key to the whole thing is to throw the ball into the least amount of coverage.

You can't guarantee it. They can camouflage their coverage. But if your quarterback has a good system of reads, he'll find something."

X X X X X
O O O O

The year after San Francisco won the Super Bowl, Washington's championship team did have a relentless running game. But the Redskins showed that even so, there still was a place for ball-control passing.

The Redskins passed to set up the run. They weren't just doing what they did best, passing to spread out the defense and create some room for a substandard running game. They were reversing the old Raiders-Steelers strategy of jabbing with the run and delivering a knockout punch with the pass. They were wearing out opposing defenses by making them pass rush, then giving the ball to running back John Riggins to bowl them over.

See how Washington turned the tables on defenses? Pass rushing had always been something they *got* to do, not *had* to do. It was the defensive linemen's reward for shutting down a running game. Just line up and go after the quarterback.

But the Redskins didn't give a defense the certainty they would pass. The Redskins could control the ball either by running or passing. They could come from behind either by running or passing. If they weren't able to establish the pass early, the defense knew their running game was good enough that they could go back to the conventional process of setting up the pass with the run.

What the Redskins did was turn ball-control passing from a weapon of necessity into a weapon of convenience. The question is no longer, "Why use it?" It is, "Why not?"

Squirming and Wriggling and Diving

... Or how to control the ball by letting it fly

The popularity of ball-control passing rose with the 49ers' success from 1979 through 1981. Ball-control passing was the first step toward the overall efficiency in NFL passing games today.

Like the running game, a ball-control passing game set up the more conventional passing game by keeping defenses from spreading out and by keeping offenses out of situations where they had to pass. But ball-control passing did more. Its shorter, simpler passes helped teams feel less edgy about putting the ball in the air, in the manner of a child learning to swim in three feet of water instead of nine feet.

Long before Bill Walsh became the NFL's matinee idol, the Minnesota Vikings had shown the value of short passes. Fran Tarkenton was without peer at flipping the ball to a nearby-running back when he read danger signs farther downfield. Ted Marchibroda's backs at Baltimore were among the league-leading receivers in the mid-seventies. Sid Gillman's quarterbacks at San Diego threw short, safe passes in the early sixties.

"Francis would always say, 'Don't stay with it if the play isn't working out. Get a plus out of it,' " says Bud Grant, Tarkenton's coach. "A lot of teams kept their backs in to block, which they sometimes weren't all that good at. We wanted them out there where you could hit them for a high percentage of completions.

Francis didn't even wait until he got chased out. As soon as he saw something in the defense he didn't like, he went to a back to get something."

Walsh was just as adamant about not wasting any downs when he was Cincinnati's offensive coordinator in 1968–75, helping Ken Anderson win NFL passing championships the last two seasons. "He'd say, 'Make the defense do its job. Make them make a tackle,' " says Bob Trumpy, the Bengals' former tight end who became an NBC announcer. At San Francisco, with the help of the rule changes, Walsh expanded the concept.

Now Walsh's offense was throwing short passes that weren't just safety valves. The 49ers threw short to *primary* receivers, and they did it quickly. As the diagram on page 42 shows, the 49ers threw to wide receivers where other teams had thrown only to backs. They would line their wide receivers up tighter than most teams and send them on short crossing routes across the middle.

They were taking advantage of the new rules. Wide receivers were able to get off the line of scrimmage more easily, so the 49ers were aiming their best receivers at the weakest pass defenders, at linebackers. Dwight Clark was perfect for them. Clark's relative lack of speed, which kept him available in the 10th round in 1979, was not such a drawback on an eight-yard route. It was more important that he was bigger than most wide receivers, 6′4″ and 210 pounds. He could navigate the congested middle of the field. He ranked third, second, and first in NFL receptions in 1980–82—first each year among wide receivers.

Clark also could run with the ball after catching it, another trait that gained value in a ball-control passing game. Walsh figured half his team's passing yards would actually be gained on the ground. That's why he drafted fullback Earl Cooper in the first round in 1980, ironically with a choice they acquired in trading the choice the Jets used on Lam Jones. "A defense is not generally designed to account for the fullback as a receiver," Walsh said even before drafting Cooper. Now he had another receiver to mismatch with linebackers. Cooper led the NFC with 83 catches as rookie.

"In a possession passing game," Walsh says, "every pass is vital. You can't drop the ball. Your backs have to have good hands. They have to be consistent receivers and good pattern people. Backs are rarely trained for that in college, so you have to teach it here."

Defenses responded to the new rules, too, many of them with eight-man coverages that left little room for receivers to ma-neuver, but San Francisco's possession passing game aimed the ball in front of all eight men. Defenses were using more special-

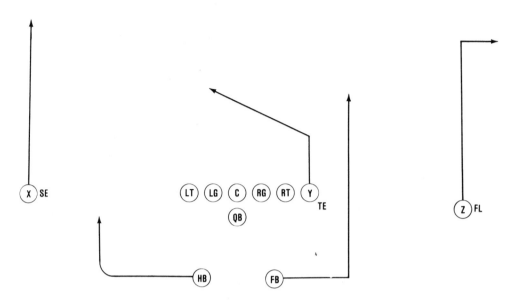

Throughout much of the seventies, the Minnesota Vikings used a short passing game that featured fullback Chuck Foreman as a frequent receiver after the wide receivers had cleared out his short area by running longer routes.

C	center	LG	left guard	RT	right tackle
FB	fullback	LT	left tackle	SE	split end
FL	flanker	QB	quarterback	TE	tight end
HB	halfback	RG	right guard		

San Francisco's short passing game since 1979 has differed from previous ones in its frequent use of wide receivers, especially split end (X) Dwight Clark, as primary targets. The 49ers often line their wide receivers up relatively close to the ball and send them on crossing routes, with a back and a tight end going farther downfield.

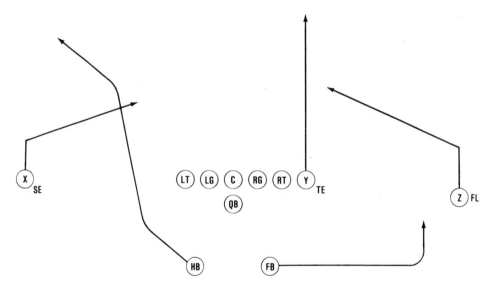

ized pass defenders, five or six defensive backs, but usually not on first down.

To coaches, first down is a game in itself. The offense wins if it gains four yards. Anything less limits its realistic options for second down. The fewer options for the offense, the easier it is to play defense.

That's why one of most important rushing statistics, something rarely kept, is the percentage of a back's or team's first-down carries of four yards or more. That can tell more about a back than his rushing average. Woody Hayes, when he was coaching at Ohio State, used to scoff at average stats by telling the story of the man who drowned in a river with an average depth of 29 inches.

First down has generally been considered a running down because pass plays couldn't be counted on to make four yards often enough. People didn't throw four-yard passes. They threw longer passes, with lower completion rates.

"They felt like they had to get 12 yards with a pass," says Grant. He didn't, but he was in a minority until San Francisco's success showed the rest of pro football what Grant already knew. A four-yard pass can be completed more than three times out of four. Not many backs can run for four yards that often. And a three-yard gain on first down isn't that much better than an incomplete pass. Either way, it's second-and-long.

"People are being successful throwing the ball, breaking modern trends. They're playing contrary to how offense has been in the past. When other people see their success, they say, 'Maybe that's not such a bad idea.' Particularly if that's what their personnel dictates."—Washington coach **Joe Gibbs**, in 1980.

"Now it's easier to pass for yards than it is to run for yards," Grant says. "Your receiver isn't getting knocked down while you're getting ready to throw. Pass blocking is easier. And if you throw the ball four or five yards to a back who can squirm and wriggle and dive, he can get you another three or four."

Ball-control passing has lived up to its name. It has helped teams control the ball. The graphs on page 44 show that not only have completions risen steadily since 1977, so have passes for first downs.

X X X X X
0 0 0 0

A new category of play emerged. "When you dump the ball to a running back, doesn't that have more the quality of a run than

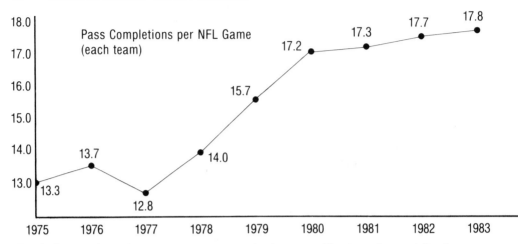

The ball-control passing game means more short-passes. They're safer, and they're completed more often. The NFL had more than a one-third increase in pass completions from 1977 to 1980.

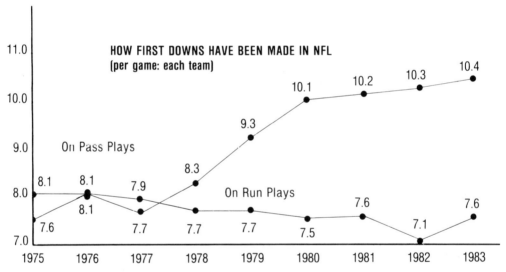

The ball-control pass was more than just a catch phrase. Teams actually began using the pass more to keep their drives going. They had run for more first downs than they passed for in 1977, but just three years later, they passed for 35 percent more first downs than they ran for.

a pass?" asks Bud Goode, a longtime statistical analyst for various NFL teams. It's not a run, certainly. It's a hybrid, although NFL statistics crews stubbornly maintain a pass is a pass is a pass. At the very least, Goode cries out for distinguishing passes to targets behind the line of scrimmage. "The NFL is obligated to keep that statistic for us," he says.

Goode is best known for his correlating winning with a team's number of rushing plays. Not rushing yards. Not rushing average.

Rushing plays. He never claimed running caused a team to win any more than winning caused a team to run out the clock—only that running and winning went hand-in-hand. And that it didn't help him do his job when the bold line between runs and passes suddenly turned gray.

In 1980, Goode noticed an old statistic gaining new significance. First downs passing per pass attempts, or: how many of your passes are making first downs? It wasn't more important than rushing plays, but it was high on Goode's chart with a bullet. Goode's conclusion? "The more you throw short successfully, that's where the passing game is at."

And why is that? Over the long haul, a team wants two things out of its passing game. It wants touchdowns, naturally. And it wants a high average gain per pass attempt. (Averages are not entirely useless statistics. It depends on what is being measured. For example, if an engineer is evaluating Woody Hayes's river as a possible power source, he would be more interested in its average depth of 29 inches than its 12-foot depth 50 miles upstream.) The average gain per pass attempt is meaningful because it tells a lot about a passing game. It rewards both a high completion percentage and long gains on passes, and it leads to touchdowns.

How can a team increase both its completion percentage and its yardage on completions? By passing to backs.

Huh? Short passes to backs help gain more yardage per completion?

Here's why. Before the ball-control passing rage, wide receivers generally averaged about 18 yards per catch, tight ends about 12, and backs about 6. Which of those figures is easier to improve? Six, of course, for the same reason a D grade is easier to improve than a B grade.

In 1983, only three NFL wide receivers with more than 20 catches had more than a 20-yard average per catch, or two yards better than the old norm. But *37* backs with more than 20 catches improved on their old norm by at least two yards. Only *three* backs averaged less than six yards a catch.

Wide receivers aren't getting 18 yards a catch anymore, but backs are more than making up for it. Both Billy Sims and James Jones averaged at least 10 yards for Detroit in 1983. Walter Payton was at 11.5, Gerry Ellis 11.6, Darrin Nelson 12.1, and they all had more than 50 catches. With less than 30 catches, Butch Woolfolk averaged 13.1 yards, Walter Abercrombie 15.0, and Curtis Dickey 20.1.

A short pass, then, is not necessarily a short play. On the other hand, a short pass almost always is easier to complete than a long pass.

X X X X X
O O O O

All this passing efficiency does not mean the run has become foolishly Neanderthal. Washington showed ball-control passing is all the more valuable in concert with a running attack. Even San Francisco, in its Super Bowl season, was among the 12 NFL teams with more runs than passing plays.

The next season, 1982, San Francisco led the league in pass attempts and passing yardage. "When you see that you're number one in passing yardage, you get suspicious," Walsh said. "It seems we're throwing about 10 passes too many each week. That is not the formula for winning."

While the 49ers' record dropped from 13–3 to 3–6, both Super Bowl teams were among the top five in rushing attempts. None of the top five teams in pass attempts even played for a conference championship.

In 1983, both Super Bowl teams ranked in the top eight in rushing attempts. Four of those eight made the playoffs. Of the top eight teams in pass attempts, only eighth-ranked Dallas made the playoffs, and not for long.

Far from dying, the run is reviving. Most league passing statistics have leveled off since 1981. One reason is the same reason the pass was so valuable in 1978. Now it's the run that represents variety.

The other reason is ball control. The ball-control passing game is wonderful for a team without a great running back, but there's no replacing Payton or Riggins as ball-control threats. And ball control has become more and more important, even if that seems a paradox when teams regularly drive 80 yards in less than a minute.

The ability to move the ball in lightning-quick drives is all the more reason to keep your opponent's offense on the bench. In one 1983 game, Payton's Bears let their opponent have the ball just three times in the second half. "The only way you can have a good defense is if you have a great running game," says the Bears' defensive coordinator, Buddy Ryan.

Ball control is important even if a team is behind, as long as plenty of time remains for catching up. San Diego had the whole second half to make up two touchdowns when it received the halftime kickoff from Miami in a 1982 playoff game. Five minutes is plenty of time for the Chargers to score two touchdowns. But they got impatient. They started throwing deep right away. Dan Fouts wound up with five interceptions, and Miami wound up winning 34–13.

Just because you *can* score quickly in eighties football doesn't mean you *have* to. If anything, it means you *don't* have to.

X X X X X
O O O O

The pass is so tempting, though. It has never looked easier. On its best days, an eighties offense looks like a backyard game of touch. First team to score 10 touchdowns wins.

Those best days have spoiled people—the Green Bay Packers' executive committee, for example. Some days the Packers made the scoreboard numbers spin, easy as pumping gas. They scored in the 40s or 50s four times in 1983, twice more in the 30s. Won all six times, too. Trouble was, their defense couldn't keep the other guys from playing touch some days, and the Packers finished 8–8 and missed the playoffs. So the executive committee fired coach Bart Starr.

Coaches get spoiled, too. Ten of the NFL's 28 starting quarterbacks when the 1983 season began were benched eventually because of performance.

At the same time passing has never looked easier, it has never been harder to be impressive. Three hundred yards in a game used to be a pie in the sky, just like 20 grand a year. People don't dream about either one anymore. What was once spectacular has become ordinary, even necessary.

In 1983, NFL quarterbacks had 66 300-yard games. Every time a quarterback started a game, the chances were better than one in seven he would pass for 300 yards. It happened almost that randomly, too. Twenty-seven different quarterbacks had 300-yard games. The Chargers, the Falcons, the Giants, the Raiders, and the Broncos each had two quarterbacks do it. Jeff Rutledge, the Giants' career reserve, passed for 300 three times.

List the top 10 passing games for 1983, and the only quarterbacks you'll see twice are Lynn Dickey and Joe Theismann. You won't see Fouts, Anderson, or Montana at all. You will, however, see Bill Kenney, Scott Brunner, and Dave Krieg.

It wasn't long ago a quarterback could be darn proud of completing 55 percent of his passes. In 1981, 12 *teams* completed more than 55 percent. In 1983 it was 20, with 12 going over 57.5 percent.

Another standard of excellence was throwing more touchdowns than interceptions. The whole NFL threw more touchdowns than interceptions in 1983. A 1–1 ratio was below average. Five quarterbacks were better than 2–1, including Dan Marino— a rookie, for Pete's sake—at better than 3–1, and Steve Bartkowski topping 4–1 (22 and 5).

Standards have changed. Excellent isn't good enough anymore,

NFL Passer Ratings

Rating Category	1977	1983	norm	exc	max
Avg. yards gained per pass attempt	6.50	7.18	7.00	9.00	12.50
Pct completed	51.3	56.9	50.0	60.0	77.5
Pct intercepted	5.7	4.4	5.5	3.5	0.0
Pct thrown for TD	4.0	4.4	5.0	7.5	11.9
Total rating	61.5	75.8	66.7	100.0	158.3

as Danny White well knows. White had the NFL's best career passer rating ever as soon as he qualified with his 1,500th pass. He finished the 1983 season with a 42–15 record as the Cowboy's four-year starter, and he also finished the season in danger of being booed out of town. White was number one for just three weeks, or as long as it took Montana to throw his 1,500th pass. Also in the top 10 are Fouts, Anderson, and Bert Jones. Half the NFL's 10 best passers of all-time played most of their careers after the 1978 rule changes.

X X X X X
0 0 0 0

The passer rating considers four statistics:

★ Yards per pass attempt
★ Percentage completed
★ Percentage intercepted
★ Percentage thrown for touchdown

Each possible statistic is assigned a value, with the points for each category weighted equally toward the passer's rating. As the chart above shows, the rating system creates standards of normalcy and excellence for each of the statistics. A passer who is normal across the board gets a rating of 66.7. The excellent rating is 100.0. But that's not the maximum rating.

The NFL, in its wisdom, has selected the memorable, round number of 158.3 for its maximum rating. A passer doesn't have to throw 50-yard touchdowns on every attempt for his coveted 158.3, either. The chart also shows the maximum standards.

In 1977, the league as a whole had a passer rating of 61.5, deservedly substandard. In 1983, the league's combined rating had climbed to 75.8, which means the league's average passer was better than all but five individuals were in 1977.

Although the rating system is designed to compare passers of different eras, current offenses clearly are outdating it. The norms for completion and interception percentages especially are taking a beating.

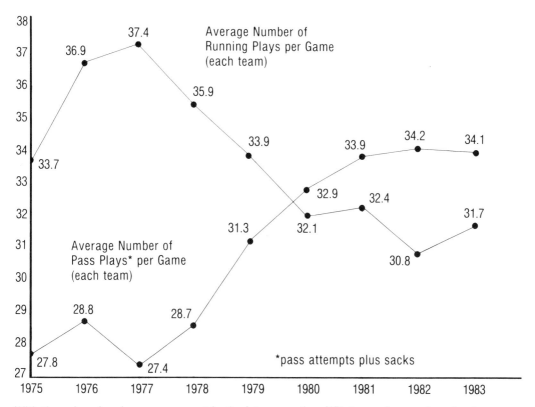

38
37 — 36.9
37.4
Average Number of
Running Plays per Game
(each team)
36 — 35.9
35
34 — 33.9   33.9   34.2   34.1
33.7
33
32.9   32.4
32 — 31.7
31.3   32.1
31 — Average Number of   30.8
Pass Plays* per Game
30 — (each team)
29 — 28.8
28.7
28
27.8   27.4   *pass attempts plus sacks
27
1975 1976 1977 1978 1979 1980 1981 1982 1983

With the rulemakers' encouragement in the late seventies, NFL teams began choosing to pass instead of run.

"For a long while, I really objected to the new rules," Sid Gillman said after the 1979 season. "I felt there had been a premium on coaching a good passing game. A good coach could get his outside ends off the line of scrimmage without help from the rules. He could design his plays well and show them how to avoid people. He could teach his quarterback how to read defenses so he would avoid throwing to the wrong areas. He could teach pass blocking. I think it's less challenging now."

The rule changes not only opened up the game, they closed the ranks. Now the best coaches had, say, a two-step head start on the pack instead of 10 steps. Nearly everybody was finding out the more you pass, the better you get. The graph above and those on pages 50–51 show just how much the NFL's passing games improved with use, and with such refinements as increasing ball-control, passing, sight adjustments, and specialized players and formations for pass receiving.

Those refinements were what brought Gillman around. Quite soon, he saw the opportunities for brainstorming were broader than before. The coaches most creative with Xs and Os had their edge back.

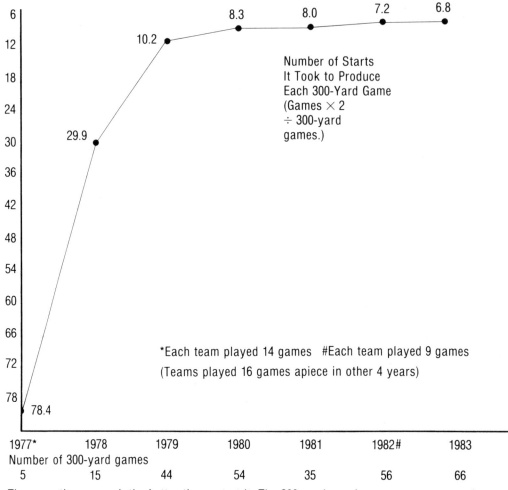

6 — 6.8

8.3   8.0   7.2   6.8

12 — 10.2

Number of Starts
It Took to Produce
Each 300-Yard Game
(Games × 2
÷ 300-yard
games.)

18

24

30 — 29.9

36

42

48

54

60

66

72   *Each team played 14 games   #Each team played 9 games
          (Teams played 16 games apiece in other 4 years)

78

78.4

1977*   1978   1979   1980   1981   1982#   1983
Number of 300-yard games
  5   15   44   54   35   56   66

The more they passed, the better they got at it. The 300-yard passing game, once a precious rarity, suddenly became almost commonplace. Leaguewide, pass completion percentages rose sharply, almost without interruption . . .

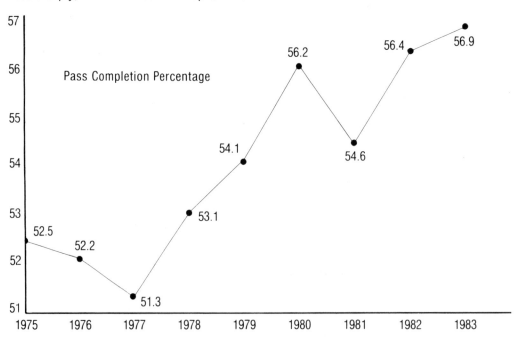

57 — 56.9

56.2

56.4   56.9

56 — 56.2

Pass Completion Percentage

55

54.1

54.6

54 — 54.1

53 — 53.1

52.5

52.2

52 — 52.2

51.3

51

1975   1976   1977   1978   1979   1980   1981   1982   1983

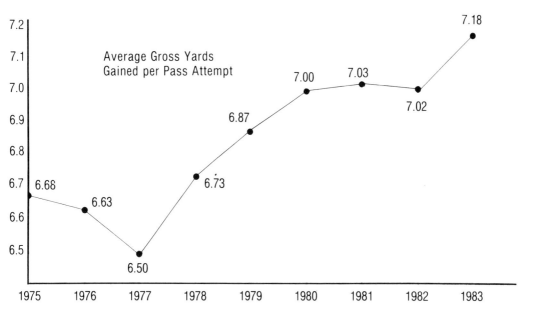

. . . as did yardage per pass attempt . . .

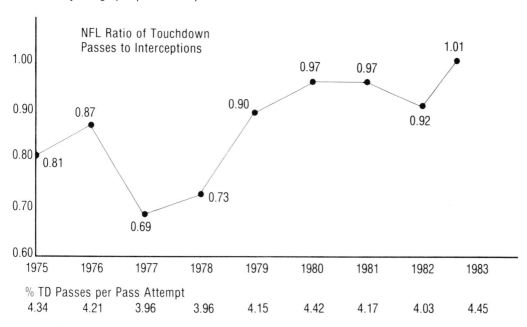

% TD Passes per Pass Attempt

| 4.34 | 4.21 | 3.96 | 3.96 | 4.15 | 4.42 | 4.17 | 4.03 | 4.45 |

. . . and the ratio of touchdown passes to interceptions dipped in the strike-shortened 1982 season, but in 1983 exceeded 1–1, which once had been a standard of excellence for individual quarterbacks.

If All the Coaches' Blackboards Were Laid End to End

... They'd finally have enough of them to draw their tricky formations and plays

The best way to complete passes consistently is to throw the pass that the defense is willing to give up. No defense can cover everything. Fran Tarkenton was taking what the defense offered when he dumped the ball off to a back. A wide receiver is taking what the defense offers when his sight adjustment has him go deep against a shallow free safety or curl in front of deeper coverage.

But taking what the defense gives you is a notion that has been taken to foolish extremes. On third-and-eight, the defense is more than happy to give up a five-yard pass.

An offense that repeatedly takes unwanted scraps from the defense has forgotten who has the ball. It happens. Some offenses still make their first priority to deprive the defense of a big play instead of making a big play themselves.

In its extreme, taking what the defense gives is reacting to the defense instead of making the defense react to the offense. It is the offense's prerogative to initiate the action. No defense can huddle up and call a left cornerback interception on two.

So the Raiders puff their chests and harrumph, "We don't take what the defense gives us. We take what we want." That is not entirely true. Even if quarterback Jim Plunkett has his heart set on throwing deep to Cliff Branch, he is more likely to throw shorter to an uncovered Todd Christensen than a blanketed Branch. What's true is this: if throwing to Branch means that much to the Raiders, they'll design the play to coax the defense out of covering him.

They'll take what they want, but they'll also make the defense give it to them.

All the Xs and Os of coaching are aimed at one goal: putting players in position to make plays. That is true on either offense or defense, although the offense also can take opposing players *out of position* to make plays.

It starts doing that by putting to use that time the quarterback spends behind the center yelling "hut hut" and a bunch of numbers. While the quarterback is yapping away, his teammates are running around to new locations, making defensive players who shadow them run, too. Even after the ball is in play, offensive players can coax defensive players out of position with tactics that coaches call misdirection, or influence blocks. Coaches like to lend those plays a certain dignity, or else they would call them sucker plays.

"One of the great things about coaching," says Washington's Joe Gibbs, "is we're evolving so fast that we change 30 to 40 percent of our offense each year." That makes for a lot of Xs and Os. Bill Walsh's San Francisco players say he doesn't stop diagramming plays in the air until April. Any napkin or envelope becomes a blackboard for the brainstorming coach.

X X X X X
o o o o

A play has to start from a formation. The players can't spread out however they please. But each play, the formation can change several times as the players shift before they take their stances and then run in motion before the snap. The only limits to those changes are the 30-second clock and the requirement for seven men to begin the play on the line of scrimmage with four men off the line (unless the referee is told a back is lining up on the line).

NFL teams use more formations each year. San Francisco, for example, used about 150 in 1983. They actually *used* that many, as opposed to just fattening the playbook with them.

One reason there are more formations now than 10 years ago is there are more substitutions. An offense doesn't replace its backs with wide receivers so the extra wide receivers can line up in the backfield.

A formation also tries to guide defensive players out of the way. Washington, for example, likes to put its two tight ends on one side and its two wide receivers on the other side. Then it sends a running play toward the wide receivers, even though the tight ends are better blockers. Why? The defense has matched the wide receivers with cornerbacks, and cornerbacks usually don't tackle as well as safeties or linebackers.

When Ken Stabler was the Raiders' quarterback, people assumed they operated with tight end Dave Casper on the left side because Stabler was lefthanded. Purely a coincidence. In fact, a favorite formation of the Raiders had both wide receivers on the right—Stabler's blind side.

The formation was effective because it matched Casper up with right linebackers who were not accustomed to battling with tight ends. It created a mismatch. On the right side, it gave the defense a choice between giving the inside receiver a pass-coverage mismatch against a safety or turning that side's run protection over to two cornerbacks. Of course, the formation was also effective because Casper, left tackle Art Shell, and left guard Gene Upshaw were all-pros who created their own mismatches. Formations can't overpower an opponent. They can only help players do it.

Even in a widely varied offense, players can be put in all the advantageous locations they need with considerably less than 150 formations. As a group, multiple formations have a different purpose. They confuse a defense, or at the very least, inconvenience it.

Doug Plank, Chicago's inordinately physical free safety from 1975 through 1982, on the Dallas Cowboys, leaders of the current trend toward multiple and shifting formations:

"I've always admired the Cowboys. They don't just try to come out and beat you physically. That won't work all the time. They seem to get more satisfaction out of getting the defense out of position. You can't be as aggressive against them. I think they create a minimum of three to five mental errors a game, which usually equates to a big play.

"It's much easier to confuse people than overpower them. More satisfying, too. It's fun to hear people shouting on the field who don't know what they're doing. And it takes a lot less wear and tear running around people than trying to go through them. You get old awful quick trying to run over people in this league."

A defense has to choose its plays with some thought about what the offense might do. Nobody gives the defense style points for a perfectly executed strong-side blitz if the offense runs to the weak side for 50 yards. So a defense needs at least a general idea about what the offense tends to do in a given situation.

We'll go into more detail later about how a defense determines offensive tendencies, but the resulting list of tendencies is sorted out by formation. On third-and-four, say, a defensive player's game plan tells him to look for one set of likely plays if the wide receivers line up on opposite sides, a different set if they're on the same side. The formation, then, is the defense's first clue to which offensive play is coming.

If the offense changes formations four or five times before the snap, it keeps changing the defense's clues. Just moving a wide receiver from one side to another could change 11 defensive players' assignments. If one of them misses the change, or makes the wrong change, that gives the offense an opening it wouldn't have had otherwise.

Too many formations can confuse offensive players, too. Penalties are called for having only six men on the line, timeouts are wasted because 10 players lined up in one formation and one lined up in another. When Denver coach Dan Reeves moved from Dallas's staff, he found it impractical to install the whole Dallas offense in one year. But generally, multiple formations actually simplify an offense. It can get by with fewer plays. The Redskins use as many formations as anyone, but they have about five running plays and five pass plays that make up most of their offense.

"Our offense isn't complex at all," says Washington wide receiver Art Monk. "It may look complex. That's the idea. When we run the same play from five different sets, it looks like five plays. But we only have to learn one. We just stick with the things we do well."

Multiple formations also give a defense logistical problems. It has to practice against all those formations in one week. It has to remember all those different lists of tendencies.

But each list is shorter. After Chicago beat San Francisco 13–3 in 1983, Bear defensive players said the 49ers had the most predictable offense they'd seen. They also said it was the most *varied* offense they had seen. So a team with lots of formations has to make sure its formations and plays don't pair up too neatly, a rut the 49ers apparently fell into when they lost four of five games in the middle of a 10–6 season.

X X X X X
O O O O

A multiple offense was never intended to confuse defenses with its sheer volume of formations. What's confusing is the change in formations before the snap, the motion. But if you're going to do a lot of moving, you need a lot of places to go. If the players kept dashing back and forth between only two formations, motion wouldn't be any more confusing than a shell game with two shells.

"I thought an offense with multiple sets was the best way to beat the best defenses of those days," says Dallas coach Tom Landry, generally considered the father of modern multiple offenses. That was in 1960, the Cowboys' first year. "We started shifting and moving then, too. It made it hard for the defense to determine what we were going to do. Of course, there's a lot more of it now, but the only advantage of multiple sets even today is to keep the defense off-balance."

Backs had been going in motion since the forties. Landry added wide receivers. He even had his linemen pop up and down from their set position, so defensive players would have a harder time seeing the motion and determining the new formation.

(Another Dallas team had a rookie coach in 1960. But it was in the wrong league, so Hank Stram's multiple offense wasn't widely recognized until his team had moved to Kansas City and won the Super Bowl 10 years later. In their third seasons, the motley expansion Cowboys were among the NFL scoring leaders and the Dallas Texans won the AFL championship.)

The Redskins, preparing for their Super Bowl against Miami, had a serious problem facing Dolphin linebacker A. J. Duhe. He had disrupted good offenses in the AFC playoffs, and the Redskins needed a way to slow down his reactions. Joe Gibbs's solution was motion. Lots of motion. He called it his explode package. Just before the snap, all eligible Redskins moved every which way. It gave the effect of a factory at the 5 o'clock whistle and might very well have given Duhe pause.

Motion was instrumental in the game's biggest play. On fourth-and-one from Miami's 43, Redskin tight end Clint Didier lined up on the left side, off the line. He went in motion toward the center, turned and headed back to the left. Cornerback Don McNeal followed him. But McNeal slipped making the turn. He was half a step late getting back to his area, which John Riggins stormed through for a touchdown.

A moment's hesitation is all the offense is looking for. Maybe it won't slow the defender's reaction time. But it might delay his recognition of the formation, his clue to the offense's play. "A lot of times you'll see defensive people still running around, trying to get into the right position when the ball is snapped," Raider cornerback Mike Haynes says. "That's when you know the motion worked."

It's especially effective if the player in motion is the tight end. The tight end is the odd man in an offense. His side is the strong side. That is important to the defense. It wants its more physical outside linebacker and safety on the strong side.

A defense rarely shifts from strong side to weak side with

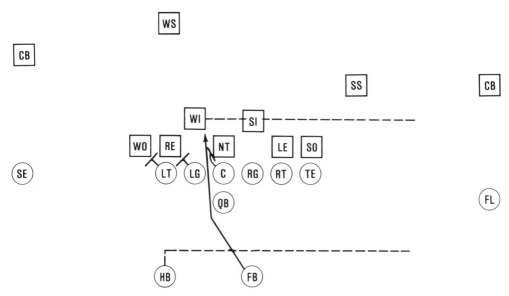

NFL teams rarely just line up and run a play without sending at least one man in motion. One reason for motion is to coax defensive players into going where they will be out of the way of the offensive play. In the diagram above, the halfback goes in motion to the right and a linebacker follows him in case the halfback is going out for a pass. Then the fullback runs to the area vacated by the linebacker. (If the linebacker hadn't followed the halfback, the quarterback could have changed the play at the line of scrimmage, calling a pass to the halfback.)

anyone but its safeties, and maybe its inside linebackers in a 3–4. It used to be standard for outside linebackers and cornerbacks to shift, too. The Bears were doing that in 1967, when they played Kansas City for the first time in an exhibition. The Chiefs made them flop six players before practically every snap and won 66–24, taking the first noticeable step toward NFL–AFL parity.

An offense can create mismatches with motion that it could not create by sending players directly from the huddle to their marks. If a wide receiver simply lined up behind a tackle, a cornerback probably would line up across from him. But if the wide receiver were to start out by the sideline, go in motion, and wind up behind the tackle just as the ball is snapped, a cornerback might not follow him. A slower linebacker might have to cover him.

Or the offense might want to coax a defender into following its man in motion. Say it's the 49er halfback Wendell Tyler. He runs from the quarterback's left toward the right sideline. The weak-side linebacker tails him. That leaves an area open for the fullback Roger Craig to run or catch a pass, as the diagram above illustrates.

Maybe the weak-side linebacker won't take the bait, but the Tyler's motion is still worthwhile. However the defense responds to motion, it is giving a hint about its pass-coverage plans. If nobody tails a halfback in motion, the defense apparently isn't covering him man-to-man. Now the quarterback has less reading to do after the snap.

So motion will, first off, limit the things a defense can do. Better yet, it might limit the defense to configurations that are vulnerable to the offense's play. And because motion causes a defense to commit itself, it might enable the offensive players to know the defense's plans even before the ball is in play.

Another advantage of motion is in its capacity to give offensive players a head start on a play. A lot of teams were sending flankers and tight ends in motion by the mid-seventies to make them harder to bump on pass coverage. They became moving targets.

A running back in motion can get a running start for a pitchout. Or a pass. Or a block. A tight end can't lead the blocking on an inside run unless he goes in motion. Motion also can bring a wide receiver toward the middle for a handoff on a reverse. Or a fake reverse.

X X X X X
O O O O

The trend toward multiple formations and men in motion is part of a larger trend toward outfoxing opponents instead of outmuscling them. That disturbs old-timers. In football's utterly macho world, it doesn't seem manly to be telling the other guy to watch out behind him and then pop him on the jaw.

The Steeler players beat that drum both times they played the Cowboys in the Super Bowl. They hated the Cowboys, many Steelers said. The point they made was: real football teams don't match wits, they bump heads. But even the Steelers are masters of one of football's most venerable sucker plays, *the trap*, as shown in the diagram at the top of page 59.

Like all influence plays, the trap turns a defensive player's quick reactions against him. It gives him a false key. Usually, the trap's pigeon is a defensive tackle. The guard across from him blocks someone else. It looks like he missed his assignment. The defensive tackle has a clear shot into the backfield. But just as he gets there, the guard from the other side bangs into the defensive tackle as Franco Harris runs by.

Now the trap has become a popular play from the shotgun formation. That makes it a double sucker play. Not only does the blocking give a defensive lineman a false key, but the whole formation—a passing formation—is a false key. Walter Payton has become one of the more frequent runners on shotgun traps, and the diagram at bottom of page 59 shows the play he turned into a 50-yard touchdown in 1983.

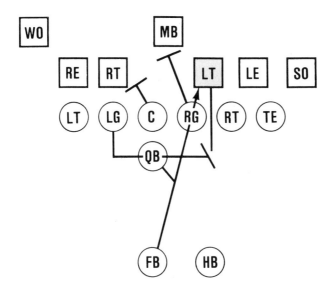

In this trap play, the shaded defensive tackle is being trapped. The guard opposite him leaves him with a clear shot into the backfield, but when he takes that clear shot, the other guard blocks him from the side. The ball carrier cuts behind the trap block.

The "long trap" from shotgun formation has almost the same blocking as the conventional trap play. It has an extra advantage in the element of surprise, coming from a passing formation on a passing down. In this diagram, the pass-rushing defensive left end takes himself out of the play by going after the quarterback, freeing the offensive right tackle to help the ball carrier farther downfield by blocking the strong safety. The shaded defensive left tackle is the victim of the trap block.

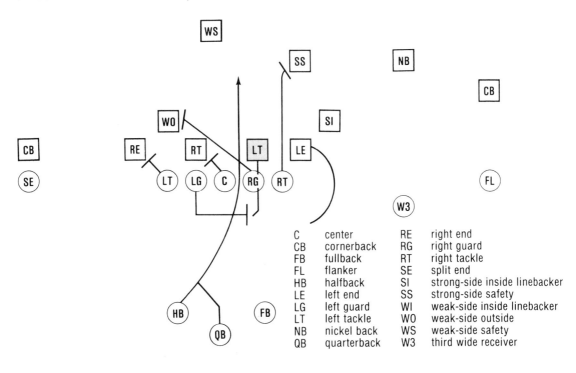

C	center	RE	right end
CB	cornerback	RG	right guard
FB	fullback	RT	right tackle
FL	flanker	SE	split end
HB	halfback	SI	strong-side inside linebacker
LE	left end	SS	strong-side safety
LG	left guard	WI	weak-side inside linebacker
LT	left tackle	WO	weak-side outside
NB	nickel back	WS	weak-side safety
QB	quarterback	W3	third wide receiver

No team built more of a reputation for coming right at a defense than Lombardi's Packers. But few teams used the play-action pass, another sucker play, more effectively. For instance, the Packers would be sitting on a 10-point lead early in the fourth quarter. On third-and-two, their linemen fire out in blocks for an off-tackle play. But Bart Starr would take the ball out of Jim Taylor's belly and fade to pass. By the time the defense realized it was not a running play, Boyd Dowler or Max McGee would be catching the touchdown pass that broke open the game. Washington did the same thing often in setting an NFL scoring record in 1983.

One of the most famous plays in Packer history was a counter play, a subtler sucker play. Both guards pulled for a sweep around right end. Bob Lilly, Dallas's all-pro defensive tackle, followed them. But instead, Chuck Mercein carried the ball over left guard, right where Lilly had vacated. He gained eight yards to the Cowboys 3 and set up Starr's winning touchdown in the famous Ice Bowl game that sent Green Bay into Super Bowl II.

Draws and screens, like play-action passes, are designed to slow down the opponent's pass rush. But unlike play-action passes, they can be used on passing downs, without the threat of the run. Both plays begin like conventional pass plays and take advantage of a heavy pass rush. The defensive linemen get only token blocking resistance, so their pass rush will take them out of position to stop either the run up the middle on a draw or the pass toward the sideline on a screen. And on both plays, the offensive linemen who didn't bother to block pass rushers can become convoys for the ball carrier downfield.

The option screen is a recently popular variation on the screen. Shown in the diagram on page 61, it provides a better chance for a big play. The flanker runs a quick route down the sideline while the rest of the offense moves for a screen pass. If the flanker is not covered, he can catch the ball at full speed 15 or 20 yards downfield. If he is covered, the outlet receiver off to the side has a blocking wall of two or three linemen in front of him.

The more gimmicky plays, with the halfback passing or the wide receiver running, also have become more popular. Payton and the Raiders' Marcus Allen threw three touchdown passes apiece in 1983. Atlanta wide receiver Billy "White Shoes" Johnson carried the ball 15 times.

Dallas no longer has the market cornered on pass plays that start with a back running into the line, and then pitching back to the quarterback. San Francisco quarterback Joe Montana took two such pitches in the 1983 NFC championship game, one after a double reverse to a wide receiver. Washington back John

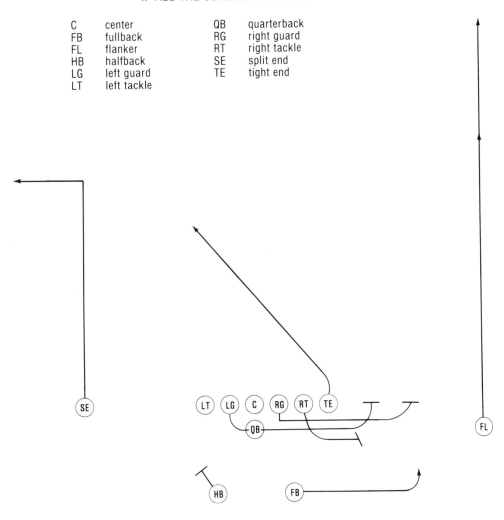

C	center	QB	quarterback
FB	fullback	RG	right guard
FL	flanker	RT	right tackle
HB	halfback	SE	split end
LG	left guard	TE	tight end
LT	left tackle		

On the option screen pass, the primary receiver is the flanker, who runs a quick route straight along the sideline. The quarterback either throws immediately to a spot ahead of the flanker or keeps the ball momentarily if the flanker is not open right away. Then the quarterback drops into his pass pocket and waits for a regular screen pass play to develop, giving the secondary receiver a wall of blockers that he would not ordinarily have when the quarterback dumps the ball off to a back.

Riggins completed a long pass in the same game. (So did a Redskin *punt returner,* although the play was called back because the pass went forward.) Cowboy quarterback Danny White and Bear quarterback Jim McMahon each caught touchdown passes in 1983. (They were legal receivers because they didn't start the plays under the center. They were single-wing tailbacks, except in shotgun formation.)

The 1981 Bengals, en route to the Super Bowl, tried a pass from a wide receiver against Houston and a triple pass against Buffalo. Neither play worked, but as coach Forrest Gregg said, "If you run the same plays all the time, it's easy for a defense to get ready and stop you." With every team passing so much, it takes more than passing on first down to be unpredictable.

Besides, even when a gimmick play doesn't work, it plants an unwelcome thought in defensive minds. *What if they do it again?* The defense might not be so quick to react to straight-ahead plays. Draws, screens, and other more conventional sucker plays can have the same effect.

These plays have nothing to do with a team's toughness. Joe Gibbs and Bill Walsh both positively relish a powerful hit. They like their tricks, but they also want their blockers putting defensive linemen on their heels. Opposing defensive players often consider the Cowboys one of the most physical NFL teams. Shell games are just so much easier than twisting arms.

Rovers, U-Backs, and Relocated Fullbacks

. . . And other fun characters from the one-back offense

If the purpose of a formation is to put players in position to make their plays, it's a good idea for pass plays to start with a lot of receivers at the line of scrimmage. A fullback needs nearly two seconds to run to the same spot a tight end can reach in one. So why not put the fullback where a tight end would line up?

Think of the second tight end in one-back formations as a relocated fullback. Coaches think of him that way. Often, a team will run the same play from a one-back set that it runs with two backs, and the second tight end has the fullback's blocking assignment. But running was not what the San Diego Chargers had in mind when they began using one-back formations regularly in 1980.

That was Kellen Winslow's first full season. He led the NFL in pass receptions, setting an all-time record for a tight end. Winslow was not a tight end in the sense that he lined up hip-to-hip with a tackle and mixed it up with defensive ends and linebackers on his way into the pass pattern. The Chargers had someone else do that. Winslow was their *second* tight end, their relocated fullback, although the way he played the position had more in common with a wide receiver. Winslow lined up somewhere between the interior line and a wide receiver, so the Chargers had 50 percent more outside receivers than other teams in their conventional formations.

Single backs didn't run much until after the Redskins hired San Diego's offensive coordinator, Joe Gibbs, to coach them in 1981. Gibbs liked the idea of using a second tight end to block the Giants' Lawrence Taylor, and other oversized blitzing right linebackers, on running plays. But the idea almost remained Gibbs's little secret. The Redskins lost their first five games. Gibbs suspected his job was in jeopardy. Quarterback Joe Theismann's job *was* in jeopardy. (There was talk of trading him to Detroit for Eric Hipple, then a second-year quarterback who had yet to start a game. Word was the Lions eventually nixed the deal.) After that fifth defeat, Theismann paid Gibbs an unexpected visit at home. They decided the Redskins were not the Chargers. They had to run. And they were going to live or die with one back and two tight ends.

The Redskins won the next week, using two backs only on short-yardage downs. They finished 8–8 in 1981. By the time they took their one-back offense to the Super Bowl the next year, they had won 19 of 23 games, but most people still hadn't noticed their strange formations. The pregame lineup on television showed two backs for the Redskins.

That mistake would not be made again. The Super Bowl is pro football's display window, and Washington's victory over Miami sold the one-back offense. More than half the NFL's teams used it

---

"I think you will see more of the one-back formation," Viking coach Bud Grant had predicted after the Super Bowl, "but not because Washington used it successfully. You'll see more of it because you get some versatility from the formation that you don't get from others."

---

in 1983, with Atlanta, Cleveland, and the Los Angeles Rams making it their offensive cornerstones, like Washington and San Diego.

"I think you will see more of the one-back formation," Viking coach Bud Grant had predicted after the Super Bowl, "but not because Washington used it successfully. You'll see more of it because you get some versatility from the formation that you don't get from others." Grant knew firsthand. He had used single backs on passing downs throughout the seventies.

"It's the only way to go," said Sid Gillman, who couldn't imagine why a coach would build his offense around anything else.

It's good for passing. It's good for running. And it's made for multiple formations and motion.

The Cowboys' terminology even calls the second tight end the

Rover. He's the man in motion. Outside toward the wide receivers. Inside to block for a run. Inside and back outside to where he started. From one side to the other side. The Redskins like to send both tight ends in motion, but they've tried combining the Rover with just about everybody except the quarterback. (The Redskins and Falcons actually call him the H-back. The Rams call him the U-back. We'll stick with the Cowboys' appellation because he does more roving than H-ing or U-ing. The Cowboys also call their basic two-tight-end formation the J-Hawk because Jay Saldi was their original Rover.)

The diagrams on pages 66–68 show just a few of countless possible formations without even moving the single back. And one-back formations accommodate a third wide receiver much more smoothly than conventional two-back formations.

There are enough formations to go a whole game without repeating one. Or to use one sizable package of formations each week, without repeating any package for several games. Just when the defense figures it has your tendencies pegged to formations, you scrap those formations and go to a new package. Washington did that at halftime in the Super Bowl against Miami.

Many of those formations have a tight end and a wide receiver on each side. Where's the strong side? Where does the defense put its strong safety? He's the better safety at stopping the run, so the offense can watch where he goes and run the other way, still to a tight end's side. "It makes the defense play honestly," Chicago halfback Walter Payton says. "You can run to either side." For a defense to be equally balanced, both safeties must be able to play the pass as well as a free safety, and play the run as well as a strong safety.

It's also easier to spread out a defense with just one back. The more it spreads out, the more area each man has to cover. "Use the whole field," is Gillman's Rule No. 1 for a passing game. Four receivers on the line scatter a defense more than three. Most defenses have felt they can't cover all four with zones. There would be too much space between zones, too much "seam" area.

"Defensive coaches will come up with ways to stop the one-back formation," Grant says. They always do. That's when you can tell whether an offense is a fad or a truly sound innovation.

"It's not a fad," says Gillman. A fad doesn't survive counter-adjustments.

The biggest apparent weakness of single backs is the lack of a second back to block blitzing pass rushers. So what? There are two ways to beat a blitz. Block all the blitzers or throw the ball before they reach the quarterback. Most teams have changed their preference from the former to the latter. Their pass plays

There are countless ways an offense can line up its players with two tight ends and one back. Some of the more popular formations are diagrammed below, with a few of them also showing the second tight end (shaded) in motion. The dotted circles show possible starting points for the second tight end before his motion, which is mapped with broken lines.

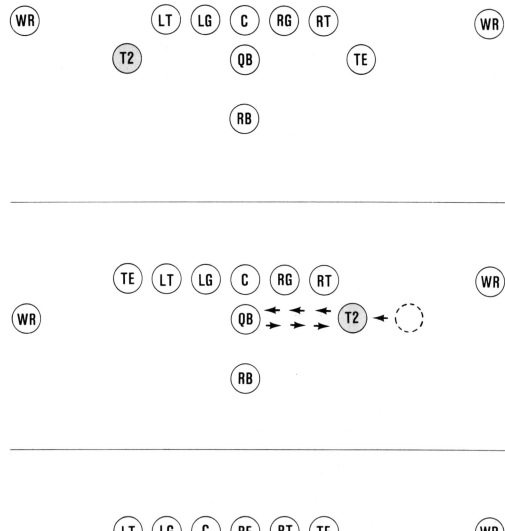

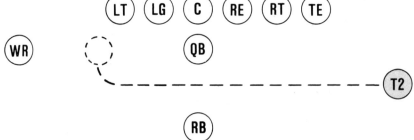

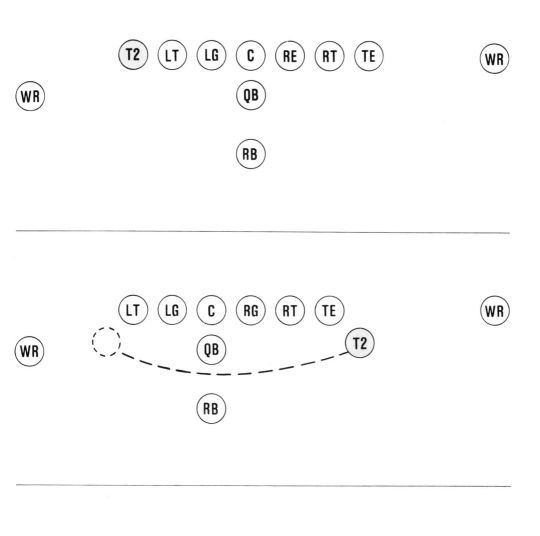

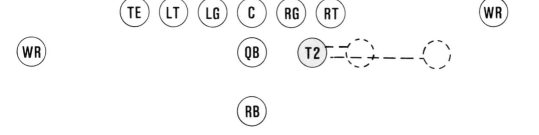

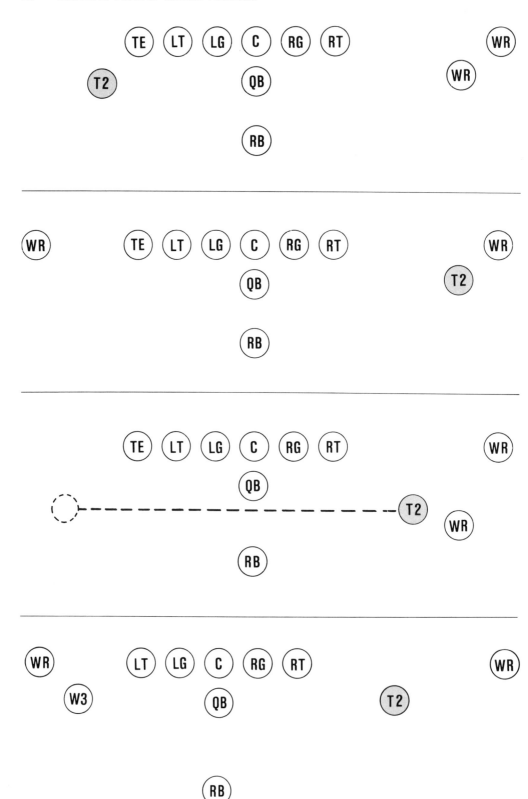

designate a hot receiver, whose job is to get open quickly against a blitz. As Brian Sipe observed at Cleveland, "If your hot receiver is right at the line of scrimmage, he's more of a threat than if he's back in the backfield." He can get open both faster and farther downfield.

On runs, a single back's lead blocker is no longer in front of him. But Matt Suhey, who has played both fullback and Rover for Chicago, says, "The blocking angles are better at Rover. Say your lead block is on a defensive tackle. If you're at fullback, he's already charging by the time you meet him. But at Rover, you get to him before he's out of his stance, and you're not taking him head-on."

X X X X X
O O O O

It's a misconception that a one-back offense's back has to be big, like Washington's John Riggins. Dallas's Tony Dorsett and Minnesota's Ted Brown could rattle around together in Riggins's uniform, but they've had success as single backs.

The back doesn't even have to be all that good. "You can get by without a—quote—super running back," Chicago coach Mike Ditka says. "What you need is a good solid football player who can pick a hole and move forward."

Sid Gillman on the one-back offense:

"That's where the future is. With four receivers up on the line, someone should get open every play. It's wonderful.

"I just think anybody who uses two backs a majority of the time—I don't see how they can win. It's a different-look game. That's what the game is all about. These coaches who are running fullback slants with two backs in the backfield have lost it."

His running plays can develop more leisurely, like an I-formation tailback's. In fact, he can be an I-formation tailback. Since the late seventies, the NFL had not been a wide-open market for college tailbacks. The pros don't use many I-formation sets because they're not good for passing, and college tailbacks don't get much experience as blockers or receivers. But who is a single back going to block for? He doesn't need to catch passes, either. Riggins caught five in 1983. "I'm in a perfect situation," Riggins says. "They don't make me do anything but carry the ball."

If the single-back is able to catch, so much the better. He doesn't need to come out on passing downs. Eric Dickerson, who caught 19 passes in four college seasons at tailback, caught 51 as a Ram rookie in 1983.

One-back offenses are redefining tight ends even more than running backs. Tight ends already are beginning to sort themselves out like power forwards and small forwards in basketball. Ozzie Newsome, Cleveland's sleek and fleet tight end, was out of position in two-back sets. He was playing power tight end. As a second tight end in 1983, he caught 89 passes.

The second tight end does not have to be a fast tight end, like Newsome and Winslow. He can be a fullback, like the Bears' Suhey and the Rams' Mike Guman. Atlanta used White Shoes Johnson, a 170-pound wide receiver. The Vikings don't call small halfback Darrin Nelson a second tight end, but that's what he is when they send him halfway to the sideline to give his sprinter's speed an open field.

Scouts had enough trouble finding enough tight ends to go around, one to a team. But that was because they were looking for tight ends who could block defensive ends and outrun safeties. In the last five years, they've found Winslow.

"If you're going to talk about Winslow, you better stop and wait a few seconds before you mention any other tight ends," says Ditka, who played tight end in five Pro Bowls and set the receiving record Winslow broke.

With two tight ends, the in-line blocker and fast receiver can come in separate packages. Eric Sievers, San Diego's conventional tight end, does little but block. Mike Barber caught 55 passes as the Rams' conventional tight end, but they usually were short ones. They got the deeper routes, Winslow's and Newsome's routes, from their second tight end, usually by replacing Guman with a third wide receiver. So the second tight end himself can come in separate packages: a fullback for lead blocking and a wide receiver for deep pass routes.

Single-back offenses are bound to affect defensive positions, too. Joe Gibbs's original intention, remember, was to block the weak-side linebackers who were turning into full-time blitzers. "You're going to start having somebody who can stand up on that weak-side end and play football instead of just blitzing," Buddy Ryan says. His answer at Chicago is to use five defensive linemen against double tight ends. Maybe that will be the next trend.

Hide and Sneak

... You can't sack a quarterback if you can't find him

To ask whether the blocking rule or the coverage rule has helped passing games more is like asking whether diet or exercise is more important for losing weight. They work together. But without the rule changes, coaches probably would have found keeping quarterbacks upright an easier chore than keeping receivers on their feet.

Quarterbacks would have unloaded the ball more quickly. Dan Fouts was doing that at San Diego under the old rules, and nearly all teams use quicker pass plays now, if only because they're throwing shorter passes. Quarterbacks don't always drop seven steps into the passing pocket, as they used to.

Fouts hardly ever drops more than five steps, sometimes only three. He is not particularly nimble afoot, but the Chargers are repeatedly among the NFL's least-sacked teams. They don't give pass rushers much time. Fouts almost never holds the ball more than 2.7 seconds.

Remember the passing window, which used to open for quarterbacks between roughly 2 and 3½ seconds after the snap. Coaching architects have widened it at both ends. Fouts doesn't always hold the ball even two seconds. It helps that receivers don't have to waste so much time picking themselves off the ground anymore, but it also helps that they're running shorter routes and more of them are starting at the line of scrimmage.

Fouts can throw long passes in a hurry, too. How long does a quarterback need to hold the ball on a sideline bomb? A sprinter at wide receiver can be 20 yards downfield in less than 2½ seconds. If the quarterback throws the ball at precisely 2½ seconds after the snap, the wide receiver will be more than 30 yards away when the ball catches up to him.

The same is true of a shorter route that isn't so straight. An *out*, for example, with the receiver running 15 yards downfield and cutting to the sideline. The quarterback knows where he's going. He doesn't have to wait for him to cut. "If the quarterback has any sense of timing, you can throw almost any pass at the end of a five-step drop," Sid Gillman says. Sometimes he can throw before the defense has set up. He can play fast-break football.

At the other end of the passing window, blockers are expected to hold off the rush for 3½ seconds. Any sack after that is blamed on the receivers for not getting open or the quarterback for not seeing an open receiver. But if the pass is scheduled to be thrown at 2½ seconds, and nobody seems to be getting open on schedule, the receivers still have a full second to ad lib their way into the clear.

They might have even longer if the quarterback has taken a five-step drop. He's harder for a pass rusher to reach there than seven steps back. "The angle is sharper. You can't go very wide around people. And the traffic is more congested," said Alan Page, who retired after the 1981 season and wondered even then why some teams persisted in sending their quarterbacks back seven steps.

Quarterbacks more mobile than Fouts can hold the ball still longer. The delayed rollout has become popular. Nobody does it better than Washington's Joe Theismann. He doesn't roll out to the sideline as soon as the ball is snapped. Then the pass rushers would know where to go. No, he goes back to the pocket first, lets the rush men waste their time chasing that way, *then* heads toward the sideline.

All this was what former Chiefs coach Hank Stram was talking about when he included the moving pocket in his famous Offense of the Seventies forecast. And it was a forecast, Stram says, not a boast. Stram was asked, before the Chiefs–Vikings Super Bowl in 1970, what some trends might be in the dawning decade. He said he expected more multiple offenses, more I-formation teams, more men in motion, and more mobile quarterbacks throwing from different places. Since all those things were already true of the Chiefs, headline writers had Stram annointing his team, "The Offense of the Seventies."

There is a lot of hard-headed machismo built into football. It has surfaced, through the years, in everything from contract negotiations and playing on unhinged knees to the superstitions that all winners established the run and no winner could have a scrambling quarterback. In 1970, it was expected for a quarterback to drop back seven steps and stay there until he finished his job or somebody knocked him down. As Stram saw it, pro football was getting so many quick defensive linemen that a lot of quarterbacks were going to get knocked down if they didn't start moving out of the way.

He was right. Roger Staubach, a third-year scrambler, led the NFL in passing and the Cowboys to the Super Bowl in 1971. The next year, Bear quarterback Bobby Douglass ran for 968 yards. In 1976, the year the NFL's sack rate peaked, the Patriots traded Jim Plunkett so they could play Steve Grogan at quarterback. Grogan ran for 12 touchdowns.

From 1971 through 1979, Staubach, Terry Bradshaw, and Fran Tarkenton—all scramblers—quarterbacked 11 of 18 Super Bowl teams. The last successful quarterback to join the NFL who wasn't a running threat was Vince Ferragamo in 1977.

The running quarterback's goal has changed over the years, from gaining yards to gaining time. Theismann and Joe Montana, the best current quarterbacks on the run, use their skill to avoid being sacked or pressured to throw a high-risk pass. They're rarely intercepted. The longer they can keep running, the harder it is for defenders to keep up with their receivers. "What you're trying to do," says Theismann, "is turn a bad situation into a big play."

X X X X X
O O O O

Quicker than the five-step drop is the no-step drop. The Cowboys have been snapping the ball directly to the pocket since 1975, letting the quarterback begin the play five yards deep. They call it their spread formation. Most places, it's called the shotgun.

At first, the shotgun didn't excite other NFL coaches any more than junk mail. The Cowboys took a lot of ridicule for sticking with a formation that eliminated the run threat, lit the fuse on pass rushers, and gave the center an opportunity to snap the ball into orbit.

Cowboy coach Tom Landry, on the other hand, was amused that other coaches thought they were kidding anybody by lining up normally when they had third-and-nine or trailed by a field goal with 53 seconds to play. Come now. How many defensive ends were going to lay back on their heels, waiting for an off-tackle dive, just because the quarterback had two backs behind him? As Landry explains, he started using the shotgun because, "I couldn't see why, in a third-down situation, you should put your quarterback under center and have him run back seven yards when everybody in the park knew you were going to pass."

These days, teams aren't so leery of letting a defense know they plan to pass. They aren't secretive about sending in a third wide receiver, or a back who hardly ever carries the ball. Nobody's worried anymore about the shotgun letting any cats out of the bag. Teams use it on second down. Mike Ditka, when he left Dallas's staff to coach the Bears in 1982, couldn't wait to use it on first down.

"It seems foolish to me that everyone waits until third down to use the spread formation," Ditka said. "That's when the defense has six defensive backs and its four best pass rushers. Why not run it on first down, when they've got their regular defense in?"

Ditka has had his team run from the shotgun more than other coaches. He treats it as just another formation in a multiple offense, shifting out of it as well as into it.

But resistance to the shotgun remains, mainly because of that infernal snap. Bill Walsh was all for it, going into the 1981 season, when the shotgun's popularity peaked with half the NFL teams using it. San Francisco's first game was at Detroit, in the league's noisiest dome. The center couldn't hear the quarterback from five yards away, he snapped at the wrong time, the ball got loose,

---

"It seems foolish to me that everyone waits until third down to use the spread formation," Ditka said. "That's when the defense has six defensive backs and its four best pass rushers. Why not run it on first down, when they've got their regular defense in?"

Detroit won the game, and Walsh ashcanned the shotgun.

It's not that hard a snap to make or to catch. It isn't supposed to be a bullet. It's supposed to flutter to the quarterback, even end-over-end, so he can catch it as absentmindedly as he would turn on a light switch. If the quarterback concentrates on the ball, he defeats the shotgun's main purpose. He isn't taking advantage of the extra second and a half of reading time Landry says it gives quarterbacks.

That's the advantage. From the shotgun, the quarterback not only can start reading the defense sooner, he has a less obstructed view. By the time the ball reaches him, he might already be able to throw it, especially since the shotgun also puts four or five receivers on the line of scrimmage.

Landry actually began using the shotgun for passing in the

early sixties. It made the blitz easier to detect and to stop. But Don Meredith was his quarterback, and Landry says, "Don never seemed comfortable back there." So Landry rolled up the shotgun and stuck it in a cubbyhole until he dusted it off for Roger Staubach, who had scrambled enough to feel comfortable passing from anywhere.

The timing was three years before the rule changes, but the shotgun laid the groundwork for one of the most controversial developments of the passing era. It was a formation perfectly suited for situation substitution.

Middle Linebackers and Family Doctors
... They're both disappearing in an era of specialization

The Pittsburgh Steelers took a lot of pride in using 20 different defensive players regularly in 1983. They were unique only in their extreme. "Teams are using so many substitutes," Sid Gillman says, "a coach walks up and down the sideline leading an entourage." One member, usually an injured player, tags along just to help the coach keep track of who's in the game and who's out.

Defensive coaches base their substitutions on the offense's substitutions. They don't just sort offensive tendencies into formations. They sort formations into personnel combinations.

Suppose a defense uses three linemen, four linebackers, and four backs on first down. On second-and-eight, the defensive coordinator sees an extra wide receiver come in for the offense. He answers by sending in a back and a lineman for two linebackers.

On third-and-six, a sixth back replaces the second linebacker, and passing-down specialists replace the remaining linebacker, a defensive end, and a safety. But if it's third-and-one, in comes the short-yardage defense with six linemen.

Those four downs alone require seven different backs, five different linebackers, and seven different linemen.

"It doesn't always make the players happy to come out," Chicago coach Mike Ditka says, "but you've got to have your best players on the field in every situation."

The only players who have stayed immune from situation substitution are the quarterback and the interior offensive linemen. "I think it's going to go so far, teams will start changing offensive linemen on long yardage," says Dallas general manager Tex Schramm. "They'll put in their better pass blockers." Already, some offensive linemen practically stand up while awaiting the snap for an obvious passing play.

And why not? It used to be unthinkable for an offensive lineman to even change the direction his toes pointed for his pass-block stance. But what's he hiding now? His team has just sent in three players who can't block a butterfly but can outrun and catch one.

Offenses have blocking backs, running backs, catching backs, and short-yardage running backs. If they're lucky, they have a back who does all four things. They have blocking tight ends, catching tight ends, and short-yardage tight ends who often are actually reserve tackles. They have wide receivers who play primarily for their blocking. They can make frequent use of as many as four different tight ends, four backs, and four wide receivers, although only five of those 12 can play at once.

Minnesota finished the 1983 season with six wide receivers, six running backs, and four tight ends, devoting nearly one-third of its roster to five positions (partly because of injuries, partly because those positions feed much of the kicking units, and partly because the Vikings had so many different roles). The Vikings had three backs catch more than 40 passes apiece. Eight other NFL teams had backs who didn't start but caught more than 20 passes. The Jets' Bruce Harper and the Redskins' Joe Washington, both nonstarters, caught 48 and 47.

Still, offenses haven't developed the variety of specialists defenses are using, with their ends who only pass rush, their ends who only stop runs, their linebackers who only blitz, their linebackers who only cover receivers, their linebackers who only stop runs, and their backs who hardly ever see runs. San Francisco's Fred Dean and Pittsburgh's Keith Willis ranked second and sixth in NFL sacks in 1983, and neither was a starter.

"You need six or seven good defensive backs," St. Louis coach Jim Hanifan said after drafting four in 1983. "Your middle linebacker may play only 12 snaps a game, and your fifth and sixth backs about 60 percent of the game." Any time injuries deplete a team's collection of defensive backs to even six, it can't use all the pass coverages it would like.

"In college, there was a big status attached to starting," says ex-Bear safety Doug Plank. "But in pro football, so many players are coming in and out, who's to say who's a starter and who's not? Reserves used to be called AYOs—all you others. Even the coaches called them AYOs. But it's just not a big deal anymore if one guy's technically a starter but the other guy is in for 80 percent of the plays."

X X X X X
0 0 0 0

It all started with the nickel defense, which George Allen took from Chicago to Los Angeles to Washington in the sixties and early seventies. Allen replaced a linebacker with a fifth defensive back when he was sure the other team would pass, or when he wanted to coax it into running. With the extra defensive back, a team could double cover both wide receivers and still have a free safety left over.

The way to get around that, offenses learned soon enough, was to bring in a third wide receiver, for either a back or a tight end. The escalation began.

In the middle seventies, the Viking defense would huddle with 13 players. That way, the offense had to call its play without knowing the Vikings' personnel. The Vikings could wait to see if the offense sent in a third wide receiver before deciding which players to keep on the field. The 13-man huddle soon became illegal.

The Cowboys drafted Tony Dorsett in 1977, and he beat out Preston Pearson at halfback. But Pearson was too good a pass catcher to leave on the bench. He played on passing downs. In 1978, he carried the ball 25 times and caught it 47 times. He compared himself with a designated hitter in baseball.

By 1979, the rule change had made pass rushing more difficult. Not everyone could do it. So teams created designated pass rushers. Some were rookies who hadn't learned to play the run, like Houston's Jesse Baker and the Jets' Mark Gastineau. Others were veterans who were less effective if they played every down, like Philadelphia's Claude Humphrey and New England's Tony McGee.

In the AFC, the better passing conference in 1979, Kansas City was the only team to keep its defense intact in nearly all situations. Some of the other teams changed from three linemen to four for better pass rushes (or vice-versa for better coverage). They all brought in at least one extra defensive back.

In the 1979 playoffs, the Bears and the Rams each used lineups with seven defensive backs. Defensive coaches were deciding the best way to neutralize the offense's new advantage was to confuse it with multiple defenses. Which required extra defensive backs. Which made possible still more coverages.

That cycle has spun to the point where many jobs in the secondary have become too complex for one player. Todd Bell, the Bears' strong safety, is a rarity. Depending on the coverage scheme, he also plays nickelback, cornerback, and outside linebacker. When he was injured for a 1983 game, four different players replaced him in various situations.

Few players are that versatile. Even if they are, their team's defense might not accommodate that versatility. As Pittsburgh's middle linebacker, Jack Lambert used to have to take on centers, cover running backs man-to-man, and tackle from sideline to sideline. Now he's an inside linebacker in the Steelers' 3–4 defense. Inside linebackers often patrol no more than a 10-yard zone.

On one hand, specialization has allowed teams to make the most of ordinary players' strengths. They have better players at each position in any situation than they did when 11 played every down. But the players, as individuals, are not better overall. They're just better at their specific, more limited assignments.

Specialization has made it easier for rookies to play right away. "You're not looking for as complete a player," Giants' general manager George Young says. "Obviously, it takes more time to develop a complete player. But if you're looking for a one-dimensional player, say a linebacker who can rush the passer, you can use him as a blitzer while he's learning to play the run and to cover receivers."

The question is, will the rookie specialist ever round out his other skills in practice, or will he merely get better at the things he already does well? The Bears' Mike Singletary became one of the NFL's few every-down middle linebackers in 1983 because he took it as an insult to be replaced on passing downs and worked on his coverage.

But what about the pass-rushing defensive end? He's already doing the most glamorous and fun thing a defensive end can do. Where's his incentive to take practice time away from pass rushing and learn to play the run? There is a growing concern in the NFL that specialization is draining the league of players who can do all the tasks generally required at their positions, of complete players.

X X X X X
0 0 0 0

To some people, situation substitution represents everything that's wrong with pro football today. It has helped inflate scores— cheapening touchdowns and glorifying 170-pound sprinters at the expense of the hard-nosed, rough-and-tumble linebackers who used to be football's trademark. It has emphasized coaching strategy at the expense of a player's individual resourcefulness. It has contributed to parity, squeezing the distance between the best and worst teams by letting less talented ones play better than the sums of their parts. And it has discouraged those teams from turning out complete players, great players, dominant players. How can a kid say his favorite player is a designated pass rusher?

Yes, pro football has become homogenized. As Mike Singletary says of his childhood idols, "I don't think there will be any more middle linebackers like Butkus or Nitschke. The whole game now is speed and quickness." Greatness, by old standards, is lost in the blur. Teams have become interchangeable components, like television sets. They all look alike.

But so do shopping centers and hotel lobbies, chain drug stores and fast-food restaurants, plastic houseplants and prefab houses. The old country inn was a quaint place to spend a night, but more people prefer the security of a Holiday Inn that will be the same in Omaha as it was in Memphis. What people really want is some old-fashioned ambience encasing their modern efficiency, like a wooden telephone with push buttons. But most things are not telephones.

When we iron out risks, some of life's color runs to gray. Sports were supposed to be exempt from such mundane verities, a respite from suffocating efficiency. It angers people to find out they're not, to find the middle linebacker has disappeared right along with soda counters, front porch swings, local beers, and doctors who make house calls.

Specialization has made football players more expendable than ever, but there always has been a tendency for team owners to view them as disposable bodies, worth not even a dime at the grocery store after they're used up. When a player is injured during practice, the team does not wait reverently for him to be carried from the field. It moves over a few yards, to avoid stepping on him, and continues practicing. There's no time for sentiment with 150 formations to prepare for. But there was no time for sentiment 20 years ago, either, when a replacement could be hired for $18,500.

The game is different, not worse. Players have grown bigger, faster, and stronger; coaches have become more imaginative.

Sure, the touchdown has been cheapened. So has the paper dollar. And who's to say, the shutout wasn't cheapened when Pittsburgh had five in 1976?

Maybe players aren't as tough as they were in the old days. Or maybe they just hit fewer opponents when they're out of bounds or turned away. Certainly, they're in better condition. The best ones start working out in February. Their bodies are million-dollar investments. They can afford to make football full-time work.

There aren't as many characters. Rick Casares isn't around to put bubble bath in the whirlpool anymore. And Doug Atkins was the last player to circle the practice field wearing a sweat suit and helmet, return to the locker room while his teammates worked out, and later report that he had been breaking in his new helmet. Football players don't laugh so much anymore. But who does?

Are there really fewer stars? Or are they just popping up in different places. Lawrence Taylor, a weak-side linebacker, is the Dick Butkus and Ray Nitschke of his day. When has pro football had an offensive player to match Kellen Winslow? Five running backs rushed for yardage in 1983 that was equivalent to more than 1,000 in a 12-game season. Walter Payton did it for the sixth time, one fewer than Jim Brown in the same number of seasons. John Riggins did it at 34, the second-oldest player ever.

The suspicion persists, though, that the game suffers because players don't have to play every down on offense or defense. Bill Walsh, who has used situation substitution to as good advantage as any coach, suggested after the 1983 season that a rule change should limit teams to one substitution each down, except on kicks. Others agree. They fear the loss of the complete player.

"It used to be a big deal to have different offensive and defensive teams," Schramm recalls of the early free-substitution days. "But when we went to two-platoon football, we developed great receivers and quarterbacks who didn't have to worry about playing defense. We developed great linebackers who didn't have to worry about offense.

"Now we have backs on offense who don't have to worry about being runners. We have nickelbacks who don't have to worry about stopping the run. Obviously, they're going to be better at what they do."

X X X X X
0 0 0 0

The players most frustrated by situation substitution are defensive specialists against the run. For doing their jobs, for leaving the offense in second-and-long, they are rewarded by being replaced.

Most of them are linebackers. It used to be important for a linebacker to have strength for defeating run blocks and quickness for covering passes. But more and more coaches are deciding that passing situations are no place for a linebacker, especially a middle linebacker.

Pro football's most enduring and endearing legends involve linebackers, especially middle linebackers. They have left a distinct mark on the game, often in blood.

Dick Butkus has practically become a common noun. Practically anybody with a wild streak has been called a butkus. The original used to call timeouts at the end of lost-cause games so he could take a few more shots at the center. He once said, jokingly, that he dreamed of heads rolling down stairways. Not incidentally, he was a complete player, ravaging offenses whether they ran or passed, at him or away from him.

Mike Curtis was not Butkus's match as a player, but if you heard someone had tackled a fan on the field or someone had said, "The next writer who asks me if I'm really an animal, I'm going to take a bite out of his arm," you probably would guess he was a middle linebacker. Same with Tim Rossovich, who amused himself off the field by eating glass or setting his hair on fire.

Jack Reynolds has been nicknamed "Hacksaw" ever since he cut a car in half after a particularly dispiriting defeat in college. Lambert has been characterized as enjoying a drink of warm blood now and then. "The Violent World of Sam Huff" was a documentary that did as much as anything to acquaint television audiences with pro football.

If he played today, how violent could Huff's world be on passing downs? He probably would come out of the game. There's the problem. Middle linebackers can't leave much of a mark on football from the bench. It pains a veteran fan to look at today's substituting and think of Butkus, Huff, Nitschke, and Joe Schmidt as situation players.

But specialization has had less to do with the obsolescence of middle linebackers than the 3–4 defense. The NFL had only seven middle linebackers in 1983. Dallas, Detroit, Atlanta, Chicago, St. Louis, Washington, and the New York Jets were the only teams playing a 4–3 defense. Lambert and Reynolds, were inside linebackers. If anything should be made illegal to save middle linebackers, ban the 3–4.

Until that happens, look to the weak-side linebacker, usually on the right side, for the new defensive heroes. That's where you'll find Taylor, the Colts' Vernon Maxwell, and the Buccaneers' Hugh Green—all rookies since 1981 and all what the coaches call impact players. Green doesn't even blitz much, but he forces turnovers and makes as many tackles on the far side of the field as he does on his own side.

They don't come out of the game for passes. They're complete players. Situation substitution isn't looting pro football of complete players as much as it's making a place for those who aren't. The complete players, like Singletary and Gastineau, will use their early situation roles as a springboard for full-time play. Any coach who isn't encouraging that doesn't deserve to have complete players.

X X X X X
0 0 0 0

Just as passing yardage has reached a plateau, the heavy traffic in substituting will reach a saturation point. Most likely, it already has. Offenses have played without huddles to keep defenses from substituting, and they're liable to do it more.

"Mainly, it keeps the other team's nickelbacks off the field," Steve DeBerg said after his Denver team had run no-huddle plays in 1983. It also can keep the defense's passing specialists *on* the field, if that suits the offense's purpose.

A less radical way to confound multiple defenses is to huddle and change formations normally, but snap the ball immediately after the final shift. Minnesota does that a lot. It lets the defense make its substitutions, but the substitutes might barely be on the field, let alone in the right places, when the ball is snapped.

The more a team substitutes, the more it risks confusing itself. That's why a team calls timeouts at the unlikeliest times. Maybe one of the substitutes didn't hear his unit called, leaving 10 men on the field. Maybe the substitutes got in, but they were the wrong bunch for matching the other team's late substitutions. Maybe the right bunch got in but lined up the wrong way.

An especially galling effect of specialized pass defenses has been the running plays they invite on third-and-eight. But that could be the first step toward running wholesale substitution back out of the game. Eric Dickerson runs for first downs against six defensive backs on third-and-eight. As Walsh predicted back in 1980, "Situation substitution will be in vogue until somebody develops a tremendous running game that can beat it."

The Sky Has Limits

... The more teams pass,
the more valuable they make the run

The one sure way to tame an opponent's passing game always has been to keep the opponent from passing. Six-back defenses can do that by making the run more attractive. But the best way to keep a team from passing the ball is to keep it from *having* the ball.

Here's what happens to a great passing team when its opponent controls the ball. It has fewer opportunities to be a great offense. It falls behind. It may grow frustrated, perhaps start pressing and throwing interceptions. Even if it keeps its cool, sooner or later the clock winds down and it *has* to pass. The great passing team became a great passing team by passing when it wasn't necessary, not by passing when the other guys' defensive linemen didn't have to worry about looking for the run. Forced to pass, the great passing team may not look so great anymore.

Look at what happened to San Diego in a 1981 game that was no more a lock than the Christians had on the Lions. The Chargers were 5–2, averaging 34 points a game; the Bears were 1–6 and averaging 15 points. The Bears controlled the ball for 48:50 of a game that went 9:30 into overtime. They had 100 offensive plays, 61 of them runs. Dan Fouts, obviously pressing, completed just 30 percent of his passes and threw two interceptions. The Chargers lost 20–17. The Bear defense had something to do with stopping the Chargers, too, but as Buddy Ryan says, "A running back and a punter are the two best friends a defense can have."

Giving the ball to a great running back is still the best way to control it. His plays use up more time than the best ball-control, passing game, and they run fewer risks. When San Diego collapsed surprisingly to a 6–10 record in 1983, it was mainly because Charger opponents had learned they could beat them by running.

Two of the first three teams to play the Chargers, the New York Jets with Freeman McNeil and the Seattle Seahawks with Curt Warner, carried the ball 51 and 56 times. They both won. The Chargers went on to lead the NFL in total yardage and passing yardage, but they lost five games when they scored no more than 14 points, a figure they had cleared in 56 of 58 previous games. In those five games, the opponents ran the ball 39, 43, 40, 37, and 36 times. In San Diego's six victories, its opponents averaged 25 running plays, with a high of 31.

The same thing happened to Green Bay, which finished a disappointing 8–8 despite ranking second in both total yards and passing yards. The Packers lost three games when they scored 14 or less, and their opponents had 45, 42, and 49 running plays.

The third-ranked team in total offense was Washington. The Redskins' yards translated to points. They never scored fewer than 23. They also led the league in defense against the run.

"I firmly believe that football kind of goes in cycles. It's like anything else. Wide ties keep coming back again. So will the running game."—**Archie Manning**, then New Orleans' quarterback, in 1980.

The main thing a ball-control offense can give a defense is rest. That helps two ways, most obviously by keeping defensive players from getting tired. But also, it helps in case the defense needs to change its plans to stop an unexpected offensive tactic, whether it's a play or a blocking scheme the offense is using on several plays.

"If the other team's offense has had a long drive," says San Diego defensive coordinator Tom Bass, "obviously, you want to make some changes. But if your offense doesn't make a first down, you don't have time. You have to go back on the field without being as prepared as you'd like."

X X X X X
O O O O

Inevitably, pro football's unleashed pass catchers have led the game back to the running backs. From 1978 through 1982, the pass accounted for a greater percentage of both plays and yards

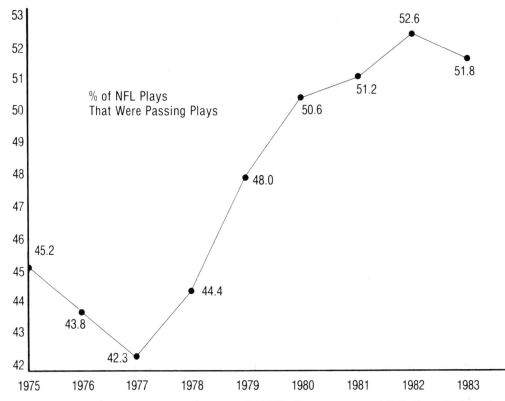

% of NFL Plays
That Were Passing Plays

45.2
43.8
42.3
44.4
48.0
50.6
51.2
52.6
51.8

1975   1976   1977   1978   1979   1980   1981   1982   1983

After steadily rising to more than 50 percent in 1982, the percentage of NFL plays that went to the air appeared to have peaked when it dropped slightly in 1983.

in the NFL each year. As the graph above and the graph on page 87 show, that trend stopped in 1983.

Handing the ball off was bound to become acceptable behavior again, and not just because it helps keep the other team from passing. The less teams ran, the more valuable a good running game became. Where it once was considered resourceful to pass on running downs, it has become resourceful to run on passing downs. Teams did that so often in 1983 that play-action passes were not uncommon on third down, and play-action passes are useful only when the defense is expecting a run.

More than anything, though, the run is coming back into vogue because defenses have become so preoccupied with the pass.

A common misconception is that a defense stops the run with its linemen and the pass with its backs. It's the other way around. "Your linemen stop the pass," says Ryan, "and your backs and linebackers stop the run." Linemen rarely are among a defense's tackling leaders. They plug the running lanes, but usually they funnel the ball carrier into a linebacker or a safety, who makes the tackle.

Specialized pass defenses don't have many linebackers to make those tackles. They have people who can cover receivers instead.

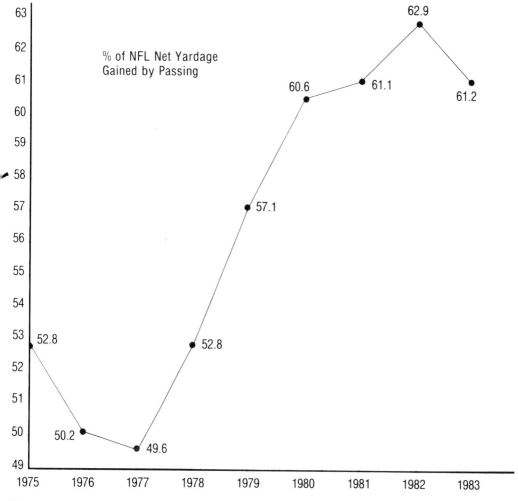

% of NFL Net Yardage
Gained by Passing

The percentage of NFL yardage gained by passing has followed much the same pattern.

So they not only encourage the offense to run, they discourage
the pass. On second-and-ten, against pass-rushing linemen and six
defensive backs, the team that selects a running play is liable to
be facing third-and-six instead of third-and-ten. It's a lot easier to
pass for six yards on third down than it is to pass for ten.

Even the defenses whose nickelbacks can tackle have geared
themselves to stopping the pass better than the run. It starts in
practice. A passing game, remember, takes more practice time
than a running game. Teams have longer practices than they did
in the days when the pass was considered a necessary evil, but
there's a limit to how long a team can practice without wearing
itself out. The total practice time hasn't always increased as much
as the entire time the offense needs for polishing its passing game.
Which leaves the defense with less practice time. In that limited
time, Ryan says, "The pass has got to take priority over run
preparation. The pass can beat you faster."

Defensive players use different techniques on run plays than on pass plays. For example, linemen want to avoid blockers if they are rushing the passer. But the lineman who does that on a running play might be taking himself out of position to make a tackle, or even to funnel the ball carrier toward a teammate.

Defenses also deploy their people differently on runs than on passes. Defensive linemen might make their initial charge at an angle that makes them difficult to pass block but easy to block for a run. The linebacker who arranges his feet for quick pass coverage might also be making himself easier to block.

So the right thing to do for stopping a pass might be the wrong thing to do for stopping a run. Which is precisely the thing a lot of defensive players are doing when someone runs for a first down on third-and-five.

The one-back offense also has helped the run. Some coaches say it creates better running lanes. And it can create even more of them from passing formations that scatter the defense across the field.

Besides, as Sid Gillman says, "Most teams don't have more than one good back anyway." From one-back formations, the one good back is the only one who carries the ball. The NFL had 16 backs run for 1,000 yards in 1983, the most ever.

Just as teams pass better as they pass more often in a season, the best backs run better as they run more often in a game. John Riggins was just one of many very good backs until the Redskins started giving him the ball 30 times a game in the 1982 playoffs. Since then, he has been a great back, and he has been his greatest in the fourth quarter. That was when he broke open the Super Bowl against Miami.

Running backs, more than other football players, rely on an instinctive feel for avoiding tacklers. They have no time for anything else. As the Raiders' Marcus Allen says, "I never stop to think about what to do. A lot of times, I don't know what I'm doing out there. I just let my instincts take over." That's why it's so hard to coach a back to greatness. That's also why the same running play that gained five yards on three tries in the first half can start going for eight or ten yards a pop late in the third quarter.

The smart offensive coach won't forget about a running play just because it didn't gain big yardage the first couple of times. Maybe the back missed a hole he'll be looking for next time. Maybe the guard just missed his block. The smart offensive coach will come back to a running play unless the defense has shown it has the play covered.

Striking Back

... Aggressive defenses join in the scoring fun

The excitement of all these 84-yard touchdown passes and 420-yard passing games and 42–38 scores in recent years is, naturally, lost on defenses. Defensive coaches will agree the game sure has gotten more exciting since the mid-seventies, but earthquakes are exciting, too. That doesn't make them fun.

Defensive units had enjoyed those 10–6 games. Those were the days. They ruled the NFL then. By the early eighties, defense was to the NFL as the free press was to the Soviet Union. It didn't really exist, as we know it, but something that looked like it was trotted out for the public's benefit, to make everything look on the up and up.

The defenses never were willing foils for the passing game. The day the rules were changed, coaches began tinkering with coverages and pass rushes, looking for a formula that would make the defense's presence felt. They finally hit on it in 1983.

Now, great defense may not be the first thing that leaps to your mind when you look at what went on around the NFL in 1983. The league had its highest and third-highest scoring weekends ever. Green Bay's 48–47 victory over Washington was the highest scoring Monday night game ever. Seattle beat Kansas City 51–48 in the third-highest scoring game played any day or night. Green Bay set a record with 49 points in the first half against Tampa Bay. The average score for a team was up from 20.7 in 1981 to 21.9, the highest since the NFL–AFL merger in 1970. And so on. At first glance, this wouldn't seem to indicate a defensive resurgence any more than the Grand Canyon shows the beauty of strip mining.

But defenses had more to do with the scoring upsurge than offenses. Really. Offenses had ridden the new rules about as far as they could take them. The change in 1983 was that defenses quit playing the stooge, quit letting offenses slap them around and hoping it wouldn't hurt much. They started to slap back. They mixed enough coverages to mix up the most experienced quarterbacks and receivers. They unleashed all-out pass rushes that made the passing pocket look like the first door to open at a Michael Jackson concert.

"We're not waiting for things to happen anymore," defensive end Ed "Too Tall" Jones said. "We're making them happen."

Sometimes they made interceptions, sacks, and fumbles happen. When they did that, defenses either scored themselves or set up easy scores for their offensive teammates.

Sometimes the aggressiveness backfired. A blitz-depleted secondary is easy pickings for the quarterback who manages to get the ball downfield. A lot of long touchdowns happen that way.

But either way, by forcing the action, defenses forced scores still higher.

"That's a good point," Bill Walsh said. "In our case, we blitzed a lot. We made a lot of defensive touchdowns on big plays. On the other hand, we've been hurt defensively by big plays. So I think the game is more an attacking game both offensively and defensively."

Walsh's 49ers were near the middle of the NFL rankings in touchdown passes allowed. But they tied for second in sacks, tied for first in return plays for touchdowns, and went to the NFC championship game.

The essence of the game has gone from making fewer mistakes than your opponent to forcing the other guy to make more mistakes than you.

Washington made its share of mistakes on defense. Only two NFL teams gave up more touchdown passes than the Redskins. But they also ranked first in interceptions and seventh in sacks and became the NFC's first-ever 14-game winner.

After sacks and interceptions had dropped steadily for four seasons, both of them were up noticeably from 1981 to 1983, sacks by nearly 20 percent. (It's hard to fit the 1982 season into a trend because the eight-week players' strike was most likely to hurt passing offenses, which require the most precision timing.) Defenses also were making the biggest plays they can make. Interceptions returned for touchdowns, a figure that had rarely varied, leaped by more than 60 percent, as the graph on page 92

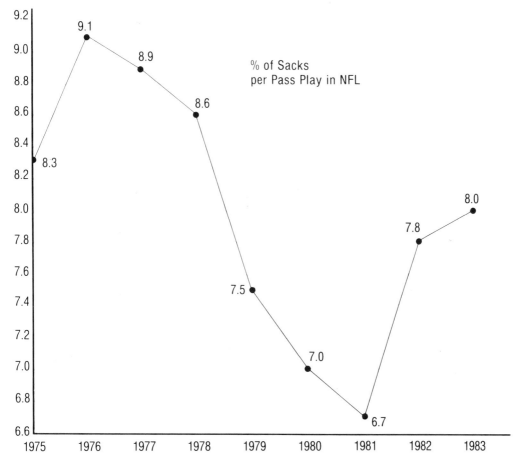

% of Sacks
per Pass Play in NFL

After a steady decline in sacks from 1976 through 1981, NFL defenses have put more emphasis on getting to the quarterback. Taking more chances, they increased the rate of sacks in 1982 and again in 1983.

shows. Pittsburgh, which had never scored more than two defensive touchdowns in 14 seasons under Chuck Noll, scored seven.

When Green Bay scored 49 points in one half, three of the seven touchdowns came on returns of a punt, an interception, and a fumble. The Packer offense just watched them. Two others were touchdown passes for 75 and 57 yards. Aggressive defenses help make that kind of thing happen, too.

If you keep rolling the dice, sometimes they come up sixes. But at least defenses were no longer sitting around with their thumbs in Christmas pies, waiting to see who they would have to tackle next. There may have been more high-scoring games in 1983, but there also were more low-scoring games, as the chart on page 93 shows. The increase in bad defensive games, shown in Chapter 4, was nothing new, and it was a small price to pay for an increase in *good* defense.

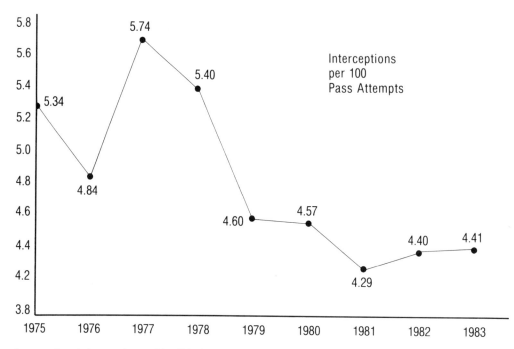

Aggressive defense also paid off in interceptions, which began increasing again after a steady decline from 1977 through 1981.

Those interceptions had an inordinate effect on the defenses' joining in on the scoring increase. Look at the sharp rise in interceptions returned for touchdowns after 1981.

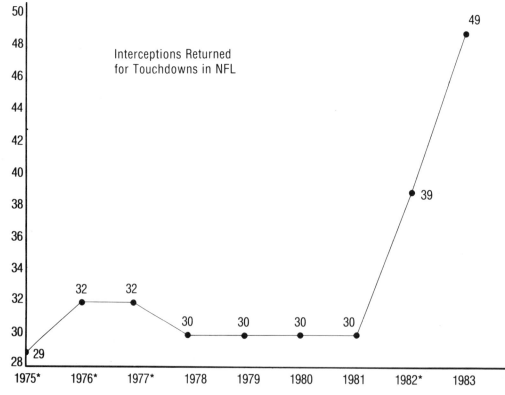

*Actual figures for shorter seasons in 1975 (25), 1976 (28), 1977 (28), and (1982) (22) are projected to 16-game season played in other years. Each team played 14 games in 1975, 1976, and 1977; 9 in 1982.

	1981	1983
Games when winning team scored 17 points or less	35	40
Games when winning team scored 14 points or less	15	20
Games when losing team scored less than 7 points	21	27
Shutouts	9	10

The 1983 NFL season was hardly memorable for its titanic defensive struggles, but they were coming back.

Once the other team has the ball, there are two ways to stop the pass. One is to knock the ball down before it reaches a receiver. The other is to knock the quarterback down before he throws the ball.

A defense tries to do both, of course, but it can't stress coverage without hurting the rush, or vice-versa. The linebacker who blitzes can't cover a receiver.

Pass coverage and pass rushing aren't independent of each other. Tight pass coverage can keep the quarterback waiting long enough for the rush to level him, and a strong rush can hurry him into throwing an interception or incompletion. But any defense has to decide whether it's going to try harder to rush the quarterback or cover the receivers, or whether it's going to go down the middle with four pass rushers and seven-man coverage.

The classic position NFL defensive coaches have taken is to rush as many people as it takes to make the quarterback dance. The rush is more apt to help the coverage than the other way around. Besides, give the receivers enough time downfield and one of them is going to get open.

But when the rules changed in 1978, defensive coaches generally worried more about the pass blockers' new help. They were afraid they weren't going to be able to plow through all those straight elbows and open hands, no matter how many men they sent. In that case, it made sense to cover with eight instead of wasting players in futile chase of the quarterback. Make him aim well, if nothing else. (As Chicago's Buddy Ryan said after a 1982 game when the Rams' Vince Ferragamo frisked his defense for 509 yards passing, second most ever in the NFL, "We might as well have sent one guy and dropped ten off for all the pressure we were giving him.")

Ryan, coincidentally, was among the minority of defensive coaches who never veered from stressing the rush after the rule changes. Most of them turned their energies to confounding quarterbacks with downfield labyrinths.

There was some sporadic blitzing, which the Steelers and the

Rams pretty much ended when they took turns ransacking each other's blitz defenses in the Super Bowl after the 1979 season. Multiple coverages started right away, too. And receivers still took a lot of hits in the legal five-yard area at the line of scrimmage. "Don't let them get downfield to that five-yard marker," was how San Diego cornerback Willie Buchanon put it. But the predominant defensive trend in 1978 and 1979 was eight-man coverage.

For a while, it looked so stifling, Chicago general manager Jim Finks said, "I think we'll see a day when the defense has to have a minimum number of players on the line of scrimmage. Perhaps a maximum number who can drop off. Against that eight-man secondary, by the mere limitations of the field, it's difficult to complete anything but little dump passes." In 1980, for the first time, both Super Bowl teams played with three defensive linemen.

One of the model teams for eight-man coverage was Tampa Bay, which turned some heads by climbing from 5–11 to 10–6 and the NFC championship game in 1979. The Buccaneers hardly ever rushed more than three. They led the league in total defense and pass defense. What people forgot to notice, though, was the Bucs' three-man rush put ample pressure on the quarterback because Lee Roy Selmon was one of the three. Against teams

---

Former Minnesota Viking coach **Bud Grant** on the changing role of defenses:

"To be effective defensively, you have to recognize that you no longer can keep the offense from throwing and catching the ball, but that you can minimize the damage that throwing and catching can do. Maybe we can't stop you, but perhaps we can force you to do a few things a little more quickly than you want to.

"It's just like the evolution of basketball, where they can't stop the other guy from shooting or making baskets because they play so well and shoot so well, but what you try to do is make him shoot from two feet farther out. Then, if you're fortunate, his percentage will drop from 60 percent to around 40 percent or 45 percent and you've got a chance to outscore him."

---

with less gifted ends, offenses learned to appreciate the advantage of giving the quarterback enough time in the pocket to set a table for four. Before long, they were devouring eight-man coverage as insatiably as they were putting away anything else the defenses cared to offer.

One fact remained. The only sure way to stop the big pass was to stop the big passer.

So eventually, as Denver defensive line coach Stan Jones puts it: "Somebody put all the things together and figured out that the difference between winning and losing is to make the offense make mistakes. Force the fumbles, or the interceptions, or the sacks. The teams that have the biggest plays, or the most big plays, usually win.

"For years, we did well with a three-man rush, until about '77. It protected-you from the long bomb. But now the thinking is more to create problems for the offense. You're seeing more blitzing, teams coming with everything. That's really the way to get to the guy."

Or as Brian Sipe puts it, from a quarterback's viewpoint, "It's like defenses threw their arms up in the air and said, 'We can't cover it. Let's go get the quarterback.' "

The blitz is less risky than it used to be, if only because offenses are making big plays even against saturation coverage. So you're going from, say, a 10 percent big-play risk to 20 percent, instead of from near zero to 20 percent. Besides, specialization has reduced the risk of the blitz. It's most common from a nickel or six-back defense. The blitzing specialist is more likely to get to the quarterback, and the coverage specialists are more likely to stay with their receivers man-to-man.

Defenses have reduced the risks further simply by learning more about the relatively new offensive habits. "I think they're finally figuring out the formations, who has to be staying in to block and who doesn't," Chicago's Mike Ditka says.

The most important revelation for defenses may have been to accept that their role isn't what it used to be.

"There was a time," says Bud Grant, "when you could win just with defense, when the defense could shut down a team to the point it became frustrating. You couldn't run, you couldn't pass, you just couldn't figure out a way to move the ball. But now the defense can't really shut the other guy down. The defense is just out there to try to minimize the effectiveness of the offense. We're putting pressure on the quarterback not with the idea that we're going to come up with eight or ten sacks a game, although we've had a couple in that area, but more to pressure them to throw quicker passes."

If the defense makes the quarterback throw in two seconds on a three-second pattern, it takes the offense's play away. If it tackles the quarterback often enough, or draws enough holding penalties, Ditka says, "You break up the spontaneity of the offense. Then it's hard to have a consistent offense no matter how many yards you get." Ditka knew that from painful experience. It was the reason the Bears ranked sixth in yardage in 1983 but just 20th in scoring.

Dallas has always been known for its structured defense. The Cowboys didn't want even one player taking his own initiative. They were afraid he would open a door for the offense. But they softened that hard line in 1983, so right linebacker Anthony Dickerson was able to blitz on his own in the last two minutes of a game the Cowboys trailed by one point. Dickerson tackled Saints quarterback Kenny Stabler in the end zone and Dallas won by a point.

Blitzing is a fairly routine chore for someone like Lawrence Taylor. The Giants' weak-side linebacker was a pass-rushing terror as a college defensive end. He's 6'3", 237 pounds, and fast enough not only to cover pass receivers, but to drag them down from behind on plays when he has blitzed. It doesn't matter if the offense knows Taylor is coming. He has even been known to wink at quarterbacks. "When Lawrence is pass rushing, it's like a cop putting sirens on top of his car," teammate Beasley Reece said when Taylor was a rookie.

For a blitzer who neglected to grow as big or as fast as Taylor, there's some value to discretion. Sometimes he'll creep up toward the line to let the offense know he's coming, but sometimes he'd rather stay back at his linebacker or safety spot and time his rush with the snap. If he charges too soon, he might drop back again and hope the offense thinks he's faking a blitz.

Sometimes a blitzer will even wait a step after the snap. That might give the back responsible for blitz protection time to decide it's safe to run his pass route. It might coax the hot receiver downfield on his planned route, so the quarterback won't have a quick outlet receiver. Blitzers even have been known to hide behind the umpire (the official in the defensive secondary), so they seem to materialize from nowhere.

It can be awfully fun, though, to give advance warning of an all-out blitz. Say, eight men coming. "I love to see the looks on offensive players' faces when they see *everybody's* coming," says Doug Plank, who blitzed often as a Chicago safety. "That's one of the few times a defense is actually calling the play." It has to be a quick pass.

On a less ambitious blitz, sending just a fifth pass rusher, the idea is either to spring someone free or to get one-on-one blocking for all the rushers. The blitzer doesn't have to reach the quarterback for a blitz to work. It's just as effective if the defensive tackle gets there because the blocker who would have double-teamed him had to pick up the blitzer.

The skill in blitzing comes when the blitzer is between the line and the quarterback. It helps to know who's assigned to block him. If the backs run pass routes, he can assume it will be an uncovered lineman (the center against a conventional 4–3 defense or a guard against a 3–4). Then it's often a race to the quarterback. A back won't usually block as well as an uncovered lineman, but he's in a better position. The blitzer wants to know whether the back is apt to block him at the chest or the knees, which he can learn by watching film.

Even if he has passed a blocker, the blitzer can't give in to the temptation to let his mind start whistling, "Oh boy, oh boy, oh boy, I'm free." Some of the most spine-tingling game film footage involves a guard's outstretched forearm and an unsuspecting blitzer's forehead. And the job isn't done just because the quarterback is in reach. Many a quarterback has ducked under the arms of a blitzer who forgot to tackle at waist level.

The problem is, there's no way to practice blitzing. It's entirely different at full speed.

Teams do practice the flip side of blitzing, the undermanned coverage. That doesn't make the experience any more pleasant for those in the secondary who get left behind. Most, if not all of them, are covering receivers one-on-one, even the wide-outs. Their margin for error isn't much bigger than a dentist's. "Those guys are depending on you to get to the quarterback fast," Plank says.

Blitzing the run, which is common but less spectacular than pass blitzing, follows much the same principle: Give up the security of some deep players for the chance to make a quick tackle. A full, run blitz is a gap defense. The defense tries to fill every hole.

There are 10 holes. If the blocking is right, and one hole goes unfilled, there aren't a lot of defensive players left over to clutter up the field past that hole.

Whether the blitz is for a run or a pass, it has to be tailored to the offensive team's blocking scheme. That's why defenses don't necessarily blitz young quarterbacks. It won't do any good if the blockers can keep the blitzers at bay.

As Ditka pointed out, defensive coaches have begun solving the latest blitz-protection schemes, which had tended toward zone blocking: each blocker responsible for an area instead of a particular player. Now it's the offensive coaches' turn to adapt their blocking. They'll do it. They always have. "In every 10 years," Walsh has said, "you're going to get two periods of heavy blitzing."

Meet Me at the Quarterback

... Pass rushers keep moving the starting blocks so they'll reach the finish line

One advantage of blitzing is to make the blockers have to guess where the blockees are coming from. It's sneaky. That element of cat burglary has not always elevated blitzing to the highest level of esteem within the pro football fraternity. Real football teams don't need to blitz. Real football teams take people on, man-to-man.

It's true that coaches would rather not resort to blitzing. "You'd never blitz or stunt if every lineman could physically beat his man," says Neill Armstrong, an assistant coach at Dallas who was Minnesota's defensive coordinator when Alan Page, Carl Eller, Gary Larsen, and Jim Marshall were physically beating their men like cake batter, down after down. Armstrong recalls games when the Vikings lined up in a straight 4–3 defense every play. They didn't need to confuse anybody. The extent of their creative pass-rush scheming was to make sure Page, Eller, Larsen, and Marshall made the team bus.

"That was when you could just sit back and watch," Armstrong says. That was also when defensive linemen were allowed to hit pass blockers in the head and pass blockers had to keep their elbows bent and hands closed.

There were no defensive linemen dancing and whooping over fallen quarterbacks. The sack wasn't so uncommon. It almost would have been more appropriate for an offensive tackle to twirl his arms and do a jig whenever the quarterback got the ball downfield. The best pass rushers made the sack look easy, as though it were something they could pick up at the corner convenience store. ("I'll have a dozen eggs, a gallon of milk, and two quarterback sacks, please.")

But the game has changed. The rulemakers have given pass blockers hands. Where the pass-rush lanes once were guarded by a swinging gate, now the rush men have to contend with deadbolt locks, key card systems, and attack dogs. No wonder they're tempted to sneak through the side window with a blitzing safety.

Defenses use blitzes to confuse opponents, just as offenses use men in motion before the snap. Either way, the opponent doesn't know where the danger is coming from. A defense can send men in motion, too. They don't go far, but linemen and linebackers can hop around, and they can wind up anywhere. They can gang up on one side of the offensive line. They can trade places after the snap, in a stunt. The best pass rusher might line up outside the offensive right tackle on one down and over the left guard on the next.

The traditional advantages of a blitz are to confuse the blockers, to outnumber them at a particular point, and to clutter up the opposing offense's practice time with an extra problem to work on. But those advantages can be enjoyed without making pass coverage such an adventure in an undermanned secondary, as defensive coaches are finding out all the time. They use stunts. They change their fronts, which are the alignments of the linemen. And from the 3–4, they can blitz a linebacker without really blitzing; they still have seven men for coverage.

Houston was one of the first NFL teams to gain notoriety for a designated blitzer, using 6'4", 245-pound outside linebacker Robert Brazile as early as 1975. But Brazile rarely moved from the left side, which usually was the strong side. The Oilers wanted him there for run support. For a weak-side blitz, unencumbered by the offense's tight end, the Oilers had to send their right linebacker.

The notion of moving a strong-side linebacker to a more advantageous blitzing lane didn't catch on until the 1980 Raiders won the Super Bowl with Ted Hendricks popping up here, there, and anywhere like some video game target. The next season, Lawrence Taylor popularized the weak-side blitzing linebacker, and the 49ers won the Super Bowl with defensive end Fred Dean rushing from different spots, proving defensive linemen didn't have to be anchored to their conventional positions either. In 1982, Miami caught the NFL's attention by going to the Super Bowl with an *inside* linebacker, A. J. Duhe, who was liable to turn up at any line or linebacker position except nose tackle. Duhe made the AFC championship victory a monument to his flexibility. When the Chargers drafted Billy Ray Smith, Jr., early in the next draft, they said they planned to use him the same way Miami used Duhe.

Those versatile pass rushers (and such other weak-side linebackers as Hugh Green and Vernon Maxwell, and movable defensive ends like Seattle's Jacob Green and Chicago's Al Harris) have one thing in common. They were undersized college linemen, many of whom stood up instead of lining up in a three-point stance. It wasn't long ago that scouts would have classified them as "Tweeners," falling between the criterion size and speed figures for linebacker and defensive end, and coaches would have worried about where to fit them into the lineup. Now they're the quick pass rushers (and in the linebackers' case, field rovers) that every team is looking for.

X X X X X
O O O O

Pro football's rage for speed and quickness, most obvious downfield, has filtered into the pits. It prompted 290-pound Dan Dierdorf, after six Pro Bowls in his 11 seasons as a Cardinal offensive tackle, to become a center in 1982.

"The way you play tackle has changed," Dierdorf said. "Speed is more important now than strength. Those defensive ends line up two or three yards wide and it's now a sprint to the quarterback."

Speed became important for offensive linemen because it became almost necessary for defensive linemen. Sure, the pass blockers could hold them. But they couldn't hold what they couldn't catch. Kansas City's defensive ends in 1983 were Mike Bell at 245 pounds and Art Still at 238, both streamlined by about 15 pounds. At Dallas, defensive tackles John Dutton and Randy White dropped their weights from 280 to 260 and 272 to the high 240s.

Detroit drafted Mike Cofer, a 235-pound college defensive end with the prototype build for a weak-side 3–4 linebacker. But the Lions, with a 4–3 defense, had no use for a weak-side 3–4 linebacker. Cofer finished his rookie season, 1983, starting at right defensive end.

"It seems like every year, this game gets quicker," says Keith Willis, Pittsburgh's 6'1", 251-pound defensive end who had 14 sacks as a part-time player in 1983.

The Steelers are a good team for charting the relative importance of speed and strength in pass rushing. Their Steel Curtain ruled the NFL when pass rushers could muscle their way into the backfield. But the game changed before the Steelers' defensive line did. In 1980, they were last in the league with 18 sacks and missed the playoffs for the first time in nine years. Since then, the Steelers have added faster defensive linemen every year. Their sack ranking has climbed to ninth, second, and seventh, their total up more than two a game from 1980 to 1983.

The Steelers also changed from rushing four linemen to rushing three linemen and a mystery linebacker. In 1982, they used a variation of the three-man line on most passing downs. It was a five-man line. They had two undersized college-ends-turned-pro-linebackers, Robin Cole and Bob Kohrs, so they put them both on the line on passing downs, kept them standing and sent in one of them. The offense could never be sure which one.

The current five-man lines are passing defenses, unlike the old five-man lines that were common until it became apparent in the early fifties that one lineman would have to drop off to cover short passes in the middle. The difference is that five-man lines in the eighties usually have five or six defensive backs behind them and that their faster ends are hybrid linebackers.

Even a conventional down lineman at the end of a five-man line is often responsible for spying a running back, checking if he runs a pass route and following him if he does. That's what Dallas's Too Tall Jones was doing when he intercepted a pass downfield against the Raiders in a 1983 Sunday night game. Al Harris has

"If you think you're going to line up four defensive linemen these days and get to the quarterback, you're wrong. You've got to have either an overpowering player or a gimmick if you're going to get to the quarterback."—**Chuck Studley**, Miami Dolphins defensive coordinator

found himself matching strides with James Lofton in the Bears' five-lineman defense, although only in a short zone.

The Bears began using their five-man line in 1978, when Armstrong became their head coach and Buddy Ryan their defensive coordinator. They played it virtually the whole game when they upset San Diego in 1981. That caught some eyes. Later that season, Cincinnati beat San Diego with a five-man line. It can work for either a 4–3 team or a 3–4 team.

So far, five-man lines haven't exactly spread through the NFL like a hot trade rumor. Not every team has a Too Tall Jones who can sack the quarterback one play and intercept a pass downfield the next. But with offenses using more double tight ends and running more on passing downs, it still might.

The five-man line is a pass defense that is stronger against the run than a nickel defense. Where the nickel beefs up coverage, the five-man line strengthens the rush. It assumes, correctly, that defensive linemen (including linebackers who were college line-men) are better pass rushers than blitzing safeties. But it still has the advantage of not letting the offense know which four (or five or six) players are rushing. Against San Diego, the Bears made Kellen Winslow block more than usual. Teams with single tight ends have found it advisable to keep both backs in for pass protection, limiting them to three pass receivers.

Conventional fronts, with three or four linemen, leave one or two of the offense's interior linemen uncovered. (For run block-ing, the area between the uncovered lineman and the first defen-sive player is called a bubble, connoting a soft spot.) An uncov-ered lineman, without a defensive lineman in front of him, is free to help on a double-team block.

For a defense with a strong inside pass rush, as Dallas and Chicago get from tackles Randy White and Dan Hampton, the five-man line makes a defensive tackle harder to double-team. It still can be done, as the diagrams on page 103 show. But the offense has to assign a lineman to each defensive lineman, even though one probably will not rush. So to double-team one defen-sive lineman, the offense must take a receiver out of its pass pat-tern. The offense has to choose between understaffing either its pass protection or its pass pattern.

X X X X X
O O O O

A less exotic way to make an offense guess where pass rushers will surface is simply to change the front without changing the number of defensive linemen. Fronts can keep changing until the ball is snapped. If that confuses the blockers enough, a pass rusher might run free, slam dunking the quarterback at the end of his fast break.

Even if the offensive linemen properly change their blocking assignments, those assignments may become more demanding. A change in fronts often unbalances the defensive line toward one side or the other and sometimes creates a more favorable matchup. The Raiders like to make a center block Howie Long, their leading sacker and a tackle in their four-man rush line, as they often did in the 1983 playoffs.

When a defensive line shifts toward the offense's strong side, it is overshifting. A shift to the weak side is an undershift. The diagrams on pages 104–105 show how defenses shift to their basic overs and unders.

Stunts have been pass-rushing tactics as long as there have been passers to rush. In the typical stunt, defensive linemen simply cross paths instead of rushing straight ahead. The hope is that maybe their blockers will lose track of one of them, or run

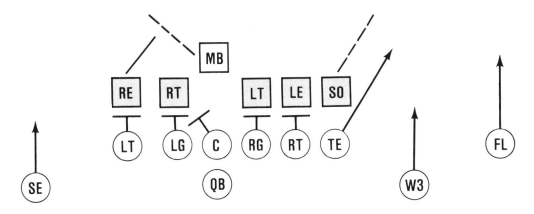

To double-team the defensive right tackle in this conventional nickel defense (with the linemen shaded and the five backs not shown), an offense merely uses its uncovered lineman, the center. It still has four pass receivers, even if the back stays in for blitz protection.

C	center	QB	quarterback
FL	flanker	RE	right end
LE	left end	RG	right guard
LG	left guard	RT	right tackle
LT	left tackle	SE	split end
MB	middle linebacker	SO	strong-side outside linebacker
NT	nose tackle	W3	third wide receiver

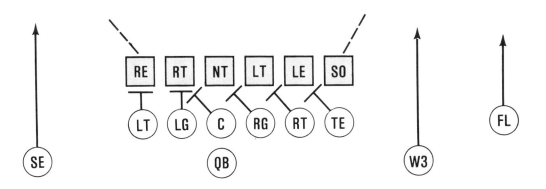

But to double-team the same defensive tackle in a five-man line (with the linemen shaded and the five backs not shown), the offense must keep one of its receivers out of the pattern. It cannot assume the defensive right end is dropping into pass coverage.

The defensive right end's responsibility depends on what the back does. The back probably will drift toward a sideline as an outlet receiver if nobody is blitzing, and the end will stay in coverage. But if the back stays in pass protection, the end could join the pass rush.

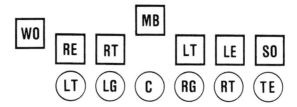

This is a basic 4–3 defense with WO being the weak-side linebacker, MB being the middle linebacker, and SO being the strong-side linebacker.

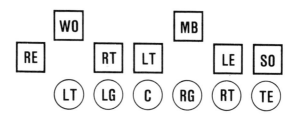

With the same personnel, the even 4–3 can have an odd front, meaning it has a man over the center. This under front unbalances the defensive line toward the weak side, with bubbles over the weak-side tackle and strong-side guard.

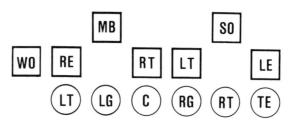

Or, the odd front can be an over, shifting toward the strong side instead.

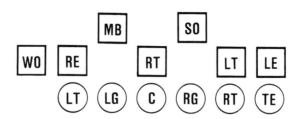

An odd front that makes the 4–3 look even more like a 3–4 is the 5–2, although one of the five linemen actually stands up as a linebacker. The modern 5–2 differs from the 3–4 only in that its left end has his hand on the ground.

C	center	QB	quarterback
LE	left end	RE	right end
LG	left guard	RG	right guard
LT	left tackle	RT	right tackle
MB	middle linebacker	SO	strong-side outside linebacker
NT	nose tackle	WO	weak-side outside linebacker

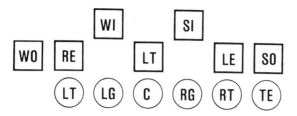

The 3–4, on the other hand, has a linebacker (SO) standing up. The inside linebackers in this 3–4 are designated WI for the weak side and SI for the strong side.

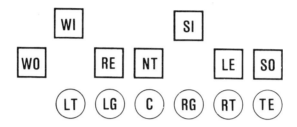

A 4–3 undershift becomes this 3–4 under if the weak-side end stands up as a linebacker.

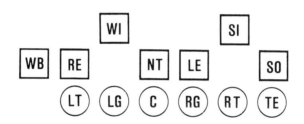

A 4–3 overshift becomes this 3–4 over if the strong-side end stands up as a linebacker. When a 3–4 team moves into an under or an over, it's called reducing weak or strong, because an end does the shifting instead of a tackle, thereby reducing the length of the line.

into each other trying to follow them. Practically any football play is enhanced when two of the opponents run into each other.

Offensive lines solved a lot of a stunt's inherent problems by zone blocking. When pass blockers are responsible for areas instead of players, the message they give pass rushers is: "OK guys, you can run all the stunts you want. We're just going to stay here and block whoever comes our way."

It isn't that simple. Pass blockers can't just stand up and wait, especially if the defensive line has overshifted or undershifted. Offenses took care of that by sliding their zones one way or another. Which gave defenses the opening they needed to bring back the stunt.

"There's a lot of science to it," Stan Jones says. "When a team with big linemen starts sliding, it can cause problems if you've got three or four men to their five or six. But if you can figure out which way they're sliding, maybe you can come in the back door with one of your men."

A particularly vogue stunt is the twist-and-loop, diagrammed on page 107. It's an end-tackle stunt designed to spring the tackle for an outside rush. The end charges first, running interference for the tackle. He fires into the offensive tackle, grabs him, and tries to push him into the offensive guard. If the end can keep two blockers busy, the tackle can run free. (Also gaining in popularity is a similar three-man stunt using both tackles and an end.)

Stunts and multiple fronts have helped put inside linemen back into the pass rush. They used to have an advantage, back when offensive linemen had their hands bound. They were closer to the quarterback. That's why Alan Page, tall and lean as defensive tackles went, wanted no part of suggestions that he might be better suited to playing end.

But when the rulemakers gave pass blockers hands, they also made them wider. Offensive coaches took that gift and varnished it by narrowing the splits between their linemen, setting them up closer together. Suddenly, there were hardly any cracks for inside pass rushers to seep through. From 1979 through 1982, there were never more than two defensive tackles among the NFL's top 20 pass rushers. What there was of a pass rush came entirely from ends and outside linebackers.

The top 20 pass rushers in 1983 included four tackles: Detroit's Doug English, Washington's Dave Butz, St. Louis's David Galloway, and Randy White. Plus Howie Long, who started at end but moved inside on most passing downs. Plus Detroit's William Gay, who began the season at end and wound up at tackle. And conspicuously absent was Dan Hampton, who either played hurt or couldn't play in all but two games. With stunts setting them free and multiple fronts making them harder to double-team, defensive tackles once again are seeing the quarterback at the end of the tunnel.

The best innovation for pass rushing, though, may have been the one that required the least juggling of Xs and Os. The specialized pass rusher is not only skilled at wading through the muck to the quarterback, he's also relatively rested whenever he tries to do it. If there is one constant that has emerged in pro football's passing era, it's that close games are most likely to go to the team with the best pass rush at the end. "It must be discouraging to an opposing offensive lineman to see a fresh Fred Dean come into the game," Chuck Studley said when he was the 49ers' defensive coordinator in their Super Bowl season. "They'd much rather he be playing the whole game, so he'd be worn down like they are."

On most defensive line stunts, two defensive linemen simply take each other's normal paths. The twist-and loop (below) is especially effective because the defensive end can actually block the offensive tackle across from him into the offensive guard, enabling the defensive tackle to loop freely around the end.

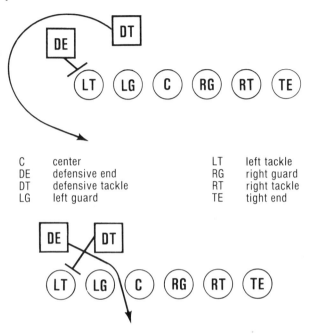

C	center	LT	left tackle
DE	defensive end	RG	right guard
DT	defensive tackle	RT	right tackle
LG	left guard	TE	tight end

A quicker stunt enables a defensive end to take an inside rush, with the defensive tackle running interference for him by blocking the offensive tackle. Sometimes a team will run this stunt on each side of the line to confuse pass blockers.

They'd also much rather block the same person all game. A pass blocker, always on the defensive, must be cautious early in a game until he gets an idea of how the pass rusher is going to try to beat him. The more new faces you can send at him, the more cautious you can make him. A team doesn't even need a Fred Dean to keep itself supplied with fresh troops. Green Bay, among other teams, has alternated entire lines, just like a hockey team.

Few things in football are glamorized more than sacking the quarterback. Defensive linemen have compared it with hitting the lottery, thumbing their noses at the boss, sex, and guest hosting "The Tonight Show." All within four seconds. It prompts grown men to dance like Snoopy.

"It's why I'm here," defensive Cedrick Hardman said as his long career wound down with the Raiders. "It's the only glamor there is on the defensive line. Other than that, I wouldn't play."

"It's like going deer hunting and you can see the big buck," says San Diego's Gary Johnson, probably the NFL's best inside pass rusher over the first five seasons with the new blocking rule.

The term itself, suggesting plundering and pillaging, could not be more appropriately graphic. Why must the Cowboys insist on calling them quarterback *traps*? Trapping is for furriers. Sacking whips a team physically and psychologically. It's as if the rules of chess permitted the person saying "checkmate" to pick up the opponent's king and throw it in his face.

For some pass rushers, it is satisfying enough to know how much impact a sack has on the game. It doesn't just cost the offense some yards and a play. It usually costs a team the ball on fourth down, and it can take away a team's nerve, its game plan, and even its quarterback. A sack can get old Mo Mentum to change uniforms faster than anything but an interception or a long kick return. And even an interception is often a sack that the offense let get out of control.

That's one reason sack statistics can be misleading. Defensive coaches also keep track of hurries, when a pass rusher makes the quarterback throw before he wants to throw and, usually, where he doesn't want to throw. Sacks don't account for the player who caves in the pass pocket and chases the quarterback into a teammate's arms. They don't account for the guy who drew double-team blocking and made it easier for his teammate to break free. (It's not a coincidence that Detroit was able to trade Al Baker, replace him with William Gay, and still have one of the league-leading sackers at right end. The Lions still had Doug English at right tackle, siphoning off blockers for whoever played right end.)

But there's something to be said for actually finishing off the quarterback. Somebody has to do it. As Miami defensive end Kim Bokamper says, "Once you've beaten your man, the quarterback is the pot of gold at the end of the rainbow."

The man who gets there first is the one the crowd notices. That's what some players like about a sack. It elevates them, however briefly, from the great unwashed oblivion of line play. With a flourish, too. "It's an exciting feeling," says Jets defensive end Mark Gastineau. "It's fantastic. It must be the way Richard Todd feels when he throws a 60-yard touchdown pass, or Wesley Walker when he catches it."

Some pass rushers find it helpful to work up a hatred for quarterbacks. It's not hard work if they think about how quarterbacks can make more money than entire defensive lines. Or how quarterbacks are cleanly immune from contact in practice while the rest of the players grovel in the mud, the sweat, and the drool.

Or how the same rulebook that practically surrounds the quarterback with an alligator-filled moat raises no objection to a defensive lineman being clobbered on the side of the knee.

To most pass rushers, though, theirs is a blue-collar job that simply allows them to punch the time clock with more gusto than most. Page was one of the NFL's best pass rushers ever, and he described the sack with no more fanfare than to call it, "the successful completion of a task." Nothing personal. Gastineau's teammate, Joe Klecko, says he doesn't hate quarterbacks. "They're probably nice guys who brush their teeth and call mom once a week. I hate what quarterbacks stand for. They stand between me and success."

The sack never was as easy as the best pass rushers made it look, even in the early seventies. It never did come in a bottle. As Page said: "You go through plan one and if that doesn't work, you go through plan two. If that doesn't work, you go through plan three. If you run through plan ten and he's still got the ball, fine. You keep going.

"Sometimes it seems as if the play is going on forever and everybody is getting a block on you. But if you keep working at it, if you don't accept that you can't get there just because it looks impossible, you'll get there at times when you shouldn't."

Page had made a sack like that the day before he said that. Two blockers played pinball with him for a while, and after he survived their fun, a back took a shot at him. "It seemed like this was going on forever," Page said. "But I kept getting closer and closer to the quarterback, and eventually I leaped and down he went."

That's how most sacks happen. Defensive linemen don't break free very often, and they can't be picky about style. Ten sacks make a good season, and ten sacks for a defensive lineman who plays every down is about one in every fifty pass plays. "It doesn't have to be pretty," Page said. "It doesn't even have to be good."

The best pass rushers, especially if they play tackle, can count on having to beat two blockers. Maybe three. Until recently, it was legal for one blocker to hit the defensive tackle in the chest, to stand him up, so the next blocker could cut him down at the legs. Now this is legal only on running plays, although it is not unheard of on passing plays. It is legal to clip between the offensive tackles, within three yards of the line of scrimmage. It's not legal to grab a pass rusher's face mask, but it's not uncommon for a blocker to drag a pass blocker by the face mask as though it were a ring through his nose.

If the offensive team is behind, or far from a first down, the pass rusher's field tilts downhill. A defensive lineman has the advantage of not having to worry about the run. He also gets to make the first move, and only he knows where it will be. When defensive linemen rhapsodize about pass rushing, that's the kind of pass rushing they mean. That's when pass rushing is fun. So a pass rusher's best friend is his own offense. Even pass rushing isn't so much fun when the defensive linemen have to expect a running play or the quarterback is unloading the ball on his third step.

"I bet you'll find the teams with the most sacks have the most potent offenses in the first quarter," says Cardinal defensive end Al Baker. "No pass rusher is so good that he can get to the quarterback consistently without expecting a pass."

For the individual pass rusher, the strategy hasn't changed. Ends line up wider sometimes, but there aren't a lot of new fancy moves for sidestepping pass blockers. "The more I played, the fewer things I tried," Page says. If one move works, why not use it all game? It helps to have something to fall back on in case one move doesn't work. The rookie defensive end who races around the tackle's outside every play is going to find the tackle waiting for him and his teammates calling him "The Colonel." He does one thing well.

Defensive linemen like to talk about how much harder their job has gotten. Who doesn't? But as Hampton says, "That's just made a sack all the more precious." And Page even found something to like about the rule change. "It means teams are passing more," he said. "So you get to rush the passer more."

Even the Earlobes Hurt

... For better or worse,
3–4 defenses have changed line play

Speaking of linemen, let's look at them a while. They're not leaning on each other, the way it seems from a distance. The moves they make are quick, precise, and powerful. So they're colliding quickly, precisely, and powerfully. "A game in the pits is like spending 60 minutes in a tumble dryer," said Roger Stillwell, a defensive tackle who played two NFL seasons and had two knee operations.

Offensive line is pro football's safest position, in terms of career expectancy. Offensive linemen may get hurt more often than their teammates, but they spend less time in the open field, where injuries get a running start. Besides, a lineman can play with almost any ailment short of a dangling limb. Rams defensive end Jack Youngblood played an NFC championship game and a Super Bowl on a broken leg.

The only things a lineman has to put up with on a regular basis are fingers in the eyes; fists to the Adam's apple; forearms to the chin; stepped-on feet; punches in the stomach (and lower); stepped-on hands; elbows and knees hitting the hard ground; elbows, knees, and neck bent assorted creative ways in pile-ups; and blows to the head from forearms, knees, and the ground. Hardly any of that is televised. Nor is the sound of pads popping, sometimes as loudly as a gunshot; nor the grunting, groaning, heavy breathing, and occasional shrieking. The "Get off my leg! My knee's gone!" from underneath a pile is lost to instant replays.

111

"You get twisted just about every way you can get twisted," says Dan Neal, a Chicago center who had virtually no Official Injuries in 11 pro seasons until his back hurt so much in 1983, he couldn't reach the ball. Not to say Neal wasn't injured before then. "Our hurts aren't anything like a wide receiver getting clobbered in midair," he says, "but ours are constant, day after day. You take a nail and hammer it long enough, eventually it's going to go through the wood. It's the same with hammering the body."

Jim Clack played ten seasons at guard and center for the Steelers and the Giants, retired, and then came back to the Giants when they needed a center to finish the 1981 season. After his return to the trenches, he realized he had been taking for granted the pinched nerves, the slightly pulled muscles, the small broken bones in his hands, the aching rib cartilage. "Those are just everyday things," he said.

During his brief furlough in the real world, Clack had seen people on crutches two days after spraining an ankle playing racketball, and he had thought to himself, "If that had happened to me playing ball, I'd have gone over to the sideline, walked around a couple times, and gone back in. That's one thing the average fan doesn't realize."

Every Monday, Clack said someone would ask him where he was sore. "I'd say, 'Ask me this: Where am I not sore?' " We're talking sprained *bodies*. For a lineman on Monday, even the earlobes and eyebrows hurt.

Let's look at his hands. That middle fingernail, the one that looks like a watercolor palette left out in the rain. He was working a double-team block with the fullback, and his hand was on the defensive man's shoulder when the fullback hit it with his helmet. He'll never be able to hold his ring and middle fingers together, not since the time that pass rusher bent the ring finger halfway to the quarterback. The little finger that won't straighten was stepped on a few years ago. So was that huge knuckle at the base of his middle finger. The knots between that knuckle and the wrist were broken bones he barely remembers.

"Dislocated fingers are pretty common now that we can use hands in pass protection," Clack said. Imagine trying to hold off 280 angry pounds with a dislocated finger. "It's one of the toughest things to play with. And your thumbs always seem to be stretched beyond where they should be. Every time you use them, you get the original pain all over again."

Now look at the lineman's stance. That's not a comfortable sprinter's stance. It's too compact for comfort. His legs aren't behind his torso, they're under it. You could almost serve tea on his back. His spine is bent 90 degrees at the neck. His knuckles and wrists are supporting more weight than some people's ankles. The body was not designed to be a perfectly balanced three-legged stool. For most people, it would hurt just holding that position five to ten seconds, let alone doing it 70 times a day. Very few retired linemen have painless lower backs.

Most of them also have kneecaps that are beginning to shred from the inside. That's from bouncing off artificial turf so often. Some artificial fields are softer than others, but artificial turf is essentially fuzzy concrete. When an elbow hits it, the turf not only rattles the joint around but tears away some skin, too. Artificial turf also is responsible for turf toe, a cute-sounding injury that is one of the most painful in sports. The toe joint is hyperextended from a sudden stop. Concrete doesn't give like dirt does.

This all happens in the normal course of doing a lineman's job. It gets worse when linemen and their coaches start dreaming up inventive ways to make an opposing lineman's job harder.

"I cringe sometimes at what I see, what happens to me, what I'm about to do sometimes," Alan Page once said. "I get squeamish."

People with weak stomachs should not focus on the nose tackle. In a basic 3–4 defense, he lines up over the center and has two uncovered blockers to either side. Uncovered blockers find ways to occupy themselves. It's quite common for a center to

---

"Being down in a stance, my hands and wrists always suffered a lot. It was easily 72 hours after a game before I felt I could eat with that hand, or write, or do anything comfortably. There's lower back pain from bending over. And there's leg pain at every position. That's more a reflection of the artificial surfaces, the almost apathy those in charge express toward players. It's probably an economic factor, but you're playing on a padded parking lot.

"Pain comes with the territory. It's something you have to deal with every day. Taking 10 or 15 minutes to get up in the morning. It's entirely different from the kind of pain a medical patient has. A football player's everyday pounding wears down the body. It may even wear down the mind."—**Dave Gallagher**, NFL defensive-tackle-turned-medical-doctor.

---

straighten up the nose tackle with his block, and for a guard to aim his helmet at the outside of the nose tackle's knee. "What they do to that guy, it's bordering on criminal," Page says.

The nose tackle doesn't have to take it. He could walk away. But pro football has a bull market on nose tackles. The nose tackle who considers resting his aching knee also has to consider losing his job to the guy who fills in for him. Besides, all in all, he likes playing football. And what else is he going to do? The only meaningful schooling he ever had most likely was in football.

Nearly all linemen have to make the decision sometime to drag their broken bodies off the field or keep throwing them into the tumble dryer. Dave Gallagher, a defensive tackle, made the less common decision one day when he was playing for the Giants with an injured knee. "I walked off the field," he says. "I didn't think it was worth it."

He's not smug about having strided above the tangled limbs of the pits. Gallagher had an advantage over most football players. He had medical school on his horizon. He could make a comfortable living without living uncomfortably.

"There are guys walking around today—or trying to walk around—who decided not to walk off the field," Gallagher says. "I don't know if they paid any more for it. Maybe they're more satisfied with what they did because they gave that much more. But they probably did irreversible harm to themselves."

X X X X X
O O O O

The 3–4 defense has not only changed line play, it has changed all seven defensive line and linebacker positions. A team might use the same people at left outside linebacker and defensive right end that it used in a 4–3 defense, but now those people have different pursuit angles, different responsibilities, different offensive players blocking them from new directions, different *viewing* angles. The old middle linebacker can't look straight across to the quarterback anymore. Now he's looking over the right guard's helmet. He's got new keys, new things to look for.

The biggest change in job description is for the poor defensive tackle who turned into a nose tackle. Better that than a pillar of salt, but not much. He's the point man of the defensive charge now, the pawn, the virgin who hurls himself into a volcano to save the rest of the defense. If he does his job well, if he's Miami's Bob Baumhower or the Raiders' Reggie Kinlaw, he can keep the center and two guards busy enough so his teammates don't have so many blockers in their faces. But keeping them busy means letting them dive at his knees and pepper him back and forth and generally wear him out.

"To play nose tackle," says Cleveland's Bob Golic, "you have to be unemployed or crazy. I was unemployed. The other part is still up in the air."

Nose tackles have, in turn, radically changed the demands of centers. "The nose guard's main job is to physically beat the heck out of the center all the time," Clack says.

It used to be commonly felt that a great athlete was wasted at center. He was the uncovered lineman against a basic 4–3. His main job was to put the ball in play and maybe to angle block a defensive tackle, but more likely to see if any other blockers needed help. The best centers of the sixties and seventies, players like Miami's Jim Langer and Minnesota's Mick Tinglehoff, had to be quick-footed but didn't have to be particularly big or strong. Now you have centers who can bench press the team's whole bench. Now you have Cincinnati drafting Outland Trophy winner Dave Rimington and leaving him at center, and Cleveland doing the same with Mike Baab, whom Detroit defensive tackle Doug English says is "as strong as nine acres of onions." Buffalo nose tackle Fred Smerlas calls New England center Pete Brock "A bulldozer with hair on it."

A panel of assistant coaches, voting on the NFL's best offensive lineman in 1983, chose a center for the first time in the award's nine years. It was Miami's Dwight Stephenson, who is quick *and* strong. It could just as easily have been Pittsburgh's Mike Webster.

If the nose tackle is the player who starts the ball rolling for most defenses, then it stands to reason an offense ought to have a center who can do more than slow him down. But the center still has to snap the ball. He has the advantage of being the only lineman who knows exactly when the play will start, but he still has to start the play with his arms back between his legs. No wonder Jack Rudnay, Kansas City's 12-year center through 1981, once gave his position as "prone" on a team questionnaire. "That has to be the most miserable job in the world," says former Bear fullback Rick Casares. "I never would have played football if I'd had to be a center."

X X X X X
0 0 0 0

In spite of all this abuse they put up with, offensive linemen as a group are among the smartest football players. They have to be. Their assignments may change every time a defensive lineman slides over. And very few of the things they do come naturally, starting with their stance.

They have to begin blocking—to come off the ball—in unison with the snap. They have to keep their butts low when their aching backs and legs want to stretch out. They have to follow intricate footwork that may fly in the face of reason. If the play is designed for the blocker to put his inside shoulder on the defensive lineman's outside shoulder, that's what the blocker has to do, even if it seems more natural to take him on nose-to-nose or outside shoulder to inside shoulder.

Most of all, they have to realize the only thing they'll ever do to arouse the fan's passion is get fingered for a penalty. Gene Upshaw, the Raiders' long-time, all-pro guard who now directs the players' union, compares offensive linemen with Paul Revere's horse. In all the hubbub heralding Revere's great ride, who would have thought to give his horse an extra lump of sugar?

To tell where a play is going, the offensive linemen are the ones to watch. A guard will let you know it's a run by firing ahead, a sweep by pulling, and a pass by backpedaling.

But he has to be careful about letting the defensive player across from him know his intentions. It doesn't matter if he starts leaning into his pass protection when his team has four wide receivers, but on second-and-two, the guard's knuckles might be the best clue a defensive tackle can find. If they're not turning white from supporting half his weight, then he's leaning back to pull or pass block, and the defensive tackle who sees it can take him out of the play by grabbing his jersey as soon as the ball is snapped.

To keep that from happening, offensive linemen generally wear jerseys so tight they seem to have come from an aerosol can. (Even their clothes are uncomfortable.) They keep their sleeves short, too, no matter what the temperature. Cincinnati's offensive linemen all went bare-armed in the minus-59 wind chill of their AFC championship game against San Diego. The Raiders have been accused of greasing their offensive linemen.

Another trick is to choose gloves and wrist bands that match the opponent's jersey color. It makes holding harder to spot, although a lineman with a blue uniform might be asking for extra scrutiny if he shows up with bright green gloves for a game against the Eagles.

The hardest thing for an offensive lineman to learn is pass blocking. Very few offensive linemen get their jollies falling back to be some pass rusher's punching bag. The run, now *that's* fun. That's when offensive linemen take the offensive, charge into a defensive lineman before he can get out of his stance. But on a pass, the blocker's first move is to retreat. The best he can do is absorb the pass rusher's punishment. It's either take that beating or turn around and holler, "Watch out!" which offensive linemen don't enjoy any more than they enjoy running up the stadium steps in full gear.

Pass blocking involves so many techniques. Keep your shoulders square to the rusher's path. Take him head-on. Keep your head lined up with your shoulders. Chin up, too; drop your head and you might as well turn around and start hollering. Hands up, cocked for that initial pop to the pass rusher's upper chest, the one that starts him staggering if it's done right. After that, don't let him get within an arm's length. Keep your feet spread, your waist and knees bent, your balance impeccable. You can't block sitting down. And above all, while everything else is just so, keep your feet moving.

It's as intricate as a golf swing, except golf balls don't hit back. The problem is, pass blocking is one of the few things in football where exuberance can't make up for a little technical flaw here or there. The pass blocker has to be aggressive, but the moment he gets too aggressive, he's opening the door for the pass rusher.

All the while, the pass rusher is remembering one thing. *Get to the quarterback.* That's all. It's not unusual for an offensive lineman to watch three hours of film a night, studying his opponent's moves. It's not unusual for a great pass rusher to watch no film at all. What he's doing comes naturally.

The hardest position for pass blocking is left tackle. Guards and centers work in close quarters. They can lose their man for an instant and he's liable to bounce off another lineman. The right tackle usually has a tight end next to him. The left tackle is all alone, working without a net, and because of it, the defense often puts its best pass rusher across from him at right end.

That's beginning to change now that fewer tight ends are blocking and more formations are putting tight ends on the left side; Mark Gastineau and Doug Betters had the most NFL sacks in 1983, both from left end. But right end is still the launching pad for Fred Dean, Curtis Greer, Lee Roy Selmon, and Ezra Johnson. It's the right end who's most likely to line up two or three yards wider than the tackle, where he might as well be pawing at the ground with smoke coming from his nostrils.

When Ted Albrecht was a young left tackle for the Bears, he shared a halftime conversation he had with his coach about his enthusiasm for playing against Selmon. "I told him my deepest secrets," Albrecht said. "I said I never wanted to be buried at sea, I never wanted to get hit in the mouth with a hockey puck, and I didn't want to go out and play that second half against Lee Roy."

Selmon has a particularly unnerving way of rushing from the outside, because he's not just out there to run a great circle route to the quarterback. He's strong enough to draw the left tackle out with him, fling him aside, and take the shorter inside path to the quarterback.

By then, the toothpaste is out of the tube. *"Watch out!"* What the left tackle has to do is stay out of that position in the first place. He has to pick the spot over his left shoulder where he can take on the pass rusher and protect both flanks, and he has to get there first. "It's a game of basketball," Albrecht says. "You're beating your man to the baseline."

The pits are not quiet, even aside from the grunting and heavy breathing. There's lots of chatter, too. Sometimes it's disarming, as in, "My, that was a nice move," or, "I'm awfully sorry for holding you back there," which can confuse and defuse a defensive lineman. But most often, says the Raiders' Howie Long, "It's vicious. Nothing said on a football field can be printed."

The idea is to intimidate the opponent. Or, since it's not terribly easy to intimidate a fully padded man weighing 270 pounds, to distract him. Get him thinking about the fight instead of the game. The Raiders' 1983 AFC championship victory over Seattle was a textbook in chatterbox distraction, but Seattle was a young team. When Lyle Alzado spent Super Bowl week promising to rip off the heads of various Redskins, the Redskins were more amused than annoyed. John Riggins even said he checked out the field for soft spots where his head could land without undue damage.

Intimidation is more effectively served with a forearm than with a tongue. Curley Culp, Houston's original prototype of a nose tackle, once decided to teach Dan Neal an etiquette lesson after Neal had rudely fooled him with a head fake. "He about killed me on the next three plays," Neal says. "He didn't care where the ball went. He just clobbered me. But if you've got somebody wasting his energy beating your head in, you're keeping him away from the ball. You've done your job."

The best intimidation is something that fits right into doing the job. A forearm to a blitzer's forehead might make him think twice about coming so rambunctiously next time, provided he wakes up enough to think clearly. Blockers do the same thing to stunting defensive linemen. And a defensive lineman can make a memorable impression on a running back when he doesn't fall for a misdirection play.

He can't do much to the quarterback anymore, though. There used to be an art to nailing the quarterback on his follow-through, getting him to think about throwing the ball too early next time without getting the referee to think about throwing the flag. But nowadays, anything close is a penalty. The only place the quarterback is fair game is in a pile. He might get his facemask tugged, or a defensive player might help himself to his feet by planting an elbow on the quarterback's chest or neck or head. There isn't much leg twisting anymore, though. One thing all football players respect is knees.

Standing Up on His Hind Legs

*... The fourth linebacker is
the evolutionary link in today's NFL defenses*

The Miami Dolphins had gone halfway through their 1972 exhibition season and almost completely through their supply of defensive ends. They had two left. They needed another one for their game against Atlanta that week. One of their young linebackers, Bob Matheson, had played some defensive end at Cleveland before coming to the Dolphins the previous year. So Bill Arnsparger, the defensive coordinator, had an idea. He would use Matheson as a defensive end, but he would leave him standing, like a linebacker.

And so was born the 3–4 defense, which in turn begat battered nose tackles and Herculean centers, designated blitzers and eight-man zone coverage; which in turn became the stage to make leading men of Ted Hendricks and A. J. Duhe, Lawrence Taylor and Hugh Green, and to turn those valiant middle linebackers of yore into a chorus of inside linebackers. All because Miami had a few defensive ends in sick bay.

Miami wasn't the first team to use an odd front, with a man over the center. The Chiefs had won a Super Bowl with an odd front three seasons earlier. (They also had stacked their linebackers, setting them up directly behind linemen instead of in the gaps, so the blockers wouldn't know which backers would fill which gaps.) "But their wide man kept his hand on the ground," Matheson said. He wasn't a linebacker.

Matheson always lined up on the weak side, as Taylor ordinarily does now, and the other linemen were opposite the tackles and the center, as in a 5–2. Matheson had two sacks in that game against Atlanta. But by the sixth and last exhibition against Minnesota, Matheson says, "We hardly used the defense. I thought it was one of the things we were going to can."

It wasn't. Miami opened the season against Kansas City, the team it had upset in the interminable Christmas playoff game the year before, in the first regular-season game in the Chiefs' new stadium. Matheson recalls using the 3–4 for 60 percent of that game, which Miami won 20–10. The Dolphins kept using the 3–4 and kept winning. They finished 17–0.

"We used it primarily against the pass, to give us a dimension of disguise," says Matheson, now a Dolphin assistant coach. If four players rushed, he was always the fourth. But he didn't always rush. After a while, he didn't always line up on the weak-side end. He sometimes lined up over the tight end or one of the guards and blitzed from there. "The way Hendricks and Duhe move around now," Matheson says. After still longer, the Dolphins tried sending other linebackers and found it gave them another way to fool the offense.

The next season, Houston and New England were using the 3–4 on first downs. To stop the run. Little by little since then, teams have been switching to the 3–4 as their basic defense, until only seven of twenty-eight NFL teams used primarily the 4–3 in 1983 (and two of them, St. Louis and Atlanta, had been 3–4 teams).

With most of the 3–4's pioneer teams, embracing the new defense had nothing to do with creative schemes for confounding offenses. It had to do with linebackers being easier to find than defensive linemen. More young, athletic males grow to 6'3" and 225 pounds than to 6'5" and 260.

The 3–4 has a better place for the 225-pound college defensive end than the 4–3, which requires more pass coverage of its linebackers. Better still, the 3–4 has nicely accommodated even smaller young, athletic males at linebacker. Philadelphia's Jerry Robinson plays inside linebacker at 6'2", 218, and he plays it very well. He's fast enough, and located centrally enough, to be a factor on either sideline and anywhere in between. It hasn't hurt the 3–4's popularity at all to be a defense emphasizing speed in an era demanding speed.

Another happy coincidence for the 3–4 is its flexibility, coming as it does in an era of multiple offensive and defensive formations. "That's the reason most people are going to it now," says Arnsparger, who left the Dolphins after the 1983 season to be head coach at Louisiana State. "You're getting all kinds of one-back offenses, three or four people on one side, two wide people on each side. They're spreading you all over the field. The 3–4 is more easily adjustable. If you've got four people with their hands on the ground, you've only got three linebackers available to move."

Four down linemen also tell the offense which four players are going to bring the principal pass rush. That's wonderful if the four linemen are good enough to spill the quarterback regularly without resorting to trickery. The best pass-rushing linemen are better than the best pass-rushing linebackers, so the current stampede to cut an offense off *before* the pass has led teams to bring back four-man lines on passing downs. But that's not for everybody. Young, athletic males still tend to stop growing before they reach 6'5" and 260.

"If you play a four-man line, your four men must dominate—I mean *dominate*—the line of scrimmage," says Kansas City coach John Mackovic. "The defensive linemen today are less dominant than they've ever been. So if you can't dominate the line, you better be able to cover."

Or to deceive the blockers, which is where the mystery blitzing linebacker comes in, as opposed to the designated blitzer. The 3–4 can go either way. "Standing up, that fourth linebacker can still rush the passer," Arnsparger says. "But he can also drop better for coverage. He can see better. He can still play good run defense on the tight end. Why would you want to have him put his hand on the ground?"

X X X X X
0 0 0 0

A 3–4 defense doesn't expect a lot of flashy plays out of its linemen. Their job is to tie up as many blockers as possible so the linebackers can make tackles without having to trip over players. In a sense, the lineman makes some conversation so the offense won't notice the linebacker taking its wallet.

The flex defense uses the same principle against running plays. It has a four-man line, but alternate linemen are two or three yards off the line of scrimmage. The diagram on page 122 shows the strong-side end and the weak-side tackle as the flexed linemen.

They don't charge with the snap of the ball. They wait long enough to get an idea where the play is going, which they can see better than the linemen with blockers in their faces, and *then* they react. Read and react, it's called. For the flexed linemen, that delayed reaction is a safeguard against being confused by a shifting, multiple offense. When he created the flex at Dallas,

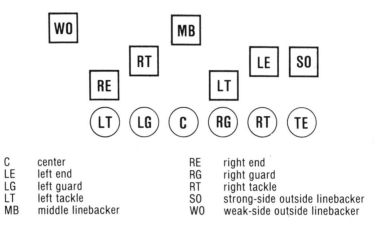

C	center	RE	right end
LE	left end	RG	right guard
LG	left guard	RT	right tackle
LT	left tackle	SO	strong-side outside linebacker
MB	middle linebacker	WO	weak-side outside linebacker

In the Flex defense, two defensive linemen are up to three yards off the line of scrimmage, where it is easier for them to see the play begin to develop before reacting to it.

coach Tom Landry didn't want his own defense getting fooled by other teams' using his offense's devices.

But mainly, Landry wanted his linebackers making tackles without having to sift through blockers. The two defensive linemen in front tie up as many blockers as possible, just as in the 3–4. So do the flexed linemen, but in a different way. They're harder to reach. An offensive lineman has to go get them. And that leaves gaps for the linebackers to fire through.

The flex has not been one of Landry's more popular innovations around the NFL. Dick Nolan, who was head coach at San Francisco and New Orleans between jobs as Landry's assistant, has been the only other coach to build a defense around it. The main objection is that it has only two actual linemen for pass rushing, even though conventional defenses designed for running downs don't send their linemen firing off the ball, either. Two other reasons are more believable:

1. The flex is complicated for defensive linemen to learn, and coaches prefer to have their defensive linemen play reckless football with a minimum of thinking.

2. The flex is a Dallas concoction, and other NFL teams are loathe to concede any of those off-the-wall Cowboy ideas can help them if they can possibly avoid it. (The Cowboys had the shotgun all to themselves for years, too.)

The Raiders particularly like to draw a bold line between themselves and the Cowboys. They like to think of their teams as being as different as black hats and white hats. But when the Raiders snuffed Washington's running game in winning the Super Bowl, their defense sprinkled some elements of the flex into their basic 3–4.

The Raiders backed nose tackle Reggie Kinlaw away from the line of scrimmage. They flexed him. In the single-back offense, remember, running plays tend to develop more slowly, with the ball carrier running to daylight instead of committing himself to a predetermined hole. Off the line, Kinlaw was able to wait, too, and cloud over that daylight at the last moment.

The remaining linemen, the ends, were to spread out and, as Lyle Alzado explained, "to stand up their offensive tackles and get our backers inside to clean up the trash." And those inside linebackers stood up at the line of scrimmage, "to keep their blockers from having a running start at them," said defensive coordinator Charlie Sumner. In other words, the Raiders took away the bubbles over the guards, but they did it with linebackers, standing up and better able to read and react than down linemen would have been.

What they used was a five-man line. But it wasn't an ordinary five-man line, with the ends standing up or dropping off for more mobility. The Raiders' five-man line had its more mobile players inside instead: the lineman opposite the center was off the line, and the linemen opposite the guards were standing up. So by the time John Riggins could get to his running hole, an inside Raider could get there first.

Two weeks earlier, the 49ers had stopped Washington's offense with a four-man line. They didn't use it the whole game. The 49ers normally use three defensive linemen. But they were using four when they rallied from a 21–0 deficit to tie the score at 21 before losing, and they may have won if they had used four linemen all game.

The one-back offense with two tight ends could dim the enthusiasm for 3–4 defenses. The reason Joe Gibbs designed Washington's offense, remember, was to attack 3–4 defenses. The 3–4 has enough advantages that it isn't likely to disappear, though. That makes the Raiders' five-man line, an adaptation of the 3–4, all the more attractive.

Between a Super Bowl and the next training camp, there is little in a Super Bowl game film that hasn't been scrutinized by NFL coaches. The Raiders weren't the first team to stop a one-back offense with a five-man line. And they certainly won't be the last to face a single-back offense with a five-man line using linebackers inside instead of outside.

Rushing the Receiver

... Pass coverage has become more aggressive, too, but with the emphasis shifting from hitting to outwitting

There are two trends in NFL pass coverage. One trend is toward more man-to-man. The other trend is toward more zone.

Which pigeonhole should the following kind of coverage go in? The strong-side linebacker is responsible for covering anybody who comes into a particular area. The first person who enters that area, the linebacker latches onto him and follows him anywhere on the field. Man-to-man? Zone? Moan?

When downfield contact was first taken out of pass coverage, defenses thought they had no alternative but to play zones. There just weren't many players who could keep up with a receiver who didn't have to climb back to his feet a couple times. But then they found out the bad news. Give a receiver room to get open, in the seams between or in front of the zones, and the quarterback can play catch with him.

The old bend-but-don't-break philosophy isn't even safe anymore. Defensive players used to be able to feel secure dropping off into zones and letting the offense play catch in front of them to their hearts' content until they got to the 20-yard line. Then they'd tighten their coverage, use man-to-man, maybe blitz, get a holding penalty or a sack, and, at worst, make the offense settle for a field goal. But in eighties football, there are too many ways the bend-but-don't-break defenses get folded, spindled, and mutilated.

1. Offenses are a lot more efficient in their short passing games, so they're more apt to get to the 20 with that kind of leeway. Before the late seventies, there was a good chance the offense would foul up on its own before the defense even had to kick into its don't-break phase.

2. It always has been easier to play pass coverage inside your own 20 because the field is smaller. Nobody worries about the bomb, and no receivers are running decoy routes way downfield to loosen things up underneath. That's still true, but the defenders can't clamp down on a receiver inside the 20 the way they once did. Man-to-man coverage means *running with* a receiver now, not beating him up. It's not easy to run with a fast person when you don't know where he's going. One wrong step, and you're *running without* him.

Besides, the illegal-chuck rule had its biggest impact on crossing routes, which are most effective for relatively short yardage. Like, say, an eight-yard touchdown pass to the tight end.

3. The chance of a zone defense giving up a long pass before the rule changes was almost nil. By the time a receiver could finagle his way into an open area behind the deep men, at least one pass rusher would have finagled his way behind the blockers. But now, since it's harder for pass rushers to slam the window shut on the end of a pass play, long passes against zone defenses are not unheard of.

They're still not common. After all, the guy playing a deep zone has close to a 20-yard head start on the receiver. That's why a popular coverage is man underneath and zone deep. It protects against the deep pass without letting the offense play pitch-and-catch in front of linebackers retreating 10 or 15 yards into zones.

But there are so many other ways to mix zone with man-to-man. Zone on the strong side, man on the weak. Zone outside, man inside. Double cover one receiver, zone the rest (the equivalent of basketball's box-and-one defense; or, for a triangle-and-two, assign men to two receivers and put the others in zones.) The diagrams on pages 126–129 show how some popular coverages look.

Even a pure zone coverage might look more like man-to-man. It's more and more common for a defender covering a zone to run with a receiver as he crosses the zone, rather than patrol the zone from its center.

So the evolution toward zone defense, which began in the late sixties and kicked into overdrive when the rules changed, is veering off in a new direction. Now the zone defender often is actively pursuing his man through the zone rather than passively

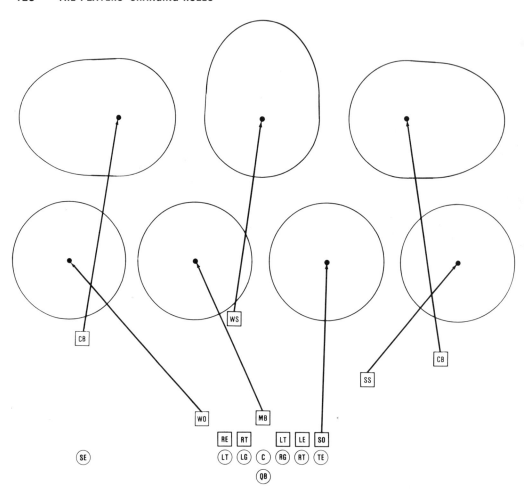

C	center	RE	right end
CB	cornerback	RG	right guard
FB	fullback	RT	right tackle
FL	flanker	SE	split end
HB	halfback	SO	strong-side outside linebacker
LE	left end	SS	strong-side safety
LG	left guard	TE	tight end
LT	left tackle	WO	weak-side outside linebacker
MB	middle linebacker	WS	weak-side safety
QB	quarterback		

This is a basic three-deep zone, with four short zones and the cornerbacks and weak safety deep. It also can be played with both safeties deep. Pass receivers are most likely to get open in the seams (between the zones) or underneath (in front of them).

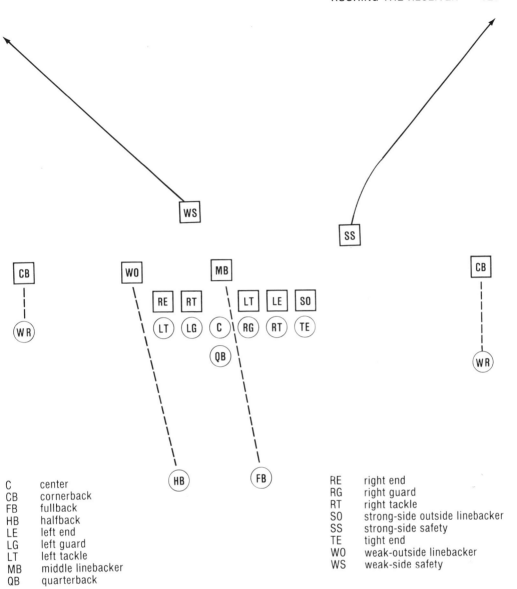

C	center
CB	cornerback
FB	fullback
HB	halfback
LE	left end
LG	left guard
LT	left tackle
MB	middle linebacker
QB	quarterback

RE	right end
RG	right guard
RT	right tackle
SO	strong-side outside linebacker
SS	strong-side safety
TE	tight end
WO	weak-outside linebacker
WS	weak-side safety

To tighten coverage of the receivers in shorter routes and still protect loosely against the deep pass, a defense can play its coverage man under and zone deep. The safeties help cover anyone who runs a long route.

waiting for the ball to be thrown before he moves. Zone coverage has become more aggressive, just like pass rushing. Defenses are even forcing the action downfield.

Combo coverages make the distinction between zone and man-to-man even fuzzier. The strong safety, for example, might help cover the tight end in some patterns, but in other patterns, he'll help with the flanker. Some teams combo the whole field, dividing it down the middle. Four defenders cover three on one

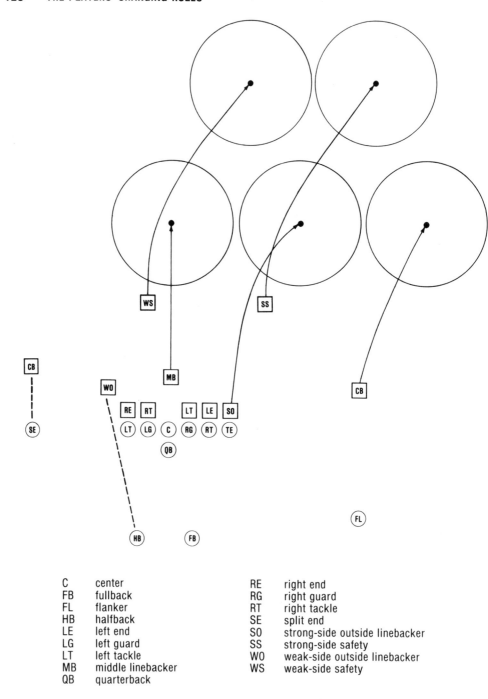

C	center	RE	right end
FB	fullback	RG	right guard
FL	flanker	RT	right tackle
HB	halfback	SE	split end
LE	left end	SO	strong-side outside linebacker
LG	left guard	SS	strong-side safety
LT	left tackle	WO	weak-side outside linebacker
MB	middle linebacker	WS	weak-side safety
QB	quarterback		

Another common mixture of zone and man coverage assigns man coverage to the weak-side receivers with five other defenders rotating toward the strong side into zones. In this kind of coverage, the weak safety and middle linebacker ordinarily would follow receivers out of their zones if the receivers ran crossing patterns to the weak side. And if motion takes the third wide receiver to the offense's left side before the snap, the defenders would rotate into weak-side zones and leave two strong-side players in single coverage.

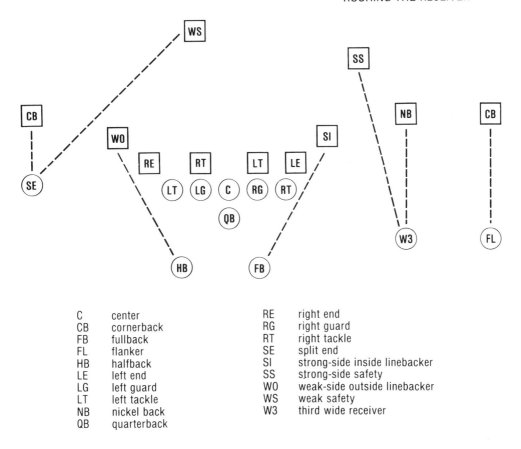

C center	RE right end
CB cornerback	RG right guard
FB fullback	RT right tackle
FL flanker	SE split end
HB halfback	SI strong-side inside linebacker
LE left end	SS strong-side safety
LG left guard	WO weak-side outside linebacker
LT left tackle	WS weak safety
NB nickel back	W3 third wide receiver
QB quarterback	

All NFL teams use nickel defenses, with five or six backs, who are faster than linebackers and better skilled in pass coverage. This nickel defense could cover man-to-man, as shown by the broken lines, with the leftover defenders blitzing, double-covering receivers, or dropping into deep zones. Or if it could play a combo coverage with four defenders covering three receivers on the strong side, and three covering two on the weak side. Or it could use any number of mixtures of zone, man-to-man, and combo.

side, three cover two on the other, but the defenders don't know precisely *whom* they're covering until the pattern starts developing. In case of a crossing route, the free safety may not even know which side he's covering.

Actually, he's the weak safety. Free safety means something else. Blame the media for that confusion, for being skittish about calling rough-and-tumble football players weak safeties. Coaches call them weak safeties, as opposed to strong safeties, because they line up across from the offense's weak side (the side without the tight end; or if there is no tight end, the side with fewer wide-outs; or, if there are two tight ends, the side with the Rover).

A free safety is always a weak safety, but a weak safety is not necessarily a free safety. He might be double covering a wide receiver. That's not free. That's having an assignment. The weak safety is a free safety only when he's playing centerfield, when he's covering the deep middle, free to lend assistance toward either sideline. That usually happens either in a three-deep zone, when no receiver comes his way, or when he's a fail-safe sentry behind man coverage.

Even a *free* safety is not always completely free. Offenses have always liked to amuse themselves by having two receivers cross in front of a free safety. Whoever he covers will be the wrong man. Long ago, a young free safety asked his coach, Weeb Ewbank, "There's two of them out there. Which one do I cover?" To which Ewbank replied, "Cover the guy they throw the ball to."

Of course, Ewbank was telling his quarterbacks, "Throw the ball to the guy they don't cover," and so was every other coach. Coaches always say that to quarterbacks. It's called reading the defense. An important part of pass coverage, then, is garbling what the quarterback is trying to read. As a defensive coach might put it, "Don't let him know which guy you're going to cover."

If there is a single trend in NFL pass coverage, it is toward *more*. More defensive backs, who can react more quickly than linebackers and therefore don't have to tip off their coverage plans as early. And above all, more coverages. Teams as varied as Washington (which still essentially uses George Allen's pre-rules change defense), Cincinnati, and Chicago (guided innovatively by Hank Bullough and Buddy Ryan) have 60 different coverage schemes at their disposal. Even the Raiders, with their reputation for playing man-to-man all the time, mix in some zones to keep quarterbacks wondering. "If they could count on us using the same coverage all the time, we'd get killed," cornerback Mike Haynes says.

The more coverages a defense uses, the more a quarterback has to consider when he reads the defense, and the more likely he is to read it wrong. The reason for reading a defense is to find out where it's vulnerable, where he should look for *the guy they don't cover*. If the quarterback misreads a defense, he wastes his limited time looking in the wrong place.

"The name of the game now is don't let the quarterback know what coverage you're in," quarterback Brian Sipe says. Or the receiver, either. Fooling him is just as good. The quarterback can waste his time just as effectively looking in the right place for a receiver who has gone to the wrong place because *he* misread the defense.

Besides mixing coverages, a defense tries to disguise them. Maybe the safeties will wait until after the snap before splitting toward the sidelines for a two-deep zone. Or the cornerback will roll up as though he's going to jam a receiver at the line of scrimmage, then drop off just before the snap. It's risky. The defensive player might not get into position on time. But it's also risky to make the quarterback's read easy.

The wider variety of coverages has made disguising them easier. Some standard keys have become obsolete. For example, if the middle linebacker dropped into a zone, that used to mean everyone was dropping into a zone. Now the middle linebacker and weak safety might be the only ones playing zones while everyone else latches onto a receiver.

What defensive coaches have decided is this: We can't cover all the receivers all the time, like we could when we were allowed to crush them like cigarette butts. We'll try, but it just isn't going to happen. But what we *can* do is confuse the quarterback into thinking his open receiver is covered. It's as good as covering him.

If the split end is open when the quarterback's read has told him to look for the flanker, is the split end really open? If a tree falls in the middle of a deserted forest, can it make any sound?

X X X X X
0 0 0 0

Multiple defenses aren't all exotic. There's room in them for basic man-to-man and ordinary zone coverage, and for coverages that fit more comfortably into either category than, say, combos. There also are some basic principles for when a defense is more likely to use zone and when it would lean toward man-to-man.

As a general rule, the closer an offense is to making a first down, the more likely the defense is to use man-to-man coverage. It can't afford to slack off and give up the short pass. So on first-and-ten, second-and-more than six or seven, and third-and-more than ten, the chance of zone coverage is 70 percent or more. It decreases to about 40 percent on third-and-six to ten yards, and to virtually nil on third-and-three.

If a defense blitzes, its understaffed secondary has to play man-to-man (which is why the blitz is most popular when five or six defensive backs are playing). If a defense has fast, skillful cornerbacks, like the Raiders, it ought to play man-to-man. Good man-to-man coverage is harder to beat than good zone coverage. But it's also harder to play.

If the quarterback eyeballs his receivers, which means he tends to stare at the one he's throwing to and ignore the rest, he diminishes the disadvantage of zone coverage. A defender can see the quarterback drawing a target on the receiver in his area and clamp down on him before the ball is in the air.

Zone coverage also is more conducive to interceptions. The defender can watch the ball more if he doesn't have to concentrate on a receiver. A good defensive back, when he expects a pass to his receiver, might lay off the receiver to give the quarterback the impression he's open, then break for the ball as soon as it's thrown.

Zone coverage usually complements three-man rushes, too. And there are times, even for an aggressive defense, when it's wise to rush just three. If four pass rushers aren't making much headway, whether because of good blocking or a slippery field, the defensive coach is apt to decide he can get a poor pass rush just as easily with three men. If you can't rush the quarterback, you'd better cover his receivers.

Philadelphia is a team that uses any number of coverages behind a three-man rush. Coach Marion Campbell's defenses are as innovative as anybody's, and he likes to use seven defensive backs, as shown in the diagram on page 133. They can run with as many wide-outs as the offense wants to unleash.

Even though defenses have grown more aggressive within coverage, jamming receivers at the line of scrimmage has tapered off. Cornerbacks still roll up to play on the line, but they're often there more to reroute the receiver than to knock him down. If the cornerback can expect help from a teammate toward the inside of the field, he'll plant himself just outside the receiver to funnel him toward the help.

A fast cornerback can roll up and simply run with a receiver. He doesn't backpedal. He turns with the receiver and stays on his inside hip, between the receiver and the quarterback. The Raiders' Lester Hayes is a marvel at this trailing or tailgating technique, which defenders use within zones as well as man-to-man.

An irony to the proliferation of coverages is that it might not have been necessary if defensive coaches hadn't fallen in love with one particular coverage in the mid-seventies. It was called the Prevent defense, not to be confused with the various prevent defenses with safeties 40 yards deep at the end of a half. The Prevent was—and is—a specific defense with five backs and three linemen. Three deep zones, five short zones.

When three pass rushers were enough for many teams to keep the quarterback's feet moving, the Prevent was a way to double-zone the wide receivers without leaving the deep middle open. Wide-outs practically disappeared from the game. In 1974, for the first time ever, a back led the NFL in receptions.

Putting wide receivers back into pro football, preferably far downfield, was one of the reasons the rules were changed. From 1973 through 1977, in five seasons, only seven times did a receiver

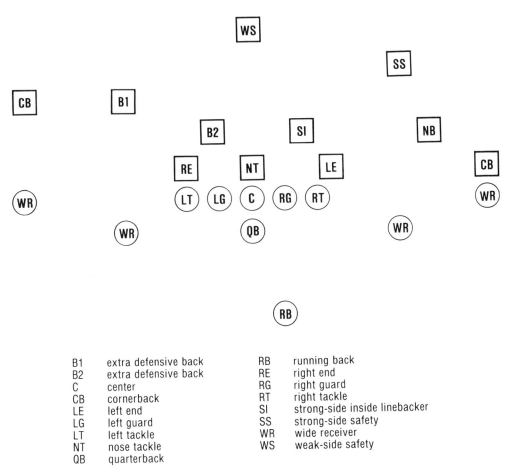

B1   extra defensive back
B2   extra defensive back
C   center
CB   cornerback
LE   left end
LG   left guard
LT   left tackle
NT   nose tackle
QB   quarterback

RB   running back
RE   right end
RG   right guard
RT   right tackle
SI   strong-side inside linebacker
SS   strong-side safety
WR   wide receiver
WS   weak-side safety

NFL teams use as many as seven defensive backs in passing downs. In this defense, against a basic four wide receiver set, the defense can cover three receivers with four men on one side, cover two with three on the other side, and still have a free safety. Or it can blitz somebody instead of having the free safety. The seven backs also should be quick enough to cover receivers man-for-man, with the leftovers helping double cover, playing deep zones, or blitzing.

catch 40 passes and average 20 yards per catch. In the next five nonstrike seasons, under the changed rules, it happened 13 times.

And backs began dropping from the lists of leading receivers, even with the popularity of ball-control passing. From 1975 through 1977, there were always at least three backs among the NFL's top six receivers. There haven't been that many since. The last year a back led the league was 1979. In 1983, the backs who caught the most passes, the Cowboys' Ron Springs and the Raiders' Marcus Allen, ranked ninth and thirteenth among all receivers.

The Race Is On

. . . For players too fast to catch

The way to beat any pass coverage is to dilute it, just like a cleaning solution or a shot of bourbon. Pass coverages become weaker by mixing them with receivers or turf. Either give a segment of the defense more receivers than it can handle, or give it more field than it can cover.

If the weak side of a secondary is designed to cover two receivers and the offense peppers it with three or four, there's a good chance one receiver won't be covered. The popular term is flooding a zone. It was more effective, though, before so many adjustments were built into pass-coverage assignments. The defenders on the nearly vacant strong side aren't just going to watch the offense gang up on the undermanned side of their secondary and chortle to themselves over the bad luck those poor mopes are having. They're going to scamper over to the other side and help out.

Overloading an area still can make a pass pattern work. Defenders don't adjust properly to everything, as 38–34 scores vididly testify. But overloading an area also might actually concentrate the pass coverage.

So the best way to attack a pass defense is to use the whole field. Spread the coverage out, stretch it like a plastic garbage bag, and beat it where it pops. That is probably the most enduring principle of passing offense, and it is more valuable than ever under rules that free receivers to run unimpeded. Great speed gets downfield in eighties football, it doesn't land in a heap at some muscular cornerback's feet.

"I know one thing," quarterback Brian Sipe says of pass receivers. "With all the new coverages, it's more important than ever to have speed." Marion Campbell calls the fastest receivers *bullets,* and more of them have been flying around NFL fields every year. Listen around draft day, and one thing every team wants is more speed.

It started in earnest in 1980, when six of the first-round choices were trackmen. Two of them, Colts halfback Curtis Dickey and Jets wide receiver Lam Jones, were world-class sprinters. They were selected second and fifth, surprisingly early at the time.

The Jets, remember, already had Wesley Walker, of whom team photographer Jim Pons said, "I have to use a wide-angle lens so Wesley doesn't run out of the picture." They were the first team to put their money on the notion that the field is big enough for two wide receivers with blazing speed. Then came the Packers, in 1981, to open their wallet for John Jefferson even though they had James Lofton. Jefferson didn't have Lofton's world-class speed, but the Packers' message was that the field was big enough for two all-pro wide receivers. That wasn't news to the Chargers, who promptly traded for Wes Chandler to replace Jefferson opposite Charlie Joiner.

The Packers didn't stop with Jefferson, either. In 1982, they drafted Phillip Epps, who ran the second-fastest 200 meters in the world that year. The fastest was run by Mike Miller, whom the Packers drafted in the fourth round in 1983 but did not keep.

The Buffalo Bills, with Pro Bowl wide-outs Jerry Butler and Frank Lewis in hand, traded up in the 1982 draft order to grab Perry Tuttle in the first round. Then the next year, they drafted Tony Hunter, a streamlined, tailor-made second tight end.

San Francisco had boosted the ante much higher before the 1982 draft. As reigning NFL champions, they signed Renaldo Nehemiah. Nehemiah had not played football since high school, but he had acceptable wide receiver speed over a high-hurdle course. On flat ground, he was the fastest man in the league. The 49ers guaranteed his contract for two years. (They had to. Unlike some NFL teams, the 49ers knew the best amateur hurdler in the world could pull in six figures a year.)

The Falcons had the same idea with sprinter Stanley Floyd, whose lower world ranking made him considerably less expensive. After Floyd didn't make it as a wide receiver in 1983, the USFL's Los Angeles Express tried him at cornerback in 1984. Somebody has to cover those offensive bullets.

That was why the Redskins spent their first-round choice in 1983 on a 5'8", 170-pound cornerback. Darrell Green was no budding Olympian, but he was among the top 25 sprinters in the world. Fast enough, as Tony Dorsett found out in the opening game when Green pulled him down from behind after a long run. Dorsett, who had broken some finish-line tapes himself, couldn't have been more surprised if a parachute had landed on him.

The first two rounds of the 1983 draft produced two wide receivers who had to make serious decisions between the NFL and training for the 1984 Olympics. Ron Brown, drafted by Cleveland, chose to keep running track. Chicago eventually signed first-round choice Willie Gault, but not until mid-training camp, after the world track championships, where Gault won a gold medal in the 4-by-100-meter relay and a bronze in the 110-meter high hurdles.

BLESTO, the scouting combine, had a verified time of 4.24 seconds for Gault in 40 yards. Four-four is blazing. Gault himself said he had run a 4.12 for one scout. Whatever, Gault was fast enough that the Bears had to speed up their quarterback's release to get the ball downfield in time to meet him. His speed generally created more inconvenience for defensive backs, though. "Three steps and they quit," said Stan Huntsman, Gault's track coach at Tennessee.

Huntsman has more than a layman's knowledge of wide receivers. He also has coached Anthony Hancock, Kansas City's first-round choice in 1982, Darryal Wilson, New England's second-round choice in 1983, and Mike Miller. Tennessee has become a Mecca for fleet wide receivers, largely because it is one of few major colleges that encourages them to pass up spring football practice for track.

It's likely to penetrate more college coaches' skulls that track training can make their players faster. Michigan safety Keith Bostic joined the track team for the first time as a college senior and surprised himself at how fast he could run. Surprised some scouts, too. Houston drafted him in the second round. As 40-yard times go down, signing bonuses go up, so even players at slower positions are liable to start flocking toward track coaches.

"It really helps me," Gault says of his track training. "Coming off the ball, I visualize myself coming out of the starting blocks and trying to accelerate and go past the defender like I was going past someone in the 100. Of course, you have to have a God-given talent to run, but I think track and field has developed that to where it is now.

"I've talked to Walter [Payton] about that. I told him if he'd had some training in track, his speed could have been down from 4.3

or 4.4 to maybe 4.2 He's very quick, but he doesn't really have that track training that teaches you how to keep everything in your body going forward. He wastes a lot of motion."

X X X X X
0 0 0 0

Gault arrived in the NFL with an advantage reserved only for those very few wide receivers who can leave a trail of singed turf. It wouldn't have mattered if his hands were a mason's delight. As his receiving coach, Ted Plumb, put it, "The thing about Willie is nobody's going to line up and say, 'This guy's supposed to run a 4.3 but I don't think he's that fast.' He has that instant respect."

The burner gives the defense a choice. Cover him with one man and take your chances, or double cover him. The chance the defense takes by single covering Gault, Lofton, Stanley Morgan, or Cliff Branch isn't so much that they can outrun any one defender. The single defender's first concern is preventing the long pass, so he's going to stay several yards upfield. But he's going to stay far enough upfield to leave the burner open longer than 7-Eleven on a 15-yard curl. The double coverage is to give the burner some company on short routes.

A secondary has seven defenders if nobody blitzes, and an offense has five eligible receivers. The defense can't double cover more than two receivers. Whom do Green Bay's opponents double? Lofton and Jefferson, obviously. Who led Green Bay in touchdown catches in 1983? Tight end Paul Coffman, with 11 to Lofton's 8 and Jefferson's 7. Double both outside receivers, and a defense lets the offense choose its matchups for a back or a tight end.

The main thing a burner does for an offense, even more than keeping it always within arm's reach of the end zone, is to stretch the defense. There's only a limited amount of space between the short zones and the deep zones. If the people in the deep zones don't see any urgent reason for playing real deep—if they don't see a single receiver who can give them whiplash running past them—then the deep zones will be that much closer to the short zones and the quarterback's passing lanes will be that much narrower.

That's why the burner doesn't necessarily have to make a lot of catches to be valuable. Just being on the field, he opens more space for the other receivers. But as Steve Largent, Seattle's relatively slow but incomparable craftsman of a wide receiver, says of a teammate's raw speed, "It helps him more than it helps anybody else."

He doesn't need to worry a lot about being jammed at the line of scrimmage, for one thing. The defensive back's margin for error is too thin for anything risky. "Once he gets by you and gets the ball, he's going to score," says Terry Schmidt, a Chicago cornerback who has to practice against Gault and play against Lofton. "Although . . . you'd be surprised how fast someone can run when he's chasing a guy to the goal line."

"You have to get out of your backpedal sooner," says Gary Green, Kansas City's Pro Bowl cornerback. "Once you do that, you're not able to cut as fast to either direction."

The fastest receivers are no less intimidating than a punch in the nose. They're distracting. They get the defender thinking about the ultimate insult, getting beaten for a long touchdown pass, instead of stopping *any* pass. As Jets safety Darrol Ray says of teammate Lam Jones, "You know he's fast, but you don't realize how fast until you're running next to him. Then it's like, 'He's walking by me.' " That's the kind of panic an offense likes to see.

Trackmen tend to gravitate toward split end, rather than flanker, but there is no right or wrong place to put your burner. The flanker is on the strong side, which is more apt to be the primary side of the pattern. And the flanker is off the line of scrimmage, which helps him avoid the jam in case the defense wants to slow a burner down by draping an old beat-him-up double zone over his side. But the split end, on the weak side, is in a better position to either draw single coverage or make the defense rotate its coverage away from the side with more receivers. The split end also has less demanding blocking assignments.

More and more, teams are moving their burners around. Gault occasionally lines up in the Bears' backfield. "They've got to find him," says his coach, Mike Ditka. "He may end up with a linebacker covering him if they don't adjust properly. And when he comes out of the backfield, he's really moving."

"Speed alone is not going to beat anybody," Green says. If a young burner doesn't run his routes to the right depth, doesn't make the right sight adjustments, or doesn't have any moves besides straight ahead, he's not likely to catch anything but a plane ticket home. "They've got a lot of stuff to learn," Schmidt says. "But you can't learn to be fast. If you go out and tell them to run deep, they know that."

X X X X X
O O O O

Nothing buzzes up a stadium like a long touchdown pass. Whether it's called a bomb, a go, a fly, an up, a home run, a streak, or a nine route, the long pass takes all the computer printouts, film reels, and multiple, four-step adjustments and dumps them back on the playground. It reminds the players this was the same game they played as children under street lights.

"It does something for you," Lofton says of the bomb. "It does something for the quarterback, and it even does something for the guys on the sidelines."

It does something for the offensive linemen and running backs, who just got a touchdown without getting pounded on for 10 or 12 plays. It does something *to* the opposing defense, which just got its face slapped in front of 60,000 people.

The bomb is a timing route, necessarily designed with less precision than, say, a 15-yard out. The receiver runs about four yards from the sideline, and he may have to chase the ball to the inside or the outside. He doesn't want to start right into his sprint. Let the defender think he's running that 15-yard out. Keep him backpedaling. When the receiver and defender are running step for step, that's the time to kick into full speed.

By then, the ball is in the air. The receiver doesn't have to see it until it's on its way down. Then it's time to judge where it will land. The best receivers can somehow go even faster, if necessary, to catch up with the end of the rainbow. The best ones wait until the last instant to give a defender any indication that they'll need to veer toward or away from the sideline, or to slow down and beat the defender again going back for the ball.

And the best ones are concentrating so hard, their vision actually slows down the flight of the ball. They know where the defender and the sideline are, but the yard lines, the cheering fans, and the scoreboard aren't even in their universe. Wide-open receivers drop passes all the time that are so easy, their minds have time to wander. For the receiver who has kept his concentration, who catches the ball and crosses the goal line, the crowd noise hits him suddenly, like a loud radio just turned on.

"It's kind of like waking up," said Golden Richards, who averaged a touchdown nearly every fifth time he caught the ball in five seasons at Dallas. "You're not aware of anything else going downfield, and then you look back from the end zone and everybody's running at you with their arms up. You don't touch the ground on the way back to the bench. At least I don't."

Dressed to Thrill

... Offenses tailor their tight end running back positions for the small and swift

Speed is not some new fascination for NFL coaches, some fad like Space Invaders or bell-bottomed pants that they simply must have but will hardly remember in two years. Speed always has been important. But bodies often come packaged with speed and size in inverse proportions, and never in pro football have there been so many reasons for favoring speed over size.

That's true at every position. We've seen the advantages of speed at wide receiver and quarterback, defensive back and linebacker, offensive lineman and defensive lineman. Except at quarterback, most of those advantages stem from the 1978 rule changes. But even before those changes, other pressures (particularly double zones and Prevent defenses) were making tight ends and running backs sleeker and fleeter. Terry Metcalf and Joe Washington, for example, were star halfbacks and kick returners in the mid-seventies.

When Cleveland drafted Ozzie Newsome a few weeks after the rules were changed, many opponents assumed he would have to move to wide receiver. He was too small to play tight end, too fast to waste there. But Cleveland played in Pittsburgh's division, where the double zone was a scourge, and a deep threat in the middle of the field would have been desirable even if the rules had not been changed.

So the Browns kept Newsome at tight end, and then watched more and more teams stumble over each other to get their hands on a tight end who could run like Newsome. He caught 351 passes in the next six years, more than any other NFL tight end.

For Cleveland's quarterback, Brian Sipe, Newsome opened up a Pandora's Box of opportunities downfield. "Teams had been able to cover us before with two-deep zones," he said, "and the five men underneath were stopping everything short. But every time you get some speed they have to respect, that takes something away from them. They can't do as many things to make it hard on you, or you'll get a mismatch. Once we got the speed to stretch those deep zones, the game made a lot more sense to me."

"When they changed the rules," quarterback Archie Manning said, "teams started to play more man-to-man coverage against the tight end. A lot of strong safeties were kind of half defensive backs, half linebackers. They just didn't have the footwork to keep up with fast tight ends. With man coverage, you've really got a hand tied behind your back if you don't have a tight end who can run and catch."

Even the fastest tight ends would be relatively slow wide receivers. But the slowest tight ends, the scaled-down tackles of the sixties and early seventies, have been left behind in pro football's downfield game of the eighties.

"When they changed the rules," quarterback Archie Manning said, "teams started to play more man-to-man coverage against the tight end. . . . With man coverage, you've really got a hand tied behind your back if you don't have a tight end who can run and catch."

Mike Ditka, whose tight-end record of 75 catches in 1965 stood for 15 years, says he always considered himself a blocker first and a receiver second. Now few teams even ask their tight ends to block defensive ends one-on-one. "You're just looking for a guy who can get in someone's way," Sid Gillman says. Ditka's tight end at Chicago, Emery Moorehead, was an oversized wide receiver who spent five years in limbo between three teams' benches and the waiver wire until Ditka decided an oversized wide receiver was just what a tight end ought to be.

In 1971, two tight ends had more than 40 catches. In 1981, there were 10. After the trend had begun, the illegal-chuck rule accelerated it by helping tight ends get off the line of scrimmage and run short crossing routes. Dave Casper, the prototype tight end of the mid-seventies, was successful largely because he was able to run the gauntlet of punching, tripping, elbowing, and grabbing from defensive ends and linebackers. "He'd still be dragging people 10 or 12 yards downfield," Tom Landry marveled.

Getting off the line is still a chore for a tight end. His first few steps are likely to involve a defensive end's elbow to his ribs, a linebacker's stand-him-in-his-tracks block to the chest, and, when he's finally striding, a sideswipe by the strong safety. Cowboy tight end Doug Cosbie says speed is not as important as "having the strength to get off the ball."

So a tight end still gets ample use out of the old, coordinated knee-and-forearm thrust to the linebacker's stomach and chin. He still has to bang down the door to the open field. But once he's in the clear, he stays in the clear. He gets a chance to run. Given that opportunity, it's nice if he can run fast.

Winslow, Newsome, Moorehead, Todd Christensen, Jimmie Giles, Joe Senser, and Tony Hunter get downfield fast enough to make defenses reconsider the idea that the wide-outs are the receivers to double cover. Their teams can stretch a defense in the middle, as well as on the sidelines. Other prolific receivers— Cosbie, Casper, Paul Coffman, Dan Ross, Mike Barber, and Russ Francis—don't look so fast alongside Newsome and Giles, but they would have been absolute lightning among tight ends ten years ago. Used with two blazing wide-outs, as many of them are, they stretch the underside of a defense.

They're accessible to the quarterback. An eight-yard pass along the hash marks is barely half as long as an eight-yard pass to the near sideline. And besides catching the ball reliably, these tight ends can keep the play alive by running with the ball.

They're tempting targets. Christensen, Newsome, and Winslow ranked 1-2-3 in NFL pass receiving in 1983. Including Ross and Senser, five tight ends accounted for 10 of the 30 spots among the top 10 receivers in 1981–83. In 1975–79, two tight ends accounted for just 4 of 53 spots (there were some tenth-place ties), and the two were Casper and Walter White, both fast for that time.

After tailoring tight ends to their passing games, NFL teams found it worked so well that they took the extra step of tailoring their passing games to tight ends. And so we have double tight ends, tight ends in motion, and part-time tight ends used as receiving specialists. Much the same thing has happened with running backs.

X X X X X
0 0 0 0

The running back who can only run has become as obsolete as the drug store that sells only medicine. Or the tight end who can only block.

"There's no place in a pro offense anymore for someone who can't catch," Gillman says.

At best, the back who can't catch is a specialist. He might be a

1,000-yard specialist, in the case of John Riggins. Or he might be a short-yardage specialist, or even a blocking specialist. At worst, on a team that doesn't choose its backs as selectively as Riggins' Redskins, the purely *running* running back becomes a draw-back.

People have said that about Earl Campbell, who only ran for more yards in his first four seasons than anyone else in NFL history. But he doesn't catch, so the Oilers have left the backs out of their passing game most of Campbell's career. They've denied themselves one of pro football's most popular plays. As Bud Grant says, "They talk about how the Vikings have an off-tackle pass."

It was not Campbell's fault the Oilers didn't go out and get a Joe Washington for passing downs, as the Redskins did within months after Gibbs took their coaching job. The Redskins got the original, but there are lots of generic Joe Washingtons floating around the NFL, more every season. His prolonged success, at 5'10" and 179 pounds, has run roughshod through the reservations scouts used to have about small running backs.

Washington isn't quite the patron saint of receiving backs, though, as Winslow is for second tight ends. While Washington was cutting down scouts' prejudices toward size, Preston Pearson

---

"It's not easy, coming in under pressure without warming up," Pearson said. "Some places it's cold and freezing and your hands are freezing. It's like being a designated hitter in baseball. Except you're not going out there unless it's third-and-eight and your team needs a first down and the other team knows as well as you do that your chances of getting the ball thrown to you are 50 percent."

---

was showing coaches how to use those little scatbacks with good hands. It was unusual—even considered somehow unnatural—to trot a new halfback onto the field for passing downs until Pearson did it in 1977–79.

"This has started a whole new facet of the game," Pearson said then. "People are going to stop saying, 'This guy's not big enough to play running back.' They're going to look for backs who can catch the ball. Backs are going to start working on their receiving in college."

In 1980, the Bills drafted Joe Cribbs (5'11", 190) and the Jets turned a journeyman running back named Bruce Harper (5'8", 177) into a 50-catch receiving back. In 1981, San Diego drafted James Brooks (5'9", 177) in the first round, even though he clearly was not likely to start ahead of Chuck Muncie. Other backs to follow Washington's and Pearson's small and swift footsteps have included the Dolphins' Tommy Vigorito (5'10", 197), the Cardinals' Stump Mitchell (5'9", 188), the Buccaneers' Michael Morton (5'8", 180), the Giants' Joe Morris (5'7", 190, second round), the Chiefs' Joe Delaney (5'10", 184, second round), the Vikings' Darrin Nelson (5'9", 180, first round), and the Broncos' Gerald Willhite (5'10", 200, first round).

Cribbs, Delaney, Nelson, and Willhite made starting lineups (as did Washington and Pearson, earlier in their careers). That's great. With a versatile player like Nelson, it means the Vikings can go from two backs to three wide receivers without shuttling in a substitute and signaling the defense to send in its nickelback. But these players don't have to start to be valuable. They have to catch passes, maybe return kicks, and threaten a big play every time they touch the ball. The 49-man rosters are amply big for that kind of luxury.

"It's not easy, coming in under pressure without warming up," Pearson said. "Some places it's cold and freezing and your hands are freezing. It's like being a designated hitter in baseball. Except you're not going out there unless it's third-and-eight and your team needs a first down and the other team knows as well as you do that your chances of getting the ball thrown to you are 50 percent."

The receiving back develops almost a wide receiver's outlook, concerning himself more with recognizing zones than with picking out running lanes. The difference, Pearson said, is "the ball gets to you differently at five yards than it does at twenty-five yards." For one thing, "at twenty-five yards, you have time to think. Which I don't."

"But I've got an advantage," Pearson said. "Most linebackers can't keep up with me. And defensive backs just aren't as strong. That's the overriding reason to use backs as receivers. They're stronger than defensive backs and quicker than linebackers."

"Nine times out of ten, you're one-on-one with a linebacker," says Atlanta's William Andrews, whose 182 catches in 1981–83 rank fourth in the NFL, first among backs. "And after you get by the congestion at the line, get open and catch the ball, then you're a running back in the open field." That's how the Raiders set the Super Bowl record for longest pass play. The pass to Kenny King against Philadelphia didn't go 15 yards. But by the time King finished running, he had an 80-yard touchdown.

"He still gets to run," Grant says of a pass-catching back. "But he doesn't have to start from so far back."

Let's Slow Down Here

... And look at what really makes a wide receiver great

Speed has as much to do with a wide receiver's success as money has to do with a person's happiness. It's a good place to start, but better not to have it at all than to have it and nothing else.

Charlie Joiner, Ahmad Rashad, Cliff Branch, and James Lofton all came into the NFL with stopwatch-popping speed, but it was their skills that made them great wide receivers: Their abilities to run precise routes, to recognize defenses, to release past the jam at the line of scrimmage, to control their bodies and change directions without slowing down, to get open and catch the ball. That's all a wide receiver has to do. Get open and catch the ball.

"Most wide receivers who are burners can only run one of two things," says Willie Buchanon, who continued to be an excellent cornerback for San Diego after losing the blazing speed he had as a young star at Green Bay. "A fly or an out. If they slow down, you know it's an out."

The burners tend to go in the first two rounds of the draft, so consider this: From 1981 through 1983, only two of the sixteen wide receivers drafted in the first two rounds started regularly as rookies. Cris Collinsworth and Gault. And Collinsworth was the only instant all-star.

Over a long period of time, about half the touchdown passes in the NFL will be for 15 yards or less. A pulling guard can sprint 15 yards in a hurry. Less than 10 percent will be longer than 50 yards, and less than one-third will be longer than 25 yards.

"You can't be slow or you're worthless," says 49er coach Bill Walsh. "But you don't need to be a world-class sprinter. If 50 passes are completed, 40 of them are going to be in the area up to 14 yards. You just don't complete that many of them downfield.

"You need to do that. You need to play for it. But in the meantime, you need to control the ball, gain yardage, and keep your defense off the field."

In pro football's era of speed, the irony is that the fastest position of all has been the most accommodating to relatively slow players. The top ten pass receivers in 1981—in terms of yardage, which favors speed more than number of catches— included Joiner, Dwight Clark, Steve Largent, and Steve Watson: four players who actually can joke about their lack of speed. Three of them never had been fast, by wide receiver standards, and Joiner, in his thirteenth season, had long since stopped trying to outrun defenders. Lofton and Kevin House were the only burners on the list.

In terms of catches, the top seven wide receivers from 1981 through 1983, were Clark, Collinsworth, Largent, Wes Chandler, Joiner, Lofton, and Watson. Lofton was the only sprinter of the group and Collinsworth the only other one who was relatively fast for a wide receiver.

As a group, wide receivers are getting faster every year. As are the best wide receivers. But the good, reliable craftsmen with no use for track spikes have not been left behind. For a number of reasons:

1. Just as the illegal-chuck rule makes it easier to get a fast receiver deep now, it also is easier to stretch pass coverage backward so there's more room for the 10–15-yard routes. It depends where the coverage is willing to pop. "The game is becoming so highly refined," says quarterback Brian Sipe, "I think you need one group of downfield receivers and one group of short-and-intermediate receivers. Almost like pinch hitters. You need to suit your personnel to the coverage."

2. Against defenses with six or seven defensive backs, faster people in coverage, Walsh says, "It's almost impossible to get the ball downfield." A burner can get there, but not without company. So, as Buchanon says, "Teams are throwing more underneath all the time." To get open underneath, a receiver needs skills, not just speed.

3. The more sophisticated an offense becomes, the more important it becomes for receivers to run disciplined pass routes. "You have to know your receiver will be where you expect him to be," Atlanta quarterback Steve Bartkowski says.

4. The receiver running a 15-yard crossing route, or even an

out, needs more time to make his fakes and his cuts than the burner running a fly. The pass-blocking and chuck rules have given him that time.

5. The reliable, short-range receiver is essential to a ball-control, passing game. "He hurts a defense by continually getting those seven, eight, 12 yards," Walsh says, "which is just about impossible with a running game."

One thing that hasn't changed is the importance of completing a pass on, say, third-and-eight. Those completions are the unheralded big plays of any game, often the plays without which the more noticeable big plays never could have happened. And, as Chiefs cornerback Gary Green says:

"The guy the cornerback looks to in those situations is the guy he knows can adjust his route to the coverage, fight his way open, and catch the ball.

"Guys like Largent and Chandler and Joiner have very good moves. That's what you need in a possession receiver. You have to ask yourself, what's more important? Speed or quickness? These guys are much quicker than the faster wide receivers."

That's generally accepted among football people, but why is it so? Is it simply that human bodies rarely come loaded with all the options, like expensive cars? As Largent suggests, "Maybe because most sprinters are long-legged, their feet aren't as quick."

"Quick feet and excellent body control are the most important things in a wide receiver. The faster you are, there are a lot of things you can do. But if you're just fast enough, you can do the things almost anybody else can do. If you've got quick feet and body control, you can get off the line of scrimmage, you can change directions, make quick cuts, put moves on people. I'd rather have a guy like Steve Largent, who can change directions, than the fastest guy in the world."—**Jerry Rhome**, Washington Redskins offensive coordinator

Or, as Sipe offers, "Maybe it's for the same reason a blind man learns to hear so well. The guys I've worked with, Reggie Rucker and Dave Logan, who are more what you'd call a thinking man's receiver, they just work harder at it." And while speed has to be a gift; moves and route running and release techniques and reading defenses and even foot quickness can be learned or developed.

"It's seldom that a gifted runner develops the science of running intermediate pass patterns," Walsh says. Why bother? In high school and college, he gets by without it.

If that's true, the more football emphasizes speed in wide receivers, the more valuable a slower, skilled receiver becomes. "So often our scouting system just doesn't account for him," Walsh says. "The typical pro scout looks for speed, height, and weight. So those players who have agility and quickness and endurance running inside routes against linebackers have to be found and developed by certain teams. Some teams never do find and develop them because they don't understand the importance of them."

X X X X
o o o o

A common accolade given to wide receivers is, "He runs good routes." So? Isn't that a little like praising an architect who "draws straight lines" or saying your accountant sure writes nice numbers? Running good routes seems to be an awfully basic thing for a wide receiver, certainly not the kind of talent that would get coaches and scouts and quarterbacks all excited.

In other words: *What can possibly be difficult about running good routes?* For a 15-yard out, you run 15 yards, turn right, and stop before you go out of bounds, right?

For one thing, there's no orange pylon out there 15 yards downfield. There are yard lines, but they're on the ground. A receiver can't be looking down and watching out for defenders and the ball. He can't even count to 15 while he's running. "Sometimes you see young guys counting it out," says Largent. But they might get bumped off their count by a defensive back, and even if that doesn't happen, they can't be counting and reading the defense at the same time. It's hard enough to read the comics while counting. As Largent says, "You've got to just *know* the right depth for your cut. The only way to get that feel is repetition."

The first place a receiver has to adjust to defenders is getting off the line of scrimmage. Again: How hard can it be to *get off the line of scrimmage?* You see the ball snapped, you stand up, and you start running.

But what if the cornerback has rolled up to the line of scrimmage, and he's standing where you want to go? In some patterns, it makes a difference whether a receiver releases inside or outside. He might get in the way of another receiver if he starts the wrong way. So the receiver may have to throw a move on the defender—or a forearm—just to get started.

And he can't be lollygagging into his route, even if nobody is in his way. "The quicker you get off the ball, the more pressure you put on a defender," Joiner says. "They hate to see you get off the ball fast. It gives them less time to think. You know where you're going. He doesn't. So you don't want him to lay back and think and maybe figure out where you're going."

All the while, the receiver is reading the defense, in case the defenders were giving him a false look before the snap. Even if his route doesn't call for a sight adjustment, changing the route according to the coverage, he can't go 15 yards and turn right if that will take him right into the cornerback's arms.

He has to know more than who's covering his area, too. On a crossing route, Packer tight end Paul Coffman says he might delay leaving the line of scrimmage to help a teammate avoid coverage over the middle. "That'll keep the linebacker in longer," he says. "If I'm in a hurry to get out there so they'll throw it to me, I might be letting one linebacker cover two receivers."

"Some guys know the coverage within two steps off the line of scrimmage," Sipe says. "They know where the defenders will be when they get to where they make their break. A receiver who doesn't have that aptitude doesn't know until he gets to his break point."

That's too late. By then, a receiver might have to slow down to decide, where do I go now? He might as well throw his hands up and surrender.

"Some guys know the coverage within two steps off the line of scrimmage," Sipe says. "They know where the defenders will be when they get to where they make their break. A receiver who doesn't have that aptitude doesn't know until he gets to his break point."

"You have to be patient," Coffman says. "Early in my career, if the defensive back was waiting outside and I had to run an out, my mind went blank. How am I going to do it?" What Coffman does now is make a move—a head fake, a false step, maybe something he has seen work against that defender on film— maybe make two or three moves. He doesn't break at 13 yards for a 15-yard route, a tempting adjustment that often enables a receiver to practice his tackling. He persuades the defender he's running an inside route. "First, you have to get him turned around. Then you go ahead and run your out."

It's easier if he has a sight adjustment. Then he can simply run away from the coverage. But in that case, he has all the more reason to diagnose the coverage early.

What a good route runner does, then, is show up at the right place at the right time, and get there alone. The quarterback can throw him the ball without even seeing him because he knows the receiver will be resourceful enough to get there. Whether it means running 20 yards and coming back for a 15-yard route or turning the defender in circles, he'll get there. As Joiner puts it, "If you're not there, you can't get the ball."

X X X X X
O O O O

Once he's in the right place at the right time, the receiver still must perform the detail of catching the ball. "The big thing for a receiver," says Redskin offensive coordinator Jerry Rhome, "is what you do when the ball is in the air. John Jefferson has a great ability to adjust to the ball's flight and catch it."

It starts with a lot of little things a receiver does when he turns to look back toward the quarterback. His body is square to the quarterback for the widest possible target. His hands are chest high with the thumbs in for a high throw; it's easier to take them down than up at the last moment. His feet are placed properly for breaking in any direction, including up.

He has to be willing to retrace his steps—to fight for the ball and even break up an interception, if necessary, but mainly to catch the ball as high as possible off the ground. "You'll see defensive backs who have a shot at an interception," Green says, "but they want to look the ball in, catch it at their chest, and run with it. And a good receiver will jump and catch the ball before it gets there."

The underthrown pass is the best one for distinguishing the great receivers. They can stop on a dime, change directions as smoothly as they would change the channels on a remote control, and go for the ball while the defensive back keeps running right on past. Branch has reached back past defenders for long gains in the Raiders' last two Super Bowls. Against Philadelphia, he beat Roynell Young, a Pro Bowl cornerback, down the left sideline and then beat him back for the underthrow. Young was closer to the ball when the two began their jumps, but in the air, Branch spun past him, controlling his body as if it were a chicken on a rotisserie spit.

Branch learned his receiving skills from Fred Biletnikof, who, along with Raymond Berry, creeps into any discussion about the greatest tactical receivers. Branch has recalled seeing Biletnikof stay on the field after practice to work on his one-handed catches, or his sore-handed, forearm-and-ribcage catches, knowing the time would come when he would need to use them instinctively.

Scouts are partial to receivers who catch the ball with their hands, like basketball players, instead of against their bodies. There are times when it's wise for a receiver to trap the ball against his chest. "Especially if you're in traffic and know you're going to get hit," Clark says. But as a rule, fingertips grip things better than ribs do.

The best hands give with the ball, absorbing it more than snatching it. Sid Gillman tells receivers to caress the ball, but aggressively, as if it were the breast of the most beautiful woman they ever saw. But for a receiver, the hands are no better than the eyes.

"The most important thing is concentration," Joiner says. "I remember I caught a pass against Detroit on my fingertips. I caught just the back end of the ball. I really thought the ball was overthrown. But I watched it all the way."

X X X X X
O O O O

Besides helping the receiver get to the ball, quickness and body control help the ball get to the receiver. Which is to say, they help the receiver get open. That's something a quarterback likes to see before delivering the ball.

Basketball has a better term for the maneuvers a player uses to separate himself from a defender. In basketball, they're called fakes. In football, they're called moves. They're really sleight-of-body tricks, and they're the reason wily receivers give defensive backs more fits than receivers who just run wild.

"They're real good actors, is what it is," Green says. "They use your quickness against you and get you leaning away from where they want to go. Even though they won't leave you in a cloud of dust, it just takes that one split second to get open."

Moves are a private shell game between the receiver and his defender. They aren't usually obvious unless an alert television director replays a receiver's whole route, which happened during a Thursday night game shortly before the 1982 strike. Frank Lewis, the Buffalo receiver who became, in 1981, the oldest receiver to gain 1,000 yards (he was 35), was running a route near the left sideline against Viking cornerback Willie Teal.

Lewis was angling away from the sideline, obviously too fast to think about changing directions. Even his head was aiming away from the sideline, leaning in front of his body. So Teal, as both ran downfield, comfortably assumed a position inside Lewis. He was still there when Lewis, in the blink of an eye, tightly turned to his left like a bobsled on a banked course, even seeming to accelerate. Showing Teal his back, Lewis was wide open when he caught the ball at the sideline.

"I think the most important thing a receiver can do is come out of his break fast and be in control," Mike Ditka says. "And catch the ball. But you see a lot of guys going full speed in their routes, but they come out of their cuts and they're not under control enough to catch the ball."

Receivers, probably more than anyone else, watch film of the people who play their position along with film of the people they're playing against. They're looking for moves they can use. Moves are not spur-of-the-moment inspirations. They're designed specifically to sell a defender on covering a route the receiver is not running. In some cases, they're even designed *not* to fool the defender. Early in his route, a receiver might throw a couple sloppy moves at a defender to get him thinking, Huh! This guy's a piece of cake.

Some moves are just flat-out trickery. Like stopping. When the defender turns briefly to check the quarterback, a smart receiver might just pull up and let the defender keep running out of the play.

Fran Tarkenton's favorite tight ends at New York and Minnesota, Bob Tucker and Stu Voigt, perfected the falling-down move. If a defender sees his man fall down, he's going to have a strong urge to leave the man and help cover someone else. Tucker or Voigt would wait to be counted out of the play, climb to their feet, and catch another first-down pass.

The man with good moves is most dangerous when he runs what's called a double-cut route. Whether it's a stop-and-go, an out-and-up, a curl-and-up, or whatever, the idea is to sell the defender on covering a short route and then to whisk past him toward the end zone. "More than anything else, you kind of lull them to sleep," Largent says.

So a receiver doesn't even have to be fast to catch a long pass. In 1981, the NFL had three touchdown passes longer than 90 yards and Steve Watson caught two of them. He caught 60 passes that year, the most for a receiver averaging 20 yards per catch since the 1970 merger (surpassed in 1983 by faster Mike Quick with 69).

Double-cut routes are most effective late in a game, after the defenders have been lulled to sleep. Largent or Watson might spend all day running 12-yard routes, letting the defense take for granted that he's going to go in or out at 12 yards but not keep going downfield. So the defense tightens its coverage, clamping down on those 12-yard routes, and it becomes harder and harder to get open.

Sipe recalls a Cleveland game when that happened to Reggie Rucker. It went into overtime and, one more time, Rucker ran a 12-yard in. Two defenders swooped onto him like pigeons on a slice of bread. As soon as the defenders had committed themselves, Rucker turned upfield. He didn't stop until he had caught the winning touchdown pass. "That's the kind of savvy you find in a veteran receiver," Sipe says.

With a double-cut route, *a slower receiver might even more easily get open deep than a flat-out burner.* If someone like Largent wants to run an out-and-go, he's more likely to get the cornerback to bite on his out move, to close in on him, than, say, Willie Gault or Kevin House. The cornerback would be more conscious of a deep route when he's covering Gault or House. He would cover him from farther upfield and stay put until the ball is in the air. It's always easier to let defensive players take themselves out of the way than to physically move them or outrun them.

The most famous double-cut route, because it was in a Super Bowl, may have been the one John Stallworth ran to score one touchdown and set up another when the Steelers beat the Rams for the 1979 championship. The Rams were one of the first teams using seven defensive backs that year and it was hard for even Stallworth, no leadfoot even by wide-outs' standards, to beat them deep. So the Steelers had designed a play (called 60 Prevent Slot Hook and Go) to give him help.

The first time they used it was three minutes into the fourth quarter, against six defensive backs, with the Rams ahead by two. Stallworth ran a 15-yard curl (or hook), attracted the pair of swooping defensive backs and dashed between them to run under a 73-yard touchdown pass. The free safety he had planned on outrunning had missed his assignment, so Stallworth was all alone. As Terry Bradshaw said, "Usually on that play, the receiver hooks and slides toward the middle. That's the way they defensed it." And the skilled receiver left the defense grabbing a handful of air.

Playing with Fire

. . . Cornerbacks find it harder
than ever to avoid getting burned

Pro cornerbacks made their living on a tightrope over an alligator swamp even before the NFL painted track lanes along its sidelines. Their mistakes showed up in lights. On the scoreboard. In front of 60,000 people, many of them boisterous, and a television audience of millions.

The position required short memories and calloused psyches because, since the forward pass became popular, only one thing has ever been certain about playing cornerback. Every cornerback knows sometime soon, maybe on the next play, another receiver will chew him up and spit him out for six points. He will have nowhere to hide his stripped soul as he returns once again from the end zone, beyond help and beneath contempt.

All that abuse was not enough, the NFL decided. The illegal-chuck rule essentially ordered cornerbacks to look but not touch, as though receivers were museum exhibits or cheerleaders, not enemy wide receivers trying to beat and humiliate them. "After five yards and one chuck, you can't give anybody a dirty look or you'll see a handkerchief," Sid Gillman says. "They can't cover anybody. They're merely able to react to the thrown ball."

For cornerbacks, one good thing came out of this. The best ones became more valuable than ever. Before the rule changes, cornerbacks in general shared the same priority as centers in the grand schemes of personnel directors: Take care of the other positions first. The cornerback could always be someone not quite fast enough for wide receiver. As long as his feet were reasonably quick, he could be taught to play zone coverage and to keep plunking and jostling receivers as they ran.

Defensive backs were the lowest-paid players, aside from kickers, largely because they were the lowest drafted. Not until 1980 did the NFL make a regular practice of snapping up five or six defensive backs in the first round, 10 or 11 in the first two. They had gone from afterthoughts to sought after. Bud Grant went so far as to say, in 1983, "Defensive backs are probably the best athletes you have on a team."

The highest draft choices, whether they played safety or cornerback in college, were tried on the corner when training camp began. That's where the pros needed great athletes. Why not throw it against the wall and see if it sticks? San Francisco's Ronnie Lott was a college safety who stuck at corner.

The colleges have been turning out better cornerbacks lately because they, too, have been passing more. But the position still has the highest surprise rate, both good and bad, for scouts. High choices wash out and Everson Walls, drafted by nobody, becomes arguably the best cornerback in the NFL.

College cornerbacks are hard to evaluate because college teams play pass defense so differently. For one thing, most scouting is done from film, and a lot of college teams play their cornerbacks so deep, they don't even show up on film. College teams don't ask their corners to play as much man-to-man as the pros require, and that's what scouts want to know most of all about a cornerback prospect. Nor do they expect corners to play the run so aggressively, another thing pro cornerbacks must do.

And the best college cornerbacks are likely to have very peaceful games. Their opponents throw to the other side. So while a pro team puts its quickest and best defensive back on the corner, where he'll need to play more man-to-man than safeties, a college team is likely to put him inside, at free safety or something called monster back, where he can pitch in on plays to either direction.

X X X X X
O O O O

The illegal-chuck rule rewrote the job description for corner-backs. As Tom Landry says, "Now that they can't harrass receivers, you see them a little faster and quicker and not necessarily as big." You see more defensive backs on a roster, too. Eight of them, once a luxury, have become a minimum for teams using six or seven at a time. And to play in the more sophisticated defenses, all defensive backs have to be smarter than in the days when a coach could simply turn them loose on receivers and say, "Sic 'em."

"I think it puts a premium on really working hard and developing the fine skills of pass coverage," Bart Starr said when he was Green Bay's coach. "And gosh, we really have some great ones in the league. I think it's a thing of beauty to see a defensive back stay with and cover a talented receiver who knows where he's going."

There's the rub. The cornerback doesn't know where the receiver is going. He has to backpedal nearly as fast as the wide receiver—who probably has more speed or his college coach would have moved him to cornerback—and all he can do is react to where the receiver is going. Or in the case of a receiver with good moves, where he *seems* to be going.

The cornerback not only doesn't know where the receiver is going, he doesn't know for sure that the receiver is going out for a pass. His mind has to be spinning as furiously as his feet, starting before the ball is snapped. Every time an offensive player goes in motion, the cornerback has to decide whether it changes the coverage scheme. And if so, how? And whether that means he has to move, too. That could happen three or four times before the ball is even in play.

Then when the ball is snapped, it's not simply a matter of drifting into a zone or tailing a receiver. While he's doing that, the cornerback has to make sure the play is going to be a pass. He has to take his eye off the receiver and check the weak-side tackle or guard, whichever player is his key. If he reads a run key—if the tackle is driving ahead or the guard is pulling—he has to come back toward the line of scrimmage to keep the play from getting outside the defense. Provided, of course, that he's sure the linemen aren't just faking the run for a play-action pass.

Once he has established the play is a pass, he still can't devote undivided attention to his receiver. He has to check out the backs, or maybe the tight end. Their routes could change his coverage responsibility. A lot of defenses adjust their coverages on the fly according to whether the backs go out in different directions, both of them go to the strong side or both go to the weak side.

The tight end's route may not change a cornerback's coverage, but it can change the way he plays his coverage. It can change his help, the positioning of his teammates. If the tight end runs an inside route, that would take the cornerback's nearest inside teammate farther away from him, so he would have to be more conscious of protecting against an inside move while he's covering his receiver or his zone. Which he has to be doing flawlessly all the time he's looking around at the off-side tackle and guard and the backs and the tight end.

There is more to playing cornerback, then, than putting one foot in back of the other and keeping the ball out of the wrong hands. A vereran may lose some speed over the years, but the experience he gains more than makes up for it. "You don't learn everything you need to know until you're too old to use it anymore," says Ross Fichtner, a fine defensive back with Cleveland in the sixties who now coaches Minnesota's defensive backs.

An experienced defensive back doesn't just read the tackle, the guard, the backs, and the tight end as instinctively as he would read a freeway exit sign. He learns to read the offense well enough to know which receivers are decoys and who merits his attention. He can tell whether a quarterback plans to throw long or short by the way he holds the ball. He can guess a receiver's route by the way he lines up (a wide receiver nearly at the sideline isn't going to have room to run an out). He even knows officials tend to overlook contact if the defender's hands are down but usually throw the flag if they're up.

The defensive back who can read an offense quickly might be able to anticipate a newly popular type of pattern in time to avoid its trap. Defensive players call the patterns illegal picks, somewhat redundantly because all basketball-style picks by receivers are illegal and somewhat hopefully because the rule is virtually impossible to enforce. What the patterns do is send one receiver (or two) on a route that will interfere with the defender trying to cover the primary receiver. Two such patterns are diagrammed on page 158. Who's to say whether the receivers are setting picks for teammates or merely running legitimate pass routes?

A faster cornerback doesn't need to know precisely when to turn out of his backpedal. He can afford to lose a step to most receivers and still catch up. But the veteran picks up that step by turning out of his backpedal an instant before the receiver accelerates upfield. He has learned to read the receiver's face, or his footwork. He has had to. When a cornerback leaves his backpedal to run with the receiver, he picks up speed but sacrifices agility. He's no longer in position to break with the receiver in either direction.

The slower-but-wiser cornerback also keeps from losing that costly step by positioning himself where the receiver wants to cut and by not buying the receiver's moves to coax him out of the way. "The hardest defensive back to play against is the one who won't look at you," says Steve Largent. "He's the hardest to control. If he's looking at the quarterback instead of you, you can put all kinds of moves on him and it doesn't matter because he's

It is illegal in the NFL for receivers to run basketball-style picks for each other, but it is almost impossible for officials to catch if the pass pattern is designed so one receiver's route interferes with the path of the defender covering another receiver. In the pattern below, the flanker (Z) goes in motion before the snap and cuts inside the tight end (Y), who runs interference for him.

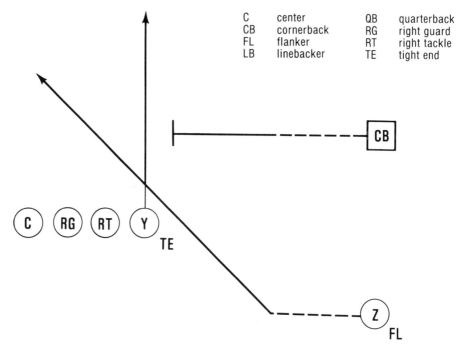

C	center	QB	quarterback
CB	cornerback	RG	right guard
FL	flanker	RT	right tackle
LB	linebacker	TE	tight end

In the pattern below, the linebacker trying to cover the fullback must fight through congestion caused by the routes of both the tight end and the flanker.

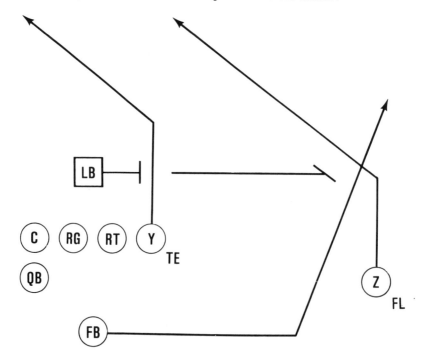

not paying any attention." Largent says Denver's Louis Wright, still among the best NFL corners after nine seasons, is one of the most frustrating in that regard.

X X X X X
O O O O

Things get hairiest for a defensive back in the instant, after he has been covering for several seconds, when he has to glance at the quarterback. It's just a quick peek, no longer than it takes a commuter to look from his newspaper to see if the bus is coming. But it's long enough for the receiver to leave him behind.

"If you peek, you're beat. That's what they tell you," says Gary Green. "While you're checking to see where the ball is, the receiver's going after it."

Green gets beaten for relatively few touchdowns, but he recalls one Largent scored against him because he peeked. Largent ran a stop-and-go route, the dreaded double-cut. "When he stopped, it was a pretty believable move," Green says. "I had good position on him. I thought the ball was coming. I peeked for just a second. When I looked back, the receiver was not there anymore."

The problem is, a pass defender cannot cover a receiver and stay oblivious to the football. He wouldn't be covering anyone if it weren't that the ball might be heading his way. "One of the real principal rules of defense is you can't play pass defense with your back to the quarterback," says Doug Plank, a safety. "You'll see it all the time, on a deep pass down the sideline, where the ball is underthrown and the cornerback keeps running while the receiver stops or slows down. That's because the cornerback wasn't watching the ball."

But still, some coaches maintain if their coverages are played perfectly, the offense can't complete a pass. Cornerbacks can't be content with quick feet and quick minds. They need four eyes and ESP, too. Because when a pass is complete, it's the man in the secondary who gets blamed.

That's not entirely fair. Nor is it fair to judge a defensive backfield solely on the number of passing yards its team gives up, which is how the NFL rates pass defenses. That figure might reveal more about how often the team gets a lead and how well it plays run defense, both of which encourage an offense to throw the ball and, naturally, to gain more passing yards than a balanced offense. As it happened, the NFL's last-ranked team in 1983 pass defense was Washington, which also usually had the lead, and had the league's best run defense.

The Redskins didn't defend the pass that badly. Their opponents' completion percentage ranked third in the league. Their opponents' passer rating was 69.4 in a year when the average was 75.8. There's more to pass defense than yardage allowed.

Passing yardage doesn't account for what a defense is trying to do, either. As defenses become more aggressive, they're more willing to give up yards for the chance of making a big play. Blitzing will cost a team passing yards while it might be winning the game. Interceptions are an important yardstick for evaluating defensive backfields, as the maligned Cowboys eagerly point out. For that matter, so are sacks. A team can't get a lot of sacks without covering receivers.

There's more to stopping the pass than knocking it down. The men in coverage need help from the men rushing the passer, just as the men rushing the passer need help from the men in coverage. Green tells of another touchdown he gave up when the pass rushers didn't help him—not to point a finger, but to illustrate a point. It was on another double-cut route, this one by Steve Watson.

"A defensive back has a clock in his mind," Green says. "You're always thinking how long you're going to have to cover before you have to look for the ball. I thought it had been enough time on this route. I thought maybe the quarterback had even been sacked. If he puts a believable move on you and you've got good position on him, you want to stay in position to follow him. So you look for the ball. I didn't think he had time for more than one move."

But he did. "When I turned around, all I saw was his back. It was time to start chasing him."

For a defensive back, those things happen. Just as a secretary will make a typo now and then. But the defensive back has no white-out. As Green says, "You can always pray the receiver will fall down or the quarterback will overthrow him."

Apple-Cheeked Generals

*... Offenses grow more sophisticated,
but quarterbacks grow younger*

Quarterbacks are the only officers among football players. They alone are privy to the daily high-command meetings, called quarterback meetings, where the dissection of next week's opponent is plotted. They alone wear white cuffs, keeping their fingernails clean as long as the enlisted behemoths in front of them do their jobs. In a game of brawn and brutality, the quarterback exists on a peninsula of intricacy and prudence.

He always has been the team leader, the one who called team meetings and spoke at pep rallies, even in leagues where his passing has been limited to the occasional play-action surprise and the desperate heave on third-and-long. The halfback may be gaining all the yards and scoring all the points, but he'll never be *the quarterback*. The football hero! Undue glory is part of the job description, as is undue scorn. The quarterback has always been the point man between his team and public reaction, shielding his fellows from boos and cheers alike.

And now, along with all that, the NFL has given the quarterback clearance to take off at will. More than carrying a team, he can pick it up by the laces and fling it to a championship. The 300-yard passer, once a by-product of hopeless defeats, has become nearly a necessity for winning. In eighties football, the quarterback can rise to greater heights than ever, and of course, can also fall with a greater thud.

"I have felt in recent years the quarterback deserves even more

161

credit," says Bart Starr, who quarterbacked the Packers to five NFL championships in the sixties and himself to the Hall of Fame. "The game has become so much more sophisticated."

Starr did not have to contend with so many different pass-coverage schemes and so many different pass-pattern adjustments to counteract the volume of pass coverage. He had so much less to look for, and the same amount of time to do it.

And yet, Starr did not become a starter until late in his fourth season. On a bad team. On good teams, it was considered hurrying a quarterback to market before he was ripe if he played regularly before his fifth season. The position took so much time to learn.

That was then. Now, at the same time the position has grown more and more complex, the fraternity of starting NFL quarterbacks has ceased to be the exclusive domain of the scarred and savvy veterans.

Look at the starting quarterbacks who finished the 1983 NFL season, listed on page 163. Of the fifteen who entered the league before 1978, back in the olden days before the rule changes, six of them served classic apprenticeships: Danny White, Joe Theismann, Ron Jaworski, Lynn Dickey, Brian Sipe, and Ken Stabler all *waited their turns.* That was part of being a quarterback. Dickey and Sipe didn't even play on particularly good teams.

"You don't have to train your quarterback five years anymore," Sid Gillman says. "They come into pro football better trained. And there's more of a need for them."

The seven older quarterbacks who started in their first two seasons played for teams that were absolutely miserable the year before. Only Steve Grogan's Patriots won more than four games. Quarterbacks like Jim Plunkett, Steve Bartkowski, and Dan Fouts (and Terry Bradshaw and Archie Manning, who were not starters in 1983) were rushed into action because their teams had nobody else.

According to the old practice of letting quarterbacks age like cheese, the 1983 season should have had several first-, second-, or third-year starters in their fourth, fifth, sixth, or seventh NFL seasons. But there were only three, and two of them, Jack Thompson and Steve Dils, were emergency fill-ins who started only because Doug Williams went to the USFL and Tommy Kramer was injured. Of the 13 younger quarterbacks starting in 1983, only Seattle's Dave Krieg had served the old-fashioned apprenticeship.

"You don't have to train your quarterback five years anymore,"

Starting NFL Quarterbacks at the End of 1983 Season

Player, team	Years of experience	Year started	Round drafted
Dan Marino, Miami	1	1	1
John Elway, Denver	1	1	1
Jim McMahon, Chicago	2	1	1
Oliver Luck, Houston	2	2	2
Mike Pagel, Baltimore	2	2	4
Neil Lomax, St. Louis	3	1	2
Eric Hipple, Detroit	4	2 (3)	4
Dave Krieg, Seattle	4	4	**
Scott Brunner, NY Giants	4	2	6
Jack Thompson, Tampa Bay	5	5*	1
Joe Montana, San Francisco	5	2	3
Steve Dils, Minnesota	5	5*	4
Bill Kenney, Kansas City	5	3	12
Vince Ferragamo, LA Rams	7	3	4
Cliff Stoudt, Pittsburgh	7	7*	5
Richard Todd, NY Jets	8	1 (4)	1
Danny White, Dallas	8	5	3
Steve Bartkowski, Atlanta	9	1 (4)	1
Steve Grogan, New England	9	1	5
Joe Theismann, Washington	10	5	4
Ron Jaworski, Philadelphia	11	5	2
Joe Ferguson, Buffalo	11	1 (5)	3
Lynn Dickey, Green Bay	11	6	3
Dan Fouts, San Diego	11	2	3
Brian Sipe, Cleveland	12	5	13
Jim Plunkett, LA Raiders	13	1 (6,10)	1
Ken Anderson, Cincinnati	13	2	3
Ken Stabler, New Orleans	15	5	2

* Indicates player who became regular starter for the first time in 1983 because of his team's emergency loss of its previous starter.
** Not drafted.

- Years of experience includes seasons on taxi squad at beginning of career and seasons in other pro leagues after first year starting in NFL.
- Number in parentheses indicates year player regained starting job after losing it for most of a season.

Sid Gillman says. "They come into pro football better trained. And there's more of a need for them."

So two years in a row, Joe Montana and David Woodley led San Francisco to Super Bowls; third-year quarterbacks playing for championships. Montana, when he started his second season, led the NFL in completion percentage. The Cardinals handed their reins to rookie Neil Lomax in 1980 and won four in a row. In 1982, the Bears' Jim McMahon set a rookie record with his passer rating and had the third-best interception percentage ever for a rookie. The Colts' Mike Pagel had the second-best.

The next year, Miami's Dan Marino blew McMahon and Pagel both out of the water (to say nothing of Woodley, who landed clear out in Pittsburgh). Marino set the rookie record for completion percentage and passer rating. He had the highest rating in the whole AFC. He started in the Pro Bowl.

A quarterback's fifth season isn't time for him to start anymore. It's time for him to finish. If he's still holding a clipboard on the sideline after five years, he might as well sit down and make himself comfortable. He has become a Back-up Quarterback.

X X X X X
O O O O

The training Gillman mentioned is one reason so many coaches are turning their teams over to kids, like keys to the family car. Marino, Pagel, McMahon, and Lomax all played on college teams that featured the pass.

Quarterback coaching has improved in the NFL, too. It had to, when teams took to the air. And the best offensive coaches, the ones with a knack for finding daylight in the jungles of multiple coverage, make things easier for quarterbacks by keeping pass receivers from getting entangled in coverage. They're the coaches who are in demand as head coaches. Joe Theismann, the NFL's Most Valuable Player in 1983, was just another college football hero before Joe Gibbs became his coach. Who knows? Marino and Montana might still be holding clipboards if they hadn't had the good fortune to be drafted by Don Shula and Bill Walsh.

Gillman has watched McMahon's school, Brigham Young, and he says, "It just tickles me. When they come out to warm up, they're throwing flare-action passes. In pregame warm-ups! They're not practicing handoffs." So McMahon arrived in the NFL with enough field sense, in his third start, to call an audible that was not even in the game plan. Picked up a first down with it, too. After BYU, how could the NFL have had any mystique for McMahon? "In fact," said teammate Gary Fencik, "maybe he's a little disappointed."

"It never got real boring," Lomax says of his rookie learning process. "But it never really was a thing where I got mentally exhausted."

Better coaching may be the reason quarterbacks are *able* to play so young, but it isn't necessarily the reason they *are* playing. These days, who can wait four years for success? Certainly not a coach with a three-year contract, especially when his owner sees other owners vaulting from last place to first faster than they can close a real estate deal. *Does the kid know our terminology yet? Then he's ready. He'll learn on the job.*

He will, too. Even the quarterbacks who served long apprenticeships took their lumps when they finally started seeing the game from behind the center. A quarterback can spend every waking moment in meetings and film study, but it can help him only so much. There's no slow-motion button in the pass pocket. To improve, a quarterback ultimately has to play. The sooner he starts playing, the faster he'll improve. "You get six or seven games under your belt, you keep getting more confident," Lomax says.

The dominance of passing attacks has tended to favor a quarterback's athletic skills over experience. The advantage goes to the younger quarterback with quicker feet and a stronger arm. He can make more of an impact on a game than when the quarterback's job was primarily handoffs, pitchouts, and leadership. His first priority now is to make the big play, not to avoid the big mistake.

Yes, reading defenses is harder. But it's harder for veterans, too. "It's sort of bringing them down to the younger quarterbacks' level," says Marv Levy, who started both Steve Fuller and Bill Kenney as young quarterbacks when he was Kansas City's coach. "They're disguising defenses so well, and they have so many different coverages, it tends to even it out." So rather than separating the men from the boys, pro football's increased sophistication has equalized them.

Quarterbacks don't call many plays anymore, either. A lot of the thinking that quarterbacks did in Starr's day, even in Bradshaw's and Manning's younger days, is being done now by the coaches. There are more decisions for quarterbacks to make now, what with reads before the snap and reads while they're dropping into the pocket and reads after they get to the pocket— all of which may be different. But veterans haven't had to make those extra decisions much longer than rookies.

The biggest obstacle for a well-coached rookie quarterback isn't his inexperience so much as his youth. As McMahon says, "It's tough to tell a nine-year veteran to shut up in the huddle."

"I was intimidated at first," Lomax says. "I wondered what it was all going to be like. Training camp, playing against pro players, traveling and all. Playing the Cowboys the first time was a big thrill for me, with all the names they have. And we played the Dolphins right away. But I had guys like Pat Tilley, Mel Gray, and Dan Dierdorf on my side. You realize these guys are your teammates, and the awe is gone pretty quickly.

"If you do well, that's how you get to be accepted as part of the team. They read about you before you get there, but you've got to show the veterans. That was one of my concerns, fitting in. I just kept my mouth shut and let my actions talk for me."

By midseason of his rookie year, Lomax's actions had the

national audience of an NFL starting quarterback. "I just went out and played that game called football," he says. "It's the same game it was in college. Of course, the players run faster and hit harder. But ours do, too."

X X X X X
O O O O

The coach who uses a young quarterback has to be patient. "You have to let them make mistakes," says Ted Marchibroda, who has nurtured Roman Gabriel, Sonny Jurgensen, and Bert Jones to greatness. You also have to scale down some coaching ambitions. Denver coach Dan Reeves admitted after benching John Elway as a 1983 rookie that he had expected Elway to learn too much of the Broncos' voluminous offense. When Elway returned to the lineup, he had fewer plays and adjustments at his disposal, but also fewer pitfalls for confusion.

As Pittsburgh's Chuck Noll says, "The coach's job is to keep things simple, no matter how complex they seem to get."

"If things are basic and elementary, it makes it easier for a quarterback to perform," says Paul Hackett, San Francisco's quarterback coach. "I think as coaches, we tend to get enamored of all the extravagant things we can do and forget we're taking away from the quarterback's ability if he has to worry about too

---

"If things are basic and elementary, it makes it easier for a quarterback to perform," says Paul Hackett, San Francisco's quarterback coach. "I think as coaches, we tend to get enamored of all the extravagant things we can do and forget we're taking away from the quarterback's ability if he has to worry about too many things. There's enough you have to worry about at quarterback even if we keep it simple."

---

many things. There's enough you have to worry about at quarterback even if we keep it simple."

One thing often overlooked is simply defining a young quarterback's goals. The turning point of Theismann's career may well have been his conversation with Gibbs the night Washington lost its fifth straight game at the beginning of the 1981 season. They discussed a seemingly basic topic: what they wanted from the Redskins' offense, a topic so basic it often is overlooked.

If a rookie quarterback is good enough to start, he probably was his college team's star. He had to make big plays happen, or they weren't going to happen. He came to the NFL considering long passes and good passes to be the same thing. Damn the torpedoes, full speed ahead. But that recklessness may not be necessary in the NFL. The quarterback may have teammates good enough to move the ball more methodically, waiting patiently for someone else to create a big play. His offense may put a premium on balancing the run with the pass, plays to the left with plays to the right, short passes with deep passes. Or maybe his team's defense is so bad, the offense's primary goal is to keep the defense out of the game.

"The thing I really had a hard time learning," Bartkowski says, "was the need in the pro game to use your mental capacities more than your physical. That's hard to accept, that you're not going to be able to just rely on your talent.

"It was hard for me to get a real grip on what we were trying to accomplish with our passing game, that we were trying to control the ball and not necessarily go for broke. The thing I was probably most guilty of was trying to force the ball downfield. I wasn't really incorporating my backs into the offense. It's pretty tough when you limit yourself with three receivers and they've got as many as eight men covering them."

Unless a young quarterback's strengths are tempered, they become weaknesses. It's good for a quarterback to be fearless, but not for him to fearlessly try to throw the ball through two defenders covering a receiver. It's good for him to be strong-armed, but not for him to try to drill a hole through the chest of a receiver 10 yards away. It's good for him to be able to run, but not to gain eight yards and risk injury when a receiver is open 20 yards downfield before the quarterback passes the line of scrimmage.

With experience, a quarterback should become both more confident and less foolhardy. The problem is, it's impossible to be sure which quarterbacks will fall on the confident side of the tightrope, and which on the foolhardy side. Theismann and Bartkowski, the NFC's leading passers in 1982 and 1983, were benched as young quarterbacks. Sipe, the NFL leader in 1980, was drafted in the 13th round. Krieg, the AFC's second-best passer in 1983, was not drafted.

Only seven first-round quarterbacks were NFL starters at the end of 1983, while twelve others rode the bench without injuries (three of the twelve were rookies, but then, two rookie first-rounders were starting. Also, two first-rounders on the bench, the Raiders' Marc Wilson and Jets rookie Ken O'Brien, were behind first-round starters). The conference-leading passers in 1983, Bartkowski and Marino, had been first-round choices, but it was the first time a first-rounder led a conference since 1978, when Bradshaw did it.

Somebody's making mistakes. Marino was the sixth quarterback drafted in 1983. In 1979, Montana was drafted after Thompson, Fuller, and Phil Simms. In 1973, quarterbacks were drafted in this order: Bert Jones, Gary Huff, Ron Jaworski, Gary Keithley, Joe Ferguson, and *then* Dan Fouts.

Too often, scouts judge quarterbacks mainly on arm strength, size, and speed in setting up. They ignore the intangibles at the position where intangibles are most important. Steve Pisarkiewicz had all the numbers when he was the first quarterback drafted in 1977 (ahead of Tommy Kramer), but he didn't last four NFL seasons and has not been able to start for any of his four teams in the NFL, CFL, or USFL. Numbers may not lie, but they can be evasive.

"There are two main criteria a quarterback must have to play in this league," says Walsh, whose coaching resume includes Ken Anderson, Fouts, and Montana. "First, he must be able to display poise under the pressure of an NFL game. He must think clearly under game stress. Second, he should possess basic intelligence. It is difficult to have longevity in the NFL without intelligence."

He's talking about football intelligence. Joe Namath's name always comes up when people talk about how quarterbacks can get by with caverns in their skulls. Thomas Henderson didn't get much argument when he said Bradshaw "couldn't spell cat if you spotted him the C and the A." But reading defenses, Namath and Bradshaw always were as brilliant as Richard Burton reading Shakespeare.

If there is an essential physical quality for quarterbacks, it's accuracy. Again, it's so obvious, it's overlooked. And accuracy is more than a high completion rate and a low interception rate. It's putting the ball where receivers can catch it without breaking stride, not where they have to turn around for it or stretch their bodies out on a defensive back's chopping block. As Falcon wide receiver Alfred Jenkins says of Bartkowski, "It's so nice when a quarterback throws the ball so the only thing you have to worry about is catching it."

X X X X X
O O O O

Even accuracy depends, to a degree, on a quarterback's poise. The quarterback who panics at seeing something unexpected downfield might rush his release. That causes the ball to sail. Which causes receivers to get sore ribs, or worse, as they're flipped out of the air.

Poise and leadership are such bulky terms, as hard to get a handle on as a refrigerator. For quarterbacks, they're best described by the ways they surface:

★ Poise is most obvious when a quarterback appears oblivious to half a ton of pass rushers closing in on him. Plunkett comes to mind, as does Fouts, of whom Joe Gibbs says, "He'll stand back there in the pocket longer than any quarterback I've seen. Dan is just a natural leader. In the huddle, he's in charge. He's as determined as any football player you'll find."

★ When the pocket breaks down and the play becomes a free-for-all, the poised quarterback is thinking on the run, often turning a bad situation into a big play. As Levy says, "There are quarterbacks who run for extra yards and there are quarterbacks who run for an extra opportunity to throw the ball. Defensively, the second kind of running is what scares me."

★ Things can go wrong before the snap, too. The poised quarterback, when he lines up with a weak-side run called against an undershifted defense, calmly calls an audible for another play. When the play messenger brings him a play for a one-back formation and two backs are in the huddle, he calls a different play instead of calling timeout.

★ Defenses especially like to disguise their coverages against a rookie quarterback. The poised one doesn't take for granted that it will be a two-deep zone when the weak safety lines up toward a sideline. So if the safety shifts into a deep-middle zone, he knows what to do.

★ A quarterback has to correct teammates who make mistakes. More than that, he has to know which ones to tongue-lash and which ones to tell, "You can do better than that."

★ Some quarterbacks, like mushrooms, thrive in the dark. But there is no place to hide under the magnifying glass of pro football fans. Richard Todd is one of countless quarterbacks who have been sincerely surprised to learn boos follow bad performances as surely as car accidents follow ice storms. And he learned it in New York City, the strongest magnifying glass in the country.

Criticism rolled off his back like darts. He took it out on reporters and, eventually, on his coach. That is not the response of a poised quarterback. A poised quarterback reacts no differently to boos than to cheers, is aroused by neither five interceptions nor five touchdown passes. Either way, he looks to next week.

★ A quarterback must be bold. He takes chances, preferably with enough knowledge to distinguish between a calculated risk and drawing to an inside straight. But if he makes a mistake, he does it wholeheartedly. There is no time in the pocket for calling a motion to a vote.

★ In the huddle, a quarterback is a salesman. He doesn't say,

"The coach wants us to run Brown Right Bob 24 Y Motion, so let's give it a whirl." He gives his teammates the impression that any play he calls is the one that's going to win the game for them. And that no game is out of reach.

From Johnny Unitas and Roger Staubach to Sipe and Kramer, there have been quarterbacks known for thriving under pressure in a game's final moments. They don't think in terms of pressure, though. "You're just doing everything you can to win a game," says McMahon.

When he was at Brigham Young, McMahon engineered one of the most stunning comebacks in football history. With 4:07 to play in the 1980 Holiday Bowl, Southern Methodist led 45–25 and BYU coach LaVell Edwards sent his punting team onto the field on fourth-and-eight. McMahon called timeout and charged at Edwards like a baseball manager arguing a balk call. "He was yelling, 'What are we gonna do? Blankin' quit?' " says Dan Plater, who was a BYU wide receiver.

Edwards reconsidered. The game ended with a 46-yard pass, McMahon's third touchdown pass in four minutes. Brigham Young won 46–45.

"No matter what the situation is, he never thinks it's hopeless," says Bear coach, Mike Ditka. For a quarterback, there is no higher

"As long as you've got the quarterback, and you've got the receivers, you can make people worry. But you have to have the quarterback,"—**George Young**, New York Giants general manager

"It's difficult to draw a profile of a quarterback. Each has his own personality. Some don't always lead by verbal or overt actions, but by productivity. This is how players are judged. By what they do on the field. If a quarterback is consistently proficient, a team can respond to him as a leader."—**Bill Walsh**, San Francisco 49ers coach

praise. Perhaps the most important trait a quarterback can have is the sort of arrogant ego that keeps him from even considering defeat, not any more than a military pilot thinks about crashing.

X X X X X
O O O O

When the Cleveland Browns fired Paul Brown as coach in 1963, they said the game had passed him by. He was, after all, still calling plays for his quarterbacks. Looking back, Brown says, "It pleases me to see that what was supposed to be passe in somebody's mind was a thing of the future."

Nearly all NFL teams call their plays from the bench now. Quarterbacks don't even mind it as much as they once did. Even in the old days, when calling plays was one of the rights and rites of quarterbacking, the quarterback who became a coach was apt to be won over to his old boss's point of view. Brown says he'll never forget a conversation with Otto Graham, the former Cleveland quarterback who had groused about Brown's calling the plays.

"He was coaching at the Coast Guard academy," Brown says. "He let his quarterback call plays, and near the end of one game, the quarterback called for a pass into the flat. The other team intercepted it for a 99-yard touchdown, and Otto told me, 'Now I know why you didn't let me call the plays.' "

More than ever, NFL coaches are reluctant to stake their futures on a quarterback's judgment. "It might be that coaches are more interested in having a feeling for their own destiny," Atlanta coach Dan Henning says of coaches' desire to select their teams' plays. The game has changed so much since the days of Graham and Sid Luckman, who fondly recalls a five-play touchdown drive in the early forties when he let each of his Bear interior linemen take turns calling a play. Not only have coaches come under closer public scrutiny since then, the game has become far more complex.

"Coaches spend so much more time with film preparation and computer printouts," Gillman says. "Can you believe a quarterback competing with Landry? With Shula? Who do you think's going to win that kind of thing?"

Still, there are valid arguments for letting the quarterback call plays. One is that the quarterback will execute his own choice of plays with more conviction. Another is that he won't have to wait around for the play, wasting part of the 30 seconds allowed between plays and perhaps losing some momentum in a good drive. But the age-old argument for letting quarterbacks call the plays is, as Luckman puts it, "I've got a better feel for the pulse of the game. I've got a good idea what the defense is doing and how to take advantage of it."

It really doesn't make a lot of difference. For the quarterback who calls the plays, the coaches have distilled the information from their hours with film and printouts, and have pumped it into the quarterback meetings. On any given down, he doesn't have more than a handful of plays at his disposal. And for the quarterback who doesn't call the plays, the coach usually gives him the freedom to take instantaneous advantage of a defensive flaw.

Coaches often say the main reason they call plays is so they can tell which plays are working and, for the ones that aren't, why they aren't. They have to know the play to know what to look for (although it would seem the quarterback could select a play and signal it to the bench as easily as a coach can select a play and signal it to the huddle).

A clear advantage for calling the plays from the elevated coaches' box is that the view there is better. The upstairs coach also is far enough away to select plays more dispassionately and objectively. And nobody's pounding on his head.

"The coach is not in physical jeopardy," Henning says. "So you can gear your scheme and plan and know it's not going to change if you lose your quarterback. You're just going to change a player, not the way your plans are executed."

Who calls the plays is a strange issue to arouse so much curiosity and controversy. As Brown points out, "Nobody says anything about coaches making the defensive calls." Ah, but quarterbacks don't play defense. Fans like to think of their quarterbacks as being special, and reducing them to telegraph operators in the play selecting somehow strips away part of their mystique.

Tinkering with Match-Ups, Playing with Matches

... The temperature keeps rising in the coaches' hot seat

After the NFL strike in 1982, it was fashionable to predict an epidemic of coaches burning out. That won't happen. Not because the hatch on the coaching pressure chamber has suddenly sprung open—it hasn't—but because the NFL head coach is a man who has reached his lifetime ambition. He isn't about to blow it by oversleeping on the cot in his office or whining about overwork.

These men didn't suddenly become workaholics the day they were named head coach. Assistant coaches don't exactly keep bankers' hours, either.

Besides, they like the job. It carries a certain amount of authority, creativity, and prestige, and it enables them to play games for a living well into middle age and beyond.

"I don't really think the demands of the job have changed," says Dan Henning, who became Atlanta's coach in 1983 after eight years as an NFL assistant. "I think the demands people have put on themselves are different. What you need is an organized approach and to realize that there are not 35 hours in a day. You have to know that, physiologically, you need a certain amount of rest and relaxation to do your best quality work."

What's happening is that coaches are trying to do what was reasonable 10 or 20 years ago, but in a different environment. It's much harder now for coaches to isolate themselves from owners' and fans' pressures than it was before nationally televised instant replays. It's much harder to assimilate every morsel of information than it was before computers and 150-formation offenses. It's much harder to exercise meaningful control over a team than it was before salaries made bigger headlines than completion percentages.

When George Allen was coaching in Washington, he wouldn't pick up the phone without turning on a film projector. It was important to him that whoever was calling found out the work never stopped for George Allen. It always has been important to Tom Landry and Bud Grant that they eat dinner at home. They may have worked after dinner, but they didn't communicate with their families by postcard.

All three have been successful. There is no formula for just how much a coach must overwork himself, or for much of anything else that has to do with coaching a winner.

"Some people think coaches are a necessary evil," says Giants general manager George Young, who has been on NFL coaching staffs and in front offices since 1968. "I used to think there wasn't much difference between coaches. But the older I've gotten, the more I think some people are better coaches, better winners, better leaders. You get an outstanding guy, and he can create an impact."

"I don't think you have to be a genius to coach football. And if you are, I think you're wasting society's time. You ought to be in something more fruitful to society."—**George Young**, New York Giants general manager

"I hear people ask all the time, 'Where did the fun go?' That element, I don't think we want to lose. Of course, winning is always the fun part of it. But it's a very physical, laborious, emotional week for a player. As a coach, you certainly don't want to give him a boring, monotonous week.
"The players make more money now, but they're better athletes than they've ever been. I find it just as fun to be around them as I ever did. I like seeing them get better and the game get better. And they're a heck of a lot better than when I played."—**Marion Campbell**, Philadelphia Eagles coach

Whatever the coach's style, coaching successfully boils down to two things:

1. Getting the most out of a team's talent.
2. Self-discipline.

Or, as Young says: "Head coaching is being a teacher and an administrator, and anybody who thinks it's anything different is silly."

Getting the most out of the players involves constructing a playbook that will deploy them properly, and using the right plays at the right time. It involves motivating them, through fear or love or pride or whatever. It involves teaching them—not only the most efficient techniques for blocking and tackling and catching and running and covering pass receivers—but also what to look for: how to read opposing offenses and defenses, and how to make the right decisions. But the first thing it involves is selecting the right players and putting them at the right positions.

One reason for the Raiders' perennial success has been their willingness to give a second chance to talented athletes whom other teams didn't want, often moving them to different positions. The most recent example is all-pro tight end Todd Christensen, who flopped with Dallas and the Giants as a second-round fullback (although Dallas did want him to switch to tight end). Kenny King, a bust as a Houston halfback, went to the Super Bowl as a Raider fullback. Lester Hayes, a fifth-round draft choice when most teams considered him a safety, has been an all-pro cornerback for the Raiders.

Several other NFL players have improved after changing positions. Some examples:

★ Bob Golic flopped as a middle linebacker at New England before anchoring Cleveland's defensive line as a nose tackle.
★ William Gay flopped as a tight end at Denver and then became one of Detroit's best pass rushers.
★ Emery Moorehead flopped as a fullback and wide receiver for the Giants and the Broncos and became the Bears' best tight end in 15 years.
★ Bill Wilkerson flopped as a defensive end in Houston and turned into a Pro Bowl guard for San Diego.
★ Mark May flopped as a tackle for Washington before starting at guard.
★ Luther Bradley was an ordinary cornerback at Detroit and a flop at Houston until George Allen brought him to the USFL, determined he belonged at free safety and watched him intercept six passes in one 1983 game.

All those players except Moorehead were drafted in the first two rounds. Coaching has as much to do with a team's drafting success as scouting. And with more teams closer in talent, the pressure to coach young players into the lineup has never been greater.

"In this day and age, if your first three choices don't make it, you haven't drafted properly," Gillman says. "And your first and second choices must play for you immediately, unless he's a quarterback. That takes some good teaching."

"The best teachers are leaders," George Young says. "They walk into a room and they affect activity. They're noticed. Their students, or any people, like to be in their presence."

That's where self-discipline comes in. All leaders have it. Self-discipline is most obvious on the sideline Sunday afternoons. It might be most important then, too. No matter how well a coach prepares his team from Monday through Saturday, if he loses it on Sunday, he wasted his time all week.

"There are coaches and there are coaches," Gillman says. "The best coaches are game-day coaches. Look at Landry. The wheels are going around all the time. His brain is constantly working. Shula. The wheels are going around. There's no screaming or yelling or ranting. No chewing out officials. You might say, 'All right, you SOB, you made a bad call,' but then you keep on going.

"When your players make mistakes, how does chewing them out during the game help you win? All that does is let the seconds tick off the clock. You don't have all day."

The best game-day coaches are ready for what's coming next. They're not screaming, "How could you clowns let that guy score!" They're thinking, *How are we going to overcome that?* They're not yelping, "Ohboyohboyohboy, we've got the lead!" They're thinking, *How are we going to keep it?* The coach who

---

"In this day and age, if your first three choices don't make it, you haven't drafted properly," Gillman says. "And your first and second choices must play for you immediately, unless he's a quarterback. That takes some good teaching."

---

throws his hat on the ground may be impressing the fans with his competitive fire, but he's missing a play or two. More than that, he is hardly encouraging his players with any sense of, "I'm still behind you. I know you can do it."

Self-discipline has to surface during the week, too. That's when the coach is an administrator. He has to organize his time and his assistants' time, his practice schedules, and his meeting schedules. Dick Vermeil, who as Eagles coach was king of the 35-hour workday, frankly admitted that coaches who worked fewer hours probably were better organized.

Aside from Sunday afternoons, self-discipline is most important in the form of equanimity when things go badly, as they eventually do for all coaches. The coach who snipes at the media is only starting a vicious circle. Worse, it's a tangential circle. What does grousing about the reports of last week's defeat have to do with winning next week's game?

When a coach blames the media or the fans for a team's losing, he only hands his players an excuse to keep losing. *Coach says it's the media's fault, not ours. We're off the hook. We don't have to get better after all.* No organization likes to apply this test to its coach, but there are few better ways to measure coaching suitability than whether he can keep his composure during a losing streak.

X X X X X
O O O O

Getting the most from the players and self-discipline come together in the single Basic Rule of coaching. The best coaches seem to agree on it:

"When I left Dallas, Tom told me one thing," Mike Ditka says, Tom being Landry. " 'When you make a decision,' he said, 'by God, live with it.' "

"You have to do what you believe in," George Allen says. "You can't listen to other people. I think if I had to give some advice to younger coaches, it would be just that. Because sooner or later, you've got to live with yourself.

"And it's not just what you do on third-and-one, either. It's which player to cut, which player to keep, which player to trade, which player to start."

After two seasons on Shula's staff and two more under Gibbs, Dan Henning said, "They didn't allow anyone to worry about what other people were thinking. They always had a realistic approach and, win, lose, or draw, they pressed on.

"Shula used to say, 'People who second-guess you are comparing what actually happened against the best possible alternative. There are so many possible alternatives, and many of them are not as good as what actually happened.' In two years with Don, I never heard him second-guess a coach or a player. If something went wrong, he just put mechanics into effect that would have a great effect on its not happening again."

In other words, a wishy-washy head coach is on his way to being a washed-up head coach.

X X X X X
O O O O

It wasn't so long ago that pro football was little more a social phenomenon than box lacrosse. Gillman remembers when the NFL was widely ignored, enabling coaches to work almost under laboratory conditions.

"I think coaching is more demanding now because of greater interest," Gillman says. "Television and the Super Bowl have made it more demanding. The Super Bowl is a great social event. Owners want to get in that thing. But only one team in the world can win it, and only two get into it.

"The thing that has come to being more than it was in the past is owner participation. Boy, that makes a hell of a difference. You look around the league, and the owners are making the decisions. Football teams should be run by football people."

Let's do look around. From 1981 to 1984, 18 NFL teams changed coaches at least once. Three of them (the Giants, Bengals, and Vikings) would have preferred to keep their coaches, who resigned. But on 12 of the other 15 teams, the owners made the changes. The Redskins, Falcons, and Jets were the only teams that left the most important football decision up to their football people, and many of the others purged their general managers along with their coaches.

That makes it hard to follow the Basic Rule of coaching. Marv Levy followed it anyway in Kansas City. He didn't go along with pressure to fill the air with footballs because he didn't have the players to win that way. In doing so, he ignored the pressure to fill the seats with fans. When fans started flocking away from Chiefs games in 1982, Levy was fired.

"It's a bigger fishbowl," Young says of the NFL. "So there's more pressure. As a coach, your character's on the line every Sunday. If your players don't make a first down or one of them fumbles, the coach is thought of as having bad character.

"People attribute greatness and great character to success. That's a fallacy of the American system. If a coach is working hard but his team's not as successful, it becomes like the Roman Coliseum. Thumbs up or thumbs down."

Consider why people buy football teams. It isn't for the money, although it has been difficult not to turn a tidy profit in the NFL. Most pro football owners buy their teams for two reasons. They get publicity that would be unheard of in their primary businesses, and they have a toy that's more prestigious to brag about with their friends than, say, a Maserati. As former player agent Jerry Argovitz has said, both before and after becoming a principal owner and president of the USFL's Houston Gamblers, "Pro football owners are the most exclusive men's club in the world."

The typical owner didn't buy his toy just to watch it run. For that, he could have bought a model train. He wants to be *involved*, wants to sit behind the wheel from time to time. That's why, for all their successes, George Allen and Hank Stram have been unable to land NFL jobs since 1978. Everywhere they've coached, they've insisted on running the show. How can an owner have any fun that way?

"Probably one of the reasons owners aren't giving that kind of authority," Allen says, "is it used to be you had to get people in the stands. You had to win. If you didn't win, you didn't make it financially." Allen isn't saying today's owners don't want to win. "Nobody wants to lose," he says. But now they don't *have* to win to make money.

NFL owners have long since isolated themselves from the demands of the marketplace, what with television networks practically guaranteeing break-even fiscal statements before the first ticket is sold. The Colts' owner, Robert Irsay, has fired a coach during a game, has called plays from the press box, has traded players without consulting his football people, has generally given the Bronx cheer to the fans of his team and, for all his management blundering, has been unable to drive down the value of his franchise. Far from it. For several years before moving to Indianapolis, Irsay was treated royally whenever he went to other cities to allow them to court his franchise.

So an NFL owner has no need to turn his team over to football experts and step out of the way. He can have his fun punching the team's control buttons, finish within a game or two of .500, and still, his name gets in the newspapers. He's the envy of all the bank presidents in town.

The owners' financial contentment hasn't been all bad for coaches, though. On many teams, it certainly eroded the coach's authority (and that of the general manager if he was different from the coach). But aside from Allen and Stram, coaches in general have found increased job security in the owners' golden goose. From the 1978 season until 1982—or between the rule changes and the strike—NFL attendance rose steadily four straight years. Fan interest and team income were at a peak. And in those four years, from the 1978–79 off-season through 1981–82, NFL teams made only 14 coaching changes. That average of 3½ per year was about half the average for the previous 10 years, when fewer teams made 67 coaching changes.

"I want the good old days," Bears general manager Jim Finks said, only half-jokingly, in 1980. Speaking from a competitive standpoint, he said, "I liked it when half the teams would have an upheaval every six months, call each other names, fire everybody, and start all over."

The best example of patience in management was on the Jets in 1981. They had dropped from 8–8 to 4–12 in 1980, and they lost their first three games in 1981. Firing coach Walt Michaels would not have been unpopular. But the Jets management took a deep breath, kept Michaels, and watched the team go 10–2–1 the rest of the season, making the playoffs for the first time in 12 years.

The 1982 strike was the first ripple in the NFL's placid economic waters since the 1978 rules changes helped reopen fans' eyes.

With the strike came the USFL and drug scandals. Suddenly, owners were being pelted with reasons not to be so patient with the coach. Eight teams changed coaches after the 1982 season, and although several were announced as resignations, only the Giants were truly sorry to see their coach depart.

X X X X X
0 0 0 0

It may turn out that the rash of coaching changes after the 1982 season was isolated. The next season, only two teams changed coaches by choice, and Cincinnati and Minnesota promoted from within, from what teams like to call their "families" after Forrest Gregg and Bud Grant resigned.

It also may turn out that the 1982 upheaval was not some once-in-a-labor-agreement's-lifetime thing. The coaching changes may have been stimulated as much by competitive hope as by economic panic.

The previous year, remember, was when San Francisco and Cincinnati went to the Super Bowl. San Francisco and Cincinnati had been the NFL's two worst teams over the 1979 and 1980 seasons. Parity had been creeping into the NFL's power structure for a few years, but never this dramatically. While Pygmalion was romping through the NFL's penthouse, light bulbs were popping in the other owners' heads like street lamps at dusk. *If they can do it, why can't we?* Now coaches were expected to consolidate those old five-year rebuilding programs into five games. Instead of making everyone happy, parity was producing all the more pressure.

"I think that's so true," Kay Stephenson said shortly after becoming Buffalo's coach in 1983. "I think the premise we have to operate on is, all we can ask for is a chance. I think that's all anybody in life is asking for anyway."

Parity has its limits. It's not as if eight teams a year are suddenly making the Super Bowl. A fourth or fifth place team might have a better crack at improving than it did 10 years ago, but the odds are still 26–2 against.

And the other side of the coin is that not only are the best teams more vulnerable, the worst teams are less vulnerable. Henning says if anything's going to burn out a coach it's "the fact that there are no breathers on the schedule. That could cause people to go into shock. There's no time to relax. It's a long time from training camp to the end of the season."

The Packers' executive committee, which governs the NFL's only publicly owned team, neglected to consider how the parity elevator goes down as easily as it goes up. The Packers finally made the playoffs in 1982, with the NFC Central Division's best record by half a game, so the committee decided before the 1983 season that anything less would be unsatisfactory for coach Bart Starr. It established a black-and-white criterion in a league where the distinction between teams has become increasingly gray. Starr was fired the day after a last-minute field goal knocked the Packers out of the playoffs.

Look at how the NFL teams shaped up going into the 1984 season. How many of them, if they were perfectly honest with themselves, had to admit they had no realistic chance to make the playoffs?

1. Houston.

That's the list.

Tampa Bay? Hey, the Bucs made the playoffs three years out of four before injuries dragged them down in 1983. The Giants? Even more injuries. The Colts? Most improved team in 1983, and that was before starting a honeymoon with a new city. The Eagles? They beat three playoff teams and gave the Cowboys and the Redskins all they wanted in their last 1983 games. The Chiefs? They can score on anybody. Even the Oilers no doubt were figuring with their maturing offensive line and new coach and quarterback (men who won five straight championships in Canada) that they could get a break here and there and leave their division behind them.

Everybody's got a shot, at least in their own minds. That has had some impact on which coaches get hired, if not a tempering effect on the urge to fire them in the first place. Four of the eight teams that changed coaches after 1982 replaced them with their own assistants. They wanted a change, but nothing radical, not when they were so close.

"If you think you're on the right track, you don't want to disrupt your personnel," says Young, who hired Bill Parcells from the Giants' staff for 1983. "Every time you bring in an outsider, he brings in his own staff and they sit down and watch film. They evaluate the personnel much differently from the staff before them. I've been on a new staff, and they say, 'You know if those players were playing well, we wouldn't be sitting here. The old coaches would still be here.'

"What you have is a palace revolt. The new coach wants to make changes. I know coaches in the league who look to new staffs whenever they want to make trades. That's where they think they can find their best bargains."

X X X X X
0 0 0 0

Another thing that has changed since Gillman's first NFL coaching job in 1955 is the coaching calendar. It no longer skips from February to July. "There isn't any off-season," Gillman says. "Years ago, it used to give you an edge, working year-round. So many coaches just left it. They went off to their boats or the golf course."

There's still time for a coach to lower his handicap in the off-season, but there is no real NFL off-season, even for many players. The Bears' Dan Hampton had a finger shaped like a dogleg after a 1983 injury, but he didn't have the simple operation to straighten it because it would have taken six weeks to heal. What about after the season ended? "I can't go six weeks in the off-season without lifting weights," he said.

When Dallas won its first Super Bowl and someone asked Bob Lilly if he thought the Cowboys could repeat in 1972, he said to ask him again around Memorial Day. He would know by then how many players had followed their off-season weight programs. The Cowboys were an exception then, but now most teams do all they can to encourage their players to stay in town for off-season programs. They help players find jobs and homes, and they give awards for attendance and performance in the weight room, where the players are urged to flex their muscles three days a week in April, May, and June.

Weightlifting doesn't work for everybody. The 49ers' Fred Dean says, "Every now and then I get an urge to lift weights. I just go somewhere and lie down until I get over it." And blockers don't kick sand in Dean's face. Cincinnati's all-pro tackle Anthony Munoz calls him the strongest defensive end he has played against.

But for more and more players, off-season weight programs build confidence right along with the muscles. And, if nothing more, they're seen as preventive maintenance. To an NFL player making an average six-figure salary, his body is an investment. He has to keep it running and glistening like a prize antique car.

Off-season programs are no longer confined to the weight room, either. Players take up martial arts, ballet, and body control exercises more endemic to gymnastics. Several teams have organized aerobics sessions.

Coaches have to organize and supervise these off-season programs. Before that, they review the previous season's film, revise their playbooks, and make their training camp schedules, right down to which film correlates with which playbook page for which meeting on which day. On many teams, coaches have become more involved in scouting, draft preparation and, especially, chasing down and signing rookie free agents who were not drafted. They have mini-camps before or after the draft, which is about May 1, and rookie camps in May.

June used to be the coaches' traditional month off, and still often is, but now a lot of teams invite their rookies to work out at their facilities a month or more before training camp. Somebody has to be around to correct mistakes, to answer questions. Veterans can't be required to begin training camp until 15 days before the first exhibition game, but they can be asked to volunteer earlier. And training camp itself is so all-consuming it's the closest a healthy person can come to stopping the world and getting off.

Then comes the season, with its miles of film and 150-formation computer printouts and weekly game plans and practices and meetings and coast-to-coast flights and dinners wrapped in waxed paper and Murine and Maalox and cots in the offices.

"The biggest problem coaches have," Landry says, "is the game has become so specialized. With all the information you get from computers and films, you could work 28 hours a day if you had it. Coaches have to work harder now because if they don't, someone else will."

Henning points out there are still 22 players on the field, "just different permutations and combinations." But so many *more* permutations and combinations.

"The biggest problem coaches have," Landry says, "is the game has become so specialized. With all the information you get from computers and films, you could work 28 hours a day if you had it. Coaches have to work harder now because if they don't, someone else will."

"Every two or three years there's a new type of offense or defense," says the Eagles' Marion Campbell, "and it requires different personnel, a different type of drafting and coaching. The game has gotten so situation oriented, it demands a lot more attention than it has in the past. You're using different personnel on practically every down."

And during the game, the coach has to make sure the right personnel is on the field. It's a small detail, but it can cost a game if a player has to line up out of position because the right one is back on the bench or worse, if only 10 players are on the field. And it's one more thing on a coach's mind besides following the game plan and talking with the upstairs coaches and some offensive (or defensive) players when they're off the field and thinking two or three plays ahead and adjusting personnel to injuries, and reacting to any surprises the other team has given him, and maybe squeezing a breath or two in edgewise.

"It all puts more pressure on the coaches," Cowboy general manager Tex Schramm says. "The game is more specialized, more sophisticated, and they have to be more intelligent. There's a lot more strategy involved. Do you send in your extra defensive backs and just rush with three? Do you blitz? One time you might stop them with seven defensive backs, but you know what the fans will say if you don't. 'Why didn't you have more guys rushing?' "

X X X X X
0 0 0 0

The euphemistic coaching catch-all, for everything from a stuffy nose or a screaming baby to drug arrests and contract disputes, is distractions. All in all, coaches probably have more tolerance for fumbles. At least fumbles, they can do something about.

"You would like to have no distractions," Stephenson says. "You would like to draft your people, sign them, and have them come to camp on time with all the veterans, with everybody happy and ready to play football. But it seems that there's more discontent these days. Everybody's making more money, but they see what other players are making and they want more. It's a snowball effect. It's not as simple as it used to be, but it's something we've all got to live with and deal with."

For an NFL coach, the USFL is a distraction along the lines of a rifle range across the 50-yard line. Coaches don't negotiate contracts anymore. (In fact, general managers who used to be players or scouts don't negotiate so many contracts anymore. NFL contracts have become so laced with annuities, loans, tax shelters, and financial mumbledy jumbo that the team without a creative CPA in on its negotiations is at a serious disadvantage.) So when a team loses a star player to the USFL, all the coach can do is watch and dig down into his depth chart.

That's what Starr had to do when the Packers allowed Mike Butler, their best defensive lineman, to sign with the USFL's Tampa Bay Bandits before the 1983 season. Without Butler, the Packers had one of the NFL's worst defenses. When the time came to find a scapegoat, the bosses didn't go looking for the guy who couldn't sign Butler. They fired Starr.

(Starr could have been more flexible about that particular distraction, though, and another one involving Pro Bowl linebacker Mike Douglass. Butler was willing to play for Green Bay in 1983 before joining the Bandits but was told he was unwelcome. And Starr suspended Douglass for a game because of comments he made to reporters.)

"You need to handle your personnel so much more individually than on a collective basis, as you used to," Landry says. "I think players have pretty much the same attitudes they've always had on the field, but there's such a basic change in the money end of the business, with the advent of agents and unions and outside business opportunities.

"As a head coach, you're handling basically problems, is what it amounts to."

That leaves less time for a head coach to be teaching on the field, although Shula, Noll, and Chuck Knox, among others, still work often with individual players. Most coaches have enough to keep them busy coaching the assistant coaches, monitoring everything, and stepping in to address emergencies.

The teaching is better, though, and not only because the coaching staffs are bigger. Twenty years ago, high school football coaches observed college coaches to improve their techniques. The best teaching was done in the colleges. Now college coaches regularly visit pro training camps to learn better techniques.

NFL coaching has become more efficient and less colorful. Coaches' faces show up on TV more than ever, but coaches seem less distinctive than ever. Who could pick, for example, Jim Hanifan out of a crowd? And he ranked 10th in head coaching seniority with the same team going into 1984, his fifth directing the Cardinals. For that matter, when do Joe Gibbs and Tom Flores stand out, except when their players are carrying them on their shoulders?

Landry, Shula, and Grant may be the last of the NFL coaching legends. Noll and Knox are in the next generation. "They're very successful, competent coaches," says Finks. "Noll has won four Super Bowls. But his name isn't a household word. Bud's is and Bud hasn't won one."

"We're tending to hire technicians more than individualists," Young says. "I don't think we have the individualist, the person as charismatic as he used to be. We've gotten away from the head coach being a medieval potentate, someone who controls the front office and the whole operation. That's one of the fruits of our society."

Indeed, there aren't a lot of business leaders reminding people of J. P. Morgan or John D. Rockefeller, either. Who is the next generation's John Wayne? The next generation's Frank Sinatra? The next generation's FDR? In dispersing images, television also shrinks them.

It isn't so much that coaches have grown smaller in stature. They're the same size. Pro football has just gotten bigger. As Gillman says, "Everything is bigger. Everything is more important."

The Cutting Room Floor

*... Game film is most useful
only after it's spliced and edited*

The NFL is bound together not by a league constitution or competitive spirit or the profit motive, but by miles and miles of film. Take away film, and pro football as we know it would fall apart.

"Our coaches say 85 percent of all the coaching they do is done on film," says Bob Friedman, the Cowboys' director of photography. The percentage might be higher for scouts, who use film to research the draft and trades. The Cowboys have a staff of part-time scouts who do nothing but grade players from film.

Say, Coach, how was your honeymoon?

I don't know. I'll have to check the film.

That joke is as much a cliche as game film itself. The popular notion is that coaches review their games over and over, meticulously gathering dossiers on each player's every false move. They don't. Film is not the coach's hairbrush, wooden spoon, or house slipper for spanking players with bad grades for lousy games. In fact, game film is history by Monday afternoon. Coaches see it once and show it once. "Game film is the least important thing we do," Friedman says.

The game film's showing is almost a social event, although the atmosphere is more funereal for those disaster flicks with Ls at the end. Winning game films are a rollicking good time. Cheers greet the big plays and, especially, the big hits, which often win a prize for the player the coaches elected the big hitter of the game.

Even the foul-ups get good-natured jeering, as opposed to the breath-holding silence that accompanies costly plays in defeats. The coaches, in better spirits after winning, are less inclined to hit the rewind button five or six times in a row to keep showing how that miserable wretch of a left tackle barely slowed down the pass rusher he was supposed to block on third-and-three when the receiver was wide open. After a win, it doesn't sting so much when the coach calls you a melon-headed hairdresser or less polite words that players have to clean up for their talks at father-and-son banquets. After a loss, there isn't a much emptier feeling than knowing your very own pratfall is about to splatter across the screen and there's nowhere to hide.

All in all, though, players like film. Game film isn't even the first kind of film that comes to mind when someone brings up the subject, they spend so much more time watching practice film and smaller, specialized reels. They're more likely to be upset with the photographer for missing one of their good plays in practice than for being a 35-millimeter tattle tale for all their mistakes. Friedman's son, Mitch, has been working for NFL teams since 1973, and he says only once has a player offered to pay him for purging a boo-boo.

It's a learning tool, players say almost unanimously of film. It teaches them how to improve themselves and what to expect from an opponent. It might even explain how that saucer-sized bruise developed on the right thigh overnight. Charged-up football players often don't appreciate how dangerous their game is until they see people clobbering them on film the next day.

Practice film might be the most important work a team photographer produces. By the time game film points out a player's mistake, it's too late. He already made the mistake in a game. Better to catch it on the film of Wednesday's practice and correct it by Sunday.

Coaches use practice film to correct themselves, too. That's where they might find out the play that looked so nice on the chalkboard doesn't work on the field. During the week, when a team simulates plays against its upcoming opponent, practice film enables coaches to make the subtle shift of a step or two that could make the difference between the outside linebacker getting blocked or merely getting sideswiped en route to an easy tackle. In training camp, practice film is the blue editing pencil for the playbook.

It also is the bluebook the coaches grade for the players' final exams. Most cuts are based on practice film.

As for game film, it's just the seed for two more useful kinds of film. From its own game film, a team makes training reels of each play it uses during the season. From opponents' game film come game-preparation reels, which give coaches their puzzle pieces for assembling game plans.

Training reels are off-season projects. "We'll take every slant 34 we ran during the season and put them all on one reel," Friedman says. "Then we'll break it down farther: all the slant 34s against four-man lines, all the slant 34s against 3–4 defenses, and so forth. We go through 400 different plays like that."

The coaching staff scrutinizes training reels to see if they suggest the playbook needs some revising on the slant-34 page. Then the reels go to training camp, where they show players how a slant 34 should look and how it shouldn't.

Game-preparation reels come together faster, keeping film men up Monday nights. They sort the next opponent's game film much the same way they sort their own film for training reels, except by situation (field position, down, distance to a first down and formation) instead of by play. The coaches need the situations from which to glean tendencies. They can't finish their game plans without these reels, so NFL teams spend six figures a year shipping film air express to each other.

NFL rules require opposing teams to exchange film of their previous three games, but teams cut deals to get as many as six films per opponent. The tendencies from all but the last game are already in the computer a week ahead of time, often fed there by a coach whose full-time job is spinning game-preparation film into computer printouts of tendencies.

More than half the NFL teams have such a coach, labeling his responsibility research and development or quality control or special assignments. Never film coach. (In fact, even the men who shoot and process the film have squeezed the word out of their titles for more highfalutin words like photographic coordinator or, if they had their way, director of cinematography.)

Occasionally, a player or coach will pluck more than general tendencies out of game-preparation film. George Halas used to study linebackers' feet for hours on end, hoping they would tell him when a blitz was coming. Or maybe the way a lineman takes his stance will signal whether the play is a pass or a run. A back might let on that he's carrying the ball by the way he sets up, or even the way he opens and closes his hand before the snap. From the end zone film, the splits of the linemen or wide receivers might tip off the next play. (Games are generally shot from both an end zone and a sideline, but the NFL requires exchanging only sideline film.)

In 1979, the Houston Oilers found something on film that

helped them upset San Diego 17–14 in a playoff game. Oiler coaches had watched film of San Diego's previous game and noticed something odd, says Wade Phillips, who has since moved to New Orleans as defensive coordinator under his father, Bum.

"Every time they ran the ball, Denver's linebackers raised their hands up in the air before the play," Phillips says. "We knew they had something. We didn't know what it was. So one of our coaches talked to one of their players."

He learned how quarterback Dan Fouts was tipping off San Diego's plays. Fouts stood with his feet squared before runs, but he staggered one behind the other before passes. Safety Vernon Perry intercepted four passes off Fouts, and the Oilers won even though Earl Campbell was hurting.

X X X X X
O O O O

When Bob Friedman started working full-time for the Cowboys, in 1971, they asked him if he wouldn't mind selling ads for the game program in the off-season. "To give me something to do," he says. Friedman had plenty to do after the next season, when Gillman arrived at Dallas as an assistant coach.

Gillman had grown up in a family that owned theaters, so he was at home around a camera. He had scouted opponents off newsreel footage when he was a college coach in the forties. Soon after he became the Rams' head coach, Gillman hired Mickey Dukich in 1956 to be the first full-time photographer for an NFL team.

Halas had a photographer shooting Bears games with a hand-held 16-millimeter camera from the Wrigley Field roof as early as 1932, and Paul Brown was the first coach to grade players off game films. But, Friedman says, "Sid was the real innovator in using film." Gillman was the first coach to break opponents' game films into the modern game-preparation reels, and he was the first to break his own film down for self-scouting. He did the editing himself. He would cut up a piece of film, attach some masking tape to it, write something on the masking tape that no one else could read and toss it into one of the garbage bags lined up against his office wall.

One night when Gillman was coaching the Oilers, a janitor made the mistake of thinking Gillman's garbage bags were full of garbage. "Sid called me at 5:30 or 6 in the morning just panicking," says Mitch Friedman, the Oilers' photographer at the time. Friedman and Gillman traced the garbage bags all the way to the dumpster. Too late.

A team photographer doesn't get to watch much of the game

he's shooting. He's not focusing on the ball so much as he's keeping 22 players in the picture. It helps if he knows a little something about both teams' tendencies, too, so he can anticipate pass plays, when he'll have to widen the picture. After the game, home or away, he immediately develops the film and splices it into offensive, defensive, and kicking reels so the coaches can start grading the film at about 6 a.m. Monday. The grades are based on one thing: Did the player carry out his assignment?

Unless the stadium is domed, the photographers work out-doors, usually high enough to feel the full force of the wind. "Electric socks are the greatest invention in the world," Bob Friedman says. Friedman was working for the Cowboys as an in-dependent contractor—an arrangement some teams still have—when they played for the NFL championship in Green Bay the day it was 13 below. He wore long underwear, insulated under-wear, long overwear, insulated overwear, and a red snow suit. He had a portable heater, too, but he had to turn it off because it was ruining the television transmission.

"I didn't think I could work with gloves on, but I learned how in Green Bay. You could pour yourself a cup of coffee and it would freeze before your cup was filled. Before I put the gloves on, my finger froze to the winding crank. I jerked it loose, and it did not bleed until I got back on the bus. I carried my camera cases back to the bus and couldn't let go of them."

Friedman still uses the same kind of camera he used then, a 1952 model, of which he guesses he has collected about 50. "I like to have spares," he says. They cost about $300 or $400, which means he could sell all 50 and have about enough money to buy one of the fancier modern machines other teams use. With either kind, though, there are still lots of ways to wind up with film that looks like it was shot down a coal miners' elevator shaft.

One sure way is to have a power failure while the film is in the processor, something that happened to Mitch after he moved from Houston to Chicago. (He called the other team for a replacement.) Mitch's brother, Max, who works for the Raiders, forgot to tighten a little screw after getting his camera back from the repair shop. The camera had no indicator to show if the shutter stayed shut, which it did for the first half of a game against Detroit. (It was a bad day for all Raiders' personnel. They were shut out for the first time in 15 years.)

X X X X X
0 0 0 0

Computers first joined the NFL in its scouting departments. Most notoriously, in the Cowboys' scouting department. As Jim

Finks says, "I don't know if the Cowboys were the first team to use computers. I know they were the first team to brag about it."

The Cowboys *are* the first team to do a lot of things that later become standard practice in NFL front offices, so maybe they were the ones who first came up with the idea computers could help coaches, too. However it happened, computers have teamed up with film to be so helpful, they've left coaches begging for mercy.

"Originally, the computer was supposed to alleviate the workload," Tom Landry says, a slight ironic chuckle in his voice. "They've caused us to work harder, of course, because they've created so much more information for us to try to absorb and use."

Computers sort and correlate the tendencies that coaches chart from opponents' game films, and there, they do save time. "I used to be up all night diagramming what computers do in no time," Marion Campbell says. "And they do it neater, too. You ask the computer a question, and you get the answer right now." No more adding up a bunch of chicken scratches and punching a pocket calculator to find out how likely the next opponent is to pass on second-and-six when it lines up with a split backfield.

The process will be even faster when NFL teams are using video tape instead of film, which will be soon. Mitch Friedman

"The only limit to the uses of video tape is your imagination. Let's take the playbook. If in the off-season, you go to a TV production house, you could actually put together a playbook on video tape. You could show the movement of players on the screen, and it would be relatively simple, compared to the many, many hours of animation that would take on film.

"Then if you get a new player during the season, you can give him a cassette and a video recorder to take home. He can grab information a lot faster that way than he could by reading a playbook."—**Mitch Friedman**, Chicago Bears' director of photography and director of NFL's pilot program for switch from film to tape.

has been pioneering the transition to tape in Chicago since the end of the 1981 season.

Film is easier and faster to edit than video tape, but only if you're making one product. With tape, Friedman can edit one game tape into five game-preparation reels, or whatever, at the same time. And it won't be long before he can program the team's computer to edit a game tape into game-preparation reels, which will have to be called game-preparation cassettes.

Tape also can be watched right away. It doesn't need to be developed. A coach working on the mechanics of a kicker or a quarterback can watch the tape with his student right out on the practice field. The NFL prohibits using moving pictures during a game, but coming back from a road game, the coaching staff could grade a game tape on the plane and sleep clear past dawn Monday morning. And, again in the not-too-distant future, tape should be possible to transmit to the next opponent over the telephone, instead of waiting for an airplane to deliver it.

Nice as those advantages are, the NFL has two other main reasons for the switch to tape. It's cheaper, and its quality is more consistent.

Color video tape costs less than one-tenth of the same amount of black-and-white film, and that's before the film is developed. And tape is reusable. Even with the start-up costs for video cameras and customized player-recorders, Friedman estimates an NFL team's tape system would pay for itself in four or five years.

There's no way tape can be as clear as film. But it can be clearer than home-viewed tapes if it's recorded at a faster speed. Friedman's tape recorder runs a standard VHS cassette all the way through in 20 minutes, or 18 times faster than a home tape recorder set for six hours.

On the other hand, video tape can't look as bad as the snowiest film. There are enough regulations now to keep NFL teams from playing dirty tricks with their film, the way they used to, but you can't legislate against sloppy processing. "The league likes things standardized," Friedman says. "Video is just another part of parity."

As far as coaches are concerned, the biggest advantage for tape might be that it can be watched with the lights on. Tape will literally bring them out of the dark ages. Those steely-eyed glares you keep seeing in the sideline close-ups of coaches? They're not glaring. Anyone who has been coaching with film for more than a few years has a perpetual squint.

From Printouts to Square-Outs

. . . How a game plan is put together—and into action

The game plan has reached out and seized America's fascination like no other sports term. It has such an efficient ring to it, and without the humdrum, gray-flannel pinstriped sound of *bottom line*, or *legislative program.* So we are pelted with economic game plans, game plans for reviving the inner city, academic game plans, political game plans. Every agenda or itinerary seems to be framed in that gloriously magical term that our most celebrated peacetime warrior, the offensive football coach, gives his plan of attack for unleashing the troops toward enemy end zones.

Basketball teams have game plans, too, as do baseball pitchers and the defensive and kicking units of football teams. But *the* game plan, the one that brings salutes from mailrooms and boardrooms alike, is the offensive game plan, the one that takes the initiative and so confidently presumes that the struggle is under control before the struggle has begun. The American capitalistic boldness of it all! Why, it's enough to bring tears of pride to the eyes of the memorial statue in the downtown city square. And to the more cynical stomachs, it is enough to bring disgust at the thought that these arrogant coaches are plugging their players into the master computer, reducing football heroes to oversized R2D2s.

Of course, the coaches who actually draw up these game plans have no such illusions. Hey, they're struggling to find something (*anything*) that will work against the other guys. That's all. If they had any smug notions about being able to map their own fates on a sheet of legal paper, they wouldn't bother with game plans—or multiple formations, sight adjustments, men in motion, or cots in the offices, either. If they thought they were that powerful or that smart, they would simply draw one play on the chalkboard Monday morning and pronounce: "This is the play with which we'll tear those guys to smithereens Sunday because it's the only play we'll need against the hapless fools who dare to compete with us."

No, the game plan is not some treasure map that, if followed precisely, will assure a victory. Nor is it a wing and a prayer, at the other extreme. It is more than a fishing expedition, more than a list of plays for lobbing randomly at the other team until it breaks. The coach who passes his game plan out to the players on Wednesday morning is sure in his heart that he has arrived at the best process for winning Sunday's game. But game plans come with no guarantees.

An offensive game plan is a collection of lists of plays, a list for each of several circumstances the offense might face during a game. A list for first-and-ten from your own 15-yard line, a list for second-and-two near midfield, a list for fourth-and-inches, a list for first-and-goal. The lists may not all be written separately. They have to fit on a card about the size of a clipboard so the coach can carry it on the sideline, and besides, a lot of plays go on more than one list.

No matter how brilliantly conceived a game plan is, no matter how thoroughly the players have learned it during the week, it's just a scrap of paper unless it is put into effect properly on Sunday. A coach has to be flexible. He can't stubbornly stick with the plays on the top of a list if they aren't working. But he also has to have the discipline, when events do not smoothly follow his plan, to move methodically down the appropriate lists in search of good plays. And the discipline, when things are going smoothly, to continue using the plays that are working.

There's a strong temptation for a coach to browse through his game plan like a kid in a bakery on his allowance day, trying one of these and one of those and one of each of those things over there. It's called grab-bagging when the coach hops desperately from list to list on a day when nothing is going right, but it can happen to a lesser extent on a good day. The coaching staff spent hours putting together a diverse, 31-flavored game plan, and it is not easy to ignore all that and make plain vanilla calls, even if those clearly are the calls that will win the game without undue risk.

The question for a coach is not: Did he change his game plan? Changing the game plan in midgame sounds exciting and creative, but the same question could be reworded: Did he panic and resort to plays his team didn't practice? No, the question is this: Did he use the right parts of the game plan at the right time?

Game plans don't change all that much from week to week, let alone from half to half. There simply isn't time to add a lot of new plays to the offense every week and run them properly. The change, week to week and sometimes half to half, is to different formations, so the defense will not be able to tell when the same old plays are coming.

So the cornerstone of any game plan is the group of plays the offense uses against every opponent. Coaches have different names for this basic group—dirty dozen or nitty gritty or super-ready list—but the idea is that the plays will work against anyone. They're the team's security blanket if the opponent surprises it with defensive maneuvers it hasn't prepared for, and they're the safe vanilla for days when victory comes with relative ease.

On top of the super-ready list come the plays best-suited for this week's opponent. From their computer printouts, the coaches can tell themselves, "In this situation, they tend to do that." Then they ask themselves, "Against that, what can we take from our playbooks that's most likely to work?" The answer goes into the game plan.

Game plans also are tailored to specific opposing players. Obviously, a passing game will draw a bead on the rookie cornerback or any other suspect defender. But more subtly, say the other team's defensive left end is not so hard to hook from the inside, but a demon to keep from pursuing toward the sideline. Against that team, end runs ought to go to the right side.

X X X X X
O O O O

For making the game plan, a team's computer printout sorts the opponent's offensive and defensive plays according to:

1. Field position. The lines of demarcation vary from team to team, but they are roughly the 5-yard lines, the 20s, and the 30s or 35s. An offense can afford to be a little bolder as it crosses each line, up to about the opponent's 20, where it enters what's called plus territory. There, the approaching goal line limits the offense's options and encourages the defense to play more tightly, perhaps more recklessly.

2. Down and distance. Within each field-position area, play selection also is governed by how leisurely the offense can afford to approach the first-down stick. The down-and-distance breakdowns are likely to be: first-and-ten, second-and-seven or more, second-and-three to six, second-and-two or less, third-and-eleven or more, third-and-seven to ten, third-and-three to six, third-and-two or less, and, perhaps, fourth-and-two or less.

So far, the offensive coach can ask his computer what the opposing defense likes to do on any down anywhere on the field. Will they blitz? Use three lineman or four? Play zone or man-to-man? How do we attack it, aside from what we ordinarily do in that situation? And the defensive coach can ask much the same things. Pass or run? To which area? Who gets the ball? To stop them, should we change the way we normally play?

3. Formation. The way the opponent lines up narrows down his tendencies even more. For example, field position and down-and-distance might not shed much light on the type of coverage a defense is likely to use, except that it will play zones with a three-man line and combos or straight man-to-man with a four-man line. Formations generally are more valuable to the defense, which can keep changing its call until the ball is snapped, but this step helps the offense establish guidelines for when to call an audible, changing its play after it lines up.

Or, in the example above, the offense might want to call two pass plays in the huddle—one designed for zone coverage, one for man-to-man—and finalize the decision at the line of scrimmage. It's called a check-with-me call, a planned audible, and it may not be narrowed down to as few as two plays in the huddle. Multiple defenses have made check-with-me increasingly popular.

After the offensive coaches determine what the opponent is likely to do, they have to decide what they want to do. One group of assistants might work on the running game, another group on the passing game, with the head coach either overseeing everything or directing one of the groups. Most likely, he'll play devil's advocate, ask his assistants why they've made their choices for the game plan and make them defend their decisions.

Within each field position–down-distance–formation breakdown, an offense has different packages of plays. It has basic runs and dropback passes, but it also has play-action passes, passes designed for nickel defenses, and deceptives, which include screen passes, draw plays, and reverses. (The packages don't all apply to each situation. An offense has little use for, say, play-action passes on third-and-long, or nickel passes for third-and-short.)

So most of the offensive play-calling is thought out before the coin flip. Choosing the play should be easier than picking one item from Column A and two from Column B in a Chinese restaurant. All situations are accounted for in the game plan. As long as the game plan is updated as the opponent's response makes certain plays look more or less desirable, the play-calling coach will usually have a play in mind for any situation. If he doesn't, nothing is more sure to start a quarterback into a slow burn than waiting for his coach to play eeney-meeney-miney-moe on the game plan while the 30-second clock is running down.

The defensive game plan is longer, often 30 to 40 pages, because a defense has less control of its own decisions. It has to react to the offense. So a defensive game plan lists the opponent's tendencies in each situation, with Our Response for each of the most common tendencies.

Say the computer printout reads, on first-and-ten in the middle part of the field, the opponent lines up in an I-formation, strong right, 80 percent of the time. And 75 percent of those plays from I-right are runs to the strong side. Now, in the huddle, the defensive call will be for a run-oriented alignment, perhaps with the linemen's charge slanting toward the offense's right. But that 20 percent of the time when the opponent lines up from a split backfield, it favors a quick inside pass to the tight end or a screen to the fullback. So if the offense shifts into a split backfield, the defensive players' game plan has told them how to adjust their defensive assignments. Their coverage will be strongest where the offense tends to pass.

What the defense is doing is playing the odds, just like a card player. If it has the right tendencies on the offense, defensive players will say afterward, "We had a good game plan. They didn't do anything to surprise us." The defensive players knew what to look for, knew where to go to stop the play. They probably weren't right all the time, just as the best card players sometimes lose. But over the long haul, provided the players are good enough to carry out their assignments, going with the odds sure is a lot better than looking around in the huddle and saying, "What now, fellas?"

An obvious question arises. How can professional football teams be so careless about developing such predictable offensive tendencies? Well, the best ones are the most careless of all. Care*free* might be a better word, because to a good offense, it doesn't matter if the defense knows what's coming. It figures it's going to make the play work anyway. The best way for an offense to win is usually to keep doing what it does best. (Quality-control coaches do consult the computer about their own offenses from time to time, though, just to make sure their tendencies haven't turned into 98 percent deadlock cinches.)

Game plans generally deal with fairly broad tendencies, rather than trying to diagnose specific surprise plays, but sometimes a coach gets a specific hunch. Charley Sumner, who directs the

Raiders' defense, had one late in the first half of the 1984 Super Bowl when he saw the Redskins line up with three wide receivers on the right side.

"Did I have a hunch? I tell you, I had a *strong* feeling that they would use that play," Sumner said of the screen pass toward halfback Joe Washington on the left. "They made a 67-yard gain on that same play against us at Washington. It led to their getting a touchdown, and that helped them come back from 35–20 to beat us. I thought they would use it again."

Playing his hunch, Sumner sent reserve linebacker Jack Squirek onto the field with instructions to tail Washington. Squirek intercepted the pass and scored the touchdown that blew the game open.

X X X X X
O O O O

The extreme in sticking to a game plan would be listing plays from 1 to 75 or so and running them one after another, like pages in a book. That would also be foolish. By halftime, the score or an injury or the other team's defense is apt to have made the game entirely different, in terms of what an offense has to do to win.

But the offense's needs aren't going to change so much in its first two or three possessions. A team still hasn't determined for sure how its opponent is going to react to what it does, and there hasn't been time for the score to get lopsided. So Bill Walsh had this idea: why not map out those first few possessions before the game, in the laboratory of his office instead of the mayhem of the sideline?

Walsh has done that for most of the 49ers games he has coached, and other teams have picked up on the idea lately. Walsh calls it scripting, moving down a play list he calls the First 25.

"Generally we live with it, and I'd say it's been more successful than not," Walsh says. "In the normal give-and-take of a game, you can probably run 18 or so of the 25. That would be the average. Not necessarily in order, but pretty close to being in order. We'll interject something as we go along, as we feel it's necessary, and if you get into special situations, you go to your lists for long yardage, goal line, or short yardage."

"I think it's a hell of a theory," Gillman says. "You say to yourself you know damn well these are the best plays we can possibly run. So let's not screw around. Let's run them right away."

It is a declaration of confidence, telling the players they perform these several plays so well that the coach doesn't care what the defense does. As Walsh says, "It does help our players get a start in the game."

The main reason athletes get butterflies early in a contest is that they don't know what's going to happen. They don't doubt if they can cope with what's going to happen, they just wonder what it will be. Scripting the first several plays doesn't give an offensive player a crystal ball, since the defense has some say in what's going to happen, too. But at least the offensive player has had a few days to think about what he'll have to do and what kind of problems he might run into. And just how troublesome can those problems possibly be, anyway? By the very act of scripting, an offense is telling its opponent, *Try and stop us.*

Often the defense does stop them, but even then, scripting serves a purpose. Every coach wants to begin a game by showcasing the most important formations in his game plan, so he can see how the defense plays against each of them. That's helpful information for the second time he uses a formation. By scripting, Walsh doesn't have to worry about forgetting something.

He also won't forget to use a particular play—one he wants to use early either because it sets the defense up for something later or because the play just looks too good against the other team's defense to risk setting aside until it's too late. The whole idea, as Walsh sees it, is he's coaching the first quarter with the dispassionate cool he had last Tuesday, insulating himself from the pressures and pitfalls of game day for as long as it's practical.

"You show good variation of run, pass—and occasional punt, I guess," Walsh says. "So you go into the game with the kind of balance you're seeking, and you have it on record so that you force yourself to have that kind of balance.

"You do repeat plays, certainly, if they're working. But you like to have a reverse, you like to have a deep pass and other things as part of the opening stages of a game, rather than hold them until the second half. By then, the score might have changed the game completely."

X X X X X
O O O O

Game plans are passed out to players first thing Wednesday. By Wednesday night, they've usually been changed. Something won't look right in practice.

Even with six days between games, football teams don't have a lot of time to practice. Mondays are for little more than screening the game film and stretching out the players' battered muscles, and Tuesdays are the players' off days, when the coaches assemble the game plans. (On a few teams, Monday is the off day.) That leaves Wednesday, Thursday, and Friday for working on the game plan. Saturday practices are short, usually involving just the kicking teams.

Practice time has been able to expand only so much to deal with the game's increasing permutations and combinations. A well-drilled squad isn't much of an advantage if it falls apart in the fourth quarter Sunday because of exhausting four-hour practices Wednesday through Friday. The time to drive players into shape is training camp. So meeting time has grown instead, often to two meetings a day, plus a daily kicking-team meeting. Even in training camp, there were coaches in 1983 who considered meeting time so important, they sometimes held extra classroom sessions instead of the traditional two-a-day practice sessions.

Even at its best, practice is drudgery. Football players like to hit their opponents and they like to win, and they can't do much of either in practice. They also find repetition as boring as the next person, even those players who have been taking blows to the head longer than they can remember. Football practice is repetition. That is its purpose. A team goes over the same thing so often as to leave a groove in each players' mind. By Sunday, every action should be reflexive.

One of a football team's less obvious problems is the number of injuries that are not apparent Sunday to Sunday. By midseason, virtually every pro football player is hurt enough that he could use a few days off. His body would feel so much better by Sunday. But if he takes those days off, his mind won't be sharp enough to give his rested body the instantaneous orders it needs. (If he takes those days off, he'll also give the coach a chance to look at someone else at his position, which is the best incentive for coming out of the trainer's room in time for practice.)

Suppose a team has four wide receivers and three of them are hurting. Two of the injured three figure to be ready to play Sunday, so it doesn't seem to be a serious handicap. But two of them aren't working with the quarterback all week, so their timing might be rusty. And the healthy one isn't getting any breathers, so he might be worn out. He's running with the first team and the scout team, imitating opponent's offense against the first-string defense. He may take a play off here and there with the scout team, but the scout team needs him almost as much as the first team.

What if the next opponent is Green Bay? The defense's cornerbacks are counting on the scout team to give them a realistic facsimile of the Packers offense. But the scout team has only one bona fide wide receiver, none on some plays. It may be using a back-up tight end or a back-up quarterback or a punter, lining them up at wide receiver to run the Packers' pass routes. The cornerbacks are tuning up for James Lofton and John Jefferson by covering a quarterback and a punter.

Competition in practice is one of those subtle things that separates winners from losers. A rookie right offensive tackle, for example, is liable to develop faster if he goes to a team with a Pro Bowl left defensive end. Even a 12th-year wide receiver, the Raiders' Cliff Branch, was delighted to have all-pro cornerback Mike Haynes join the team in 1983. "He helps me tremendously in practice," Branch said. "I'm a guy who's never satisfied. You might beat your man every day in practice, but it might not be like that in the game. Now I'm practicing against the best."

The Redskins had the NFL's best defense against the run in 1983. Why? "We're so physical against the run," defensive end Dexter Manley said. "We practice against the Hogs."

X X X X X
O O O O

By Saturday night, the game plan should be woven into the players' minds as tightly as their phone numbers. Mentally and physically, they're as ready as they're going to be for Sunday's game. Now the emotional preparation begins.

Most teams sequester their players in hotels even before home games. It's one more way for the players to think of themselves as a family—an exercise in Let's Pretend that sometimes stops just short of transporting the players in an elongated station wagon with paneled sides. There isn't a lot to separate the talent from one NFL team to another these days, and a warm, kindred spirit among teammates can indeed spur a team to play beyond its capabilities. (Or is it that the kindred spirit develops *because* the team is playing over its head? Probably a little of both.)

Another reason for staying in hotels Saturday night is to avoid the distractions that might crop up in the home of a player's real family. It's easy to make the case, though, that the hotel is more distracting than the home, especially since teams generally aren't concerned enough about their players' good-night's sleep to provide them with single rooms. Insomnia and nausea are not uncommon for football players on Saturday night, and neither is conducive to a restful night for one's roommate.

Maybe the real reason for pregame hotels is bed checks. The coaches can't very well prowl from suburb to suburb, ringing doorbells to make sure their charges are safely tucked in at 11 P.M.

Little is expected of a player on Saturday night, usually just a short team meeting and the bed check. The meeting is generally lighthearted, but the Cowboys gave written tests to the players in

1983. The meeting is often the first time the whole team has sat down together since it watched the game film Monday. During the week, offenses and defenses go their separate ways. But now, they can gather again to watch their opponent's highlight film. It's mildly entertaining, but at the same time, it shows the opponent at its best and most likely reminds the players of its reverses and flea-flickers and any other tricks it might pull the next day.

Whatever a team does on Saturday night, it wants to keep the itinerary reasonably constant from week to week, and it wants the pregame countdown to focus the players' concentration on tomorrow's game. The 49ers went through a stretch, from 1982 well into 1983, when they lost nine of ten home games and won eight of nine road games. That isn't supposed to happen, especially for a team playing a lot of road games at 10 A.M. on the clocks back home. But the way Walsh explained it, "When players are on the road, they don't have much to think about except the game." So he juggled the 49ers' Saturday schedules for home games, "taking up more of the players' time trying to make it more like a road game." The 49ers won their last four home games in 1983 (and lost three of their last four road games).

For a lot of players, there is a greater feeling of togetherness at the Sunday morning chapel service than at the Saturday night meeting. Game day has begun, the stomach butterflies have started flapping their wings, and even players who aren't terribly religious have said it comforts them to look around the room and see their teammates, other men sharing the same excitement, the same nervousness, the same fears of injury or defeat. Chapel service is early. It's before the pregame meal, which is four hours before game time, or 8 A.M. in seven cities in the Central time zone.

Some teams also perform the ankle-taping ritual before the meal. Taped ankles are as much a part of the game costume as shoulder pads and face masks, and often a player risks getting fined if he even practices without taped ankles. Some do anyway. They figure if the ankle is rigid, the only place on the leg with any give is the knee, and most players would gladly trade a knee injury for ten ankle injuries. So they leave their ankles untaped to protect their knees. If there have been any medical studies on either theory, they haven't been widely publicized.

Pancakes have become more popular than steak for pregame meals. Pancakes land more gently on twirling stomachs, and they fit better into the dietary regimen of loading up with carbohydrates for the 24 hours before a game.

At the locker room before a game, time creeps ahead like rush-hour traffic. Players have their own pregame routines, all designed to prepare themselves for willingly offering their bodies to be pounded on by other large, strong men.

One might be reviewing his game plan, pop quizzing himself. One might be walking aimlessly through the shower stalls. One might be throwing up. One might be sitting under a table, staring almost catatonically. One might be chain-smoking in the back of his locker. One might be reading a magazine. One might be sleeping. One might be reading the Bible. One might be sitting with a towel over his head, imagining himself doing all the things he'll be expected to do. One might be listening to music. One might be restlessly cruising the room, making wisecracks or nervous chit-chat, carefully picking his targets from among other nervous extroverts rather than intense introverts. It is not recommended, for example, to snatch the towel off a teammate's head and snap his behind with it.

Superstitions are common. This sock has to go on first, that shoulder pad has to be laced first, the same person has to pull the jersey down over the pads. More than superstitions, they are pieces of a structured ritual, comforting constants on a day that could go haywire without warning. This is a delicate instrument, the game-time psyche each player is assembling. It can't be too loose. It can't be too tight.

Game faces are more than a cliché. Some players wear them, *need* them in order to leave their more jovial personalities behind. The game face doesn't slip on like a mask, but consumes a player in an almost werewolfian transformation. The face tightens, even reddens, from jawbone to eyebrows. The player's concentration might be so intense by game time that he wouldn't recognize his wife and children two feet away.

There is no absolutely proper atmosphere for a pregame locker room. It shouldn't be too loud, but it shouldn't be quiet enough to hear the team's spirits drop, either. The emotion shouldn't be low, but it shouldn't be so high that it will be spent by halftime. Even the warm-up drills are not reliable predictors for how a team will play.

The coach has time to talk to the players between warm-ups and the player introductions, but he knows better than to deliver a Knute Rockne go-get-'em speech. He might do no more than turn the floor over to the chaplain giving the team prayer.

"The worst part of football is those moments before the game," Doug Plank says. "That's the worst thing to put your body through. It's like you're going to the electric chair. That is how out of whack your body gets. It's like you're going into battle and you don't know if you're going to return."

That's Led Reft Firty Thor?

*. . . Getting a play to the huddle
isn't as easy as it seems*

For one year, in 1956, the NFL allowed quarterbacks to wear wireless earphones in their helmets so coaches could tell them directly which plays to call. "It never really worked," Paul Brown says. "People had a lot of fun with it, if you know what I mean."

They sure did. Jack Faulkner, the Rams' administrator of football operations, was on the Rams' coaching staff then and recalls a day in Detroit when the Rams picked up the Lions' calls on a citizens-band radio. Brown remembers the Giants claiming they did the same thing to his signals on a day when he wasn't even using the wireless. By the next season, that experiment was over and coaches had to go back to more conventional ways of getting their plays to the huddle.

There are only two. The coach can either signal his play or send it to the huddle with a messenger. Signals are faster. Even Renaldo Nehemiah and Willie Gault can't deliver plays to a huddle at the speed of light. But messengers can carry more information.

An offensive play, even in the shorthand of football terminology, can be quite a mouthful. For example: Green Left, Z Motion, Dive 28, G Twist on two. Let's look at what that means:

1. Green Left is the formation, green telling how the players line up and left being the strong side, where the tight end lines up. Most formations are named by colors.

2. Z Motion describes the man in motion before the snap, the flanker in this case. A more intricate code for motion might tell the team how to move through three different formations before snapping the ball in Green Left.

3. Dive is the series in the playbook, indicating everybody's blocking assignment.

4. 28 is the obvious part of the play, telling the halfback to run wide around left end.

5. G Twist is a variation on the blocking assignments for the dive series.

6. Two is the snap count. The play will begin the second time the quarterback says, "Hut."

Ideally, a coach can say, "Green Left, Z Motion, Dive 28, G Twist on two" to a play messenger and assume the messenger will say the same thing to the quarterback, who will say the same thing to the other offensive players in the huddle. But as Sid Gillman says, "Nothing's perfect. There might be a mix-up even communicating it to the guy next to you who signals it in to the huddle."

A play messenger should be able to remember ten words in his team's terminology—a language he speaks as fluently as English—for as long as it takes to run from the sideline to the huddle. He has practiced delivering plays all week, at least. But ever since he started playing football, he has been trained to hear the name of a play and immediately think of his own assignment. Now he has to put off translating the play into his own assignment, unless he knows the playbook well enough to translate his assignment back into the whole play. The quarterback does not want to hear a play messenger pull into the huddle and announce, "That play where I come back in motion and help double-team block on their strong-side backer."

The messenger wouldn't even try to do that. He would try to remember the play, but he might miss just one word. He might say "Bob 28" instead of "Dive 28." Yeah, that sounds right. The team has a "Bob" series. But it doesn't have any G Twist" blocking variation in its "Bob" series, or maybe "Bob 28" can't be run from a Green Left formation. So the messenger has delivered a play that is not in the playbook.

Or maybe it's the formation that confuses the messenger. Maybe he tells the quarterback "Blue Left" and gets everything else right. That play is in the playbook. But a blue formation requires two backs, and there is only one back in the huddle because the formation is supposed to be green.

A sharp quarterback may be able to catch those mistakes. He has spent more time studying the game plan than the messenger, so maybe, while he's freezing the messenger with a glare, he can figure out what that miserable, breathless fool really means. But maybe he can't, or maybe he is running out of time on the 30-second clock, and the quarterback has to step back in front of 60,000 people and call a timeout that everybody knows his team might need at the end of the half.

Still, at least the quarterback who calls timeout has *caught* the mistake. It could have been worse. He could have called the nonexistent play the messenger gave him. He could have lined everybody up and already said his first "Hut" when suddenly it dawns on him, while a big "3" is on the 30-second clock, that *we don't have this play.*

Or worse, yet, maybe the messenger's only mistake was to call a formation that put the halfback on the quarterback's left instead of on the quarterback's right. Now, the halfback can run around left end if he starts to the left of the quarterback, but only on a pitchout. And Dive 28 is a handoff. So the quarterback knows what the messenger means. He knows the game plan didn't have any pitchouts for this situation. He calls the right play. Everything's fine. Except for one thing: *the halfback heard the messenger.*

By the time the quarterback called the right play, the halfback was already thinking about the pitchout he was going to take around left end. As the play begins, the halfback is halfway to the sideline when the quarterback turns around to hand him the ball. So there's the quarterback, holding the ball out for no one in particular, as though it's a handbill he's distributing at the airport. Before he realizes the halfback isn't going to take the ball, a defensive tackle reaches out and hits his arm. The ball bounces loose. The defensive tackle sees it all the way. He gets to it before anyone else. There's no one to stop him from scoring a touchdown. All because the messenger said the wrong color.

This doesn't happen often. But messengers do make mistakes, maybe once a game. "You get caught up in the heat of the battle, and you remember the numbers but you forget what they mean," says Gene Hickerson, one of Paul Brown's famous messenger guards with the Cleveland Browns of the fifties and sixties.

Hickerson had a safety valve in case he forgot a play. He had Jim Brown in the huddle. "I remember we were playing the Cards in 1959, and I forgot the play," Hickerson says. "I just called Jim Brown on a running play. He broke it for about a 25- or 30-yard run. Paul Brown never said anything about it."

Coaches spend a lot of time simplifying their terminology, both to make plays easy for a messenger to remember and to help get the play off in the allotted 30 seconds. They'll boil ten words down to eight. Or they'll let the quarterback add the garnish to the basic play. He knows the game plan. If he hears Dive 28, he knows the formation, motion, and blocking variation the coaches want with it, and he can certainly call a snap count.

A lot of times, a coach will assign numbers to the most common plays in the game plan, so instead of "Green Left, Z Motion, Dive 28, G Twist," all the quarterback has to hear is "Number 6." The adhesive tape wrapped aroung his wrist tells him which play is Number 6.

It's a good idea, seemingly foolproof. But remember what Gillman said. *Nothing's perfect.* In their 1983 opener, the Bears called a play off their numbered list, Play 17. That's how the call arrived at the huddle: Play 17. And the first thing quarterback Jim McMahon thought of was Play 17 from the playbook, not Play 17 from his numbered list. Both plays were passes, but Play 17 from the playbook was not a good pass for the situation. McMahon's pass was intercepted.

X X X X X
O O O O

If a coach is going to use messengers, the first thing he has to decide is whom to shuttle in and out of the game. Usually the messengers will play a position where nobody was able to clearly win the starting job. A coach isn't going to shuttle one of his best players. But through the years, the two most popular positions for shuttling have been guards and wide receivers.

"I decided to alternate guards," says Brown, one of the first coaches to use messengers, "because they weren't involved in touching the football or in the quarterback's cadence, the more intricate aspects."

Shuttling guards has an obvious drawback. As Hickerson says, "It's a 50-yard sprint. Any time you got into the game, you were tired."

"I'd put my best defensive lineman on them," Faulkner says of messenger guards. "They'd already be worn out."

That's not a problem for wide receivers. They're used to running. They can deliver the play faster, and they may find shuttling actually more restful than playing every down. As Hickerson says, "They're right on the sideline anyway. They don't have anywhere to run."

But as Brown points out, wide receivers have more intricate jobs. Their timing with the quarterback must be precise, and they need continuity in their private game with defensive backs. A wide receiver might need to run half a dozen convincing curl routes before a cornerback will fall for his fake curl move on a route to the sideline. He can't set up the cornerback for a move if he's not playing.

Besides, wide receivers are less likely to be interchangeable.

What if it turns out that one wide receiver keeps missing all the third-down plays? Chicago started shuttling tight ends instead of wide receivers after Gault kept winding up on the sideline when they called long pass plays.

Whoever delivers plays has to remember one thing. He'll be back on the sideline shortly, standing next to a coach who doesn't like surprises. Brown enjoys telling a story about guard Lin Houston delivering a play to quarterback George Ratterman:

"Houston went in with a play, and told George the play. Now George was something of a jokester. He answered back, 'I don't like that play. Go get another one.'

"Well, Houston turned right around and started running back to the sideline. He was about six feet out of the huddle when he turned around again, went back to George and said, 'Go tell him yourself.'

"Now I'm on the sideline. I don't know what's happening in the huddle, but all of a sudden I saw the whole football team out there laughing. I never thought anything was very funny during a football game, so I couldn't understand this. But when they told me about it later, I got a laugh out of it, too."

X X X X X
O O O O

The quarterback has the floor in the huddle. Players cannot come back to the huddle chattering, "Throw it to me. I was open," or "Give it to me," or "Run it to my side." A quarterback might entertain a specific suggestion while he's waiting for a messenger, but ordinarily, the time for players to share their ideas is when the defense is on the field.

The 30 seconds between plays seems to keep shrinking, especially with multiple men in motion who may need several seconds to run around before the ball is snapped. That's why the play call has to be concise, and it has to be ready even before the ball has been spotted from the previous play. "If the coach doesn't give you the play, you can't run it in," Hickerson says.

"We were in Baltimore one time, and Paul Brown couldn't think of a play. So I called a couple plays. Or I suggested them. He called one."

Active players are reluctant to talk about garbled messages or sideline indecision, probably because it sounds so much more inept to call an incomplete play than to throw an incomplete pass. It's not as if the other team is trying to tackle the play messenger.

Wasting a timeout or taking a five-yard delay penalty seems to be football's equivalent of taking a called third strike or missing two free throws. It looks so helpless. *What could be simpler than getting a play to the huddle?* But doing it fast enough gives even the best-coached teams problems. That is the main reason teams are replacing messengers with hand signals.

X X X X X
O O O O

"Hand signaling is more prevalent right now because time is so essential," says Faulkner, who prefers signals over messengers. "Signals are quicker and more efficient."

Even if there were no 30-second clock, a quarterback would want to know the next play as soon as possible. "Now the machinery can begin to work," Gillman says. "He can start thinking: What are my reads if it's a pass? Under what conditions do I call an audible if it's a run? That's the reason a quarterback loves to call plays. He can start thinking right now about what he has to do if something goes wrong."

The quarterback also has more time to react if something goes wrong. Instead of breaking the huddle with 10 seconds on the 30-second clock, barely enough time to line up and run a couple men in motion, he breaks the huddle with 18 seconds left. He has more time to call an audible.

Another advantage of signaling plays is it doesn't require substitution. Maybe the team wants to keep its best 11 players in the game. Or maybe, in the case of a defense, it wants to see the other team's substitutions before making its own. (Or maybe an offense wants to delay its substitutions, so when the defense answers with *its* new players, they might not reach their positions before the ball is snapped.)

Coaches play waiting games with each other all the time. Chicago defensive coordinator Buddy Ryan has pulled this trick on both Philadelphia and Detroit: First he sends in the personnel for, say, a 5–1–5 defense. He does it early enough for the offense to counter with substitutions to attack it. Then, just as the offense is leaving its huddle, Ryan changes players again. Now Chicago's nickel defense is on the field, and the offense is set to go against a five-man line. The offense has to waste a timeout.

Defenses almost always use hand signals. They're in as big a hurry as the offenses, except at the late end of the 30-second clock instead of the early end. And a defensive call is much shorter. It has only two or three elements:

★ The front, which indicates the alignment and everyone's responsibility against the run;
★ The pass coverage; and
★ The blitz, if there is one.

The problem with offensive hand signals is that an offensive play is so much more involved. That problem alone is reason enough for many coaches to use messengers. "A messenger can give information you just can't give with a signal," says Kansas City coach John Mackovic. "It's hard to make a signal that says, 'Watch out for the blitz.' Or 'look out' for anything. For any kind of alert, you need a messenger."

"You put more demands on your quarterback when you're signaling," Faulkner says. The quarterback not only has to remember all the signals, he has to remember which formation and which blocking scheme goes with each play. A coach rarely signals more than the play and the motion.

The quarterback—and whoever makes the huddle call for the defense—also has to be able to *see* the signal. It isn't that the sideline is so far away. Even for a goal-line play, the coach can get within 142 feet of the huddle; a second basemen in baseball can read a catcher's much smaller finger signals from 127 feet away. The problem for a football player is *finding* the right coach among 50 or so people on the sideline. That's why signal-calling coaches often wear brightly colored jackets, even on the hottest days.

But the coach can't be too obvious, either. "I think any time you use signals, there's a risk that they'll be stolen," says Tom Bass, who gives signals to San Diego's defense. San Diego uses two signaling coaches to confuse the other team. More often, a coach will use an indicator, just like baseball coaches: he'll flash a dozen different signals but none of them mean anything until he touches his cap, or his belt, or whatever the indicator is.

A football coach can make the signal even harder to steal if he wants. After the indicator, he can give the signal for a front, then throw in garbage signals for two or three more fronts before signaling the coverage. And, to be certain, a team will change its signals every two or three weeks.

"Three or four or five years ago, we stole some signs," Faulkner said in 1983. "Nowadays, I don't think it happens much. They're more careful."

"You'd have to film them and study them," New Orleans' Wade Phillips says. OK, so you hire a free-lance photographer to film a team's signals the week before you play them. And you figure them out. And the team uses the same signals against you.

Even then, says Ryan, "By the time you get it to your players, it would be too late to do much good." When Ryan was with the Jets, they figured out an opponent's blitz signal. All quarterback Joe Namath had to do was listen for a whistle on the sideline. Someone would blow it every time a blitz was on. "But Joe couldn't hear the whistle," Ryan says.

The blitz signal would be the best one for an offense to steal. For a defense, the signals for draw or screen would be the most helpful. "Even just knowing whether they're going to pass or run would be nice," Gillman says.

"I think if you went to enough trouble, you could break down someone's signals," Mackovic says. "But you'd have to be 100 percent right. Don't tell them a run is coming when they're going to fake a run and pass. That's worse than not having anything. I think usually, it's best for your players just to play the game."

X X X X X
O O O O

Whether the signals arrive by land or by air, the bench has to be organized. Possible substitutes have to stay close enough to the coach to hear when their unit reports. He doesn't have time to say, "You, you, and you. Get in there for 86, 25, and 43." It has to be enough for the coach to say "nickel," and the nickelbacks head for the huddle. Teams do so much substituting, sometimes one assistant coach will be in charge of making sure the right people are in, the right people are out, and 11 players are on the field.

The players who enter the game have to say which players they're replacing. A tight end, for example, might be replacing either a back, a wide receiver, or another tight end. If nobody leaves, it's a penalty for 12 men on the field. If two players leave, the penalty is having to play with 10. It cost the Redskins an extra point in their Super Bowl against the Raiders.

But sometimes a team gets away with a mistake. Sometimes the offense that runs a nonexistent play confuses the defense so much, the play gains big yardage. One time, it gained the biggest possible yardage.

Dallas was playing Minnesota in the last game of the 1982 season. With the Cowboys on their own 1-yard line, coach Tom Landry sent a tight end into the game to replace a wide receiver. The wide receiver left the huddle. Fullback Ron Springs, who thought the tight end was replacing him, also left the huddle.

Only ten Cowboys lined up. Quarterback Danny White didn't realize that until he turned around to hand the ball to Springs, who was nowhere in sight. Desperate to avoid a safety, White gave the ball to Tony Dorsett, the only back. Dorsett ran for a 99-yard touchdown.

Dots and Dashes among Xs and Os

... Players converse in code from the huddle to the snap

The audible has long been glorified as the switch a quarterback can flip to take the offense out of automatic pilot. Here's where the quarterback takes charge, where he shows all that poise, mettle, savvy, and whatnot, all those indescribably judicious qualities that earned him a seat on football's white steed in the first place. Here (finally!) the quarterback is no longer wired to the bench. He's *calling his own play.* And not only that, he's calling his own play at the line of scrimmage, thinking on his feet with the clock ticking down right in his face and the crowd screaming in his ears. He's just standing there, calm as can be, changing plays as nonchalantly as changing lanes on a Sunday drive, absolutely putting one over on those defensive players (who would no doubt have become quarterbacks themselves if they were smart enough to figure out what's going on).

At least that's how the scenario is usually painted. That's the picture-postcard version.

"We'll call the plays from the bench," the coach says, "but of course, the quarterback will still be allowed to call an audible any time."

So we have the image of a quarterback at the line of scrimmage, tight game, big third-down play. He's sizing up the situation and getting ready to say, "Hut!" and—suddenly—red lights and bells go off in his mind. Something's not right. The quarterback doesn't like the looks of that strong safety. He's creeping up, and the play from the bench doesn't call for anyone to block him if he blitzes.

In a flash, the playbook is spread out in the quarterback's mind, as if on microfilm. Quickly, he scans it. Aha! The perfect play. Smoke is practically coming out of his ears by now, as he barks the signals to both sides of the offense (always, he *barks* the signals, never hollering or yelling or calling them out). All the time, he manfully resists the urge to tip off his secret by giggling in anticipation.

The quarterback's audible has reined the fullback in from the pass pattern to keep the safety at bay. It has sent the tight end on a post pattern, where he can plunder the real estate the safety has abandoned in the middle of the field. The tight end has single coverage from the strong-side linebacker. He gets behind the linebacker. He's open. He catches the ball. There's nobody in front of him. Touchdown! We Win!

In the locker room afterward, the quarterback praises the linemen and the fullback for blocking and the tight end for catching the ball, and it just sort of slips out, in the middle of his monologue, that he changed the play at line of scrimmage. Yup, it was an audible. Oh, that coy devil.

But wait. Let's look at this play through the quarterback's facemask. This was not some creative masterpiece he just pulled off. He could show it to you, right there in the game plan: on a strong safety blitz, we audible to a post for the tight end. He's still feeling proud and maybe even a little tingly about the play. It *did* win the game. He's proud he was able to do everything by the book. He recognized the blitz, called the right audible, and threw a complete pass that went for a touchdown. Everything worked.

But he's not proud of any heroic initiative he took. He didn't pull a fast one on anybody. He was only doing what he was supposed to do. In fact, if he hadn't called the audible and the safety had sacked him, he would have had a lot of explaining to do once the coach was within earshot.

Even when he calls an audible, the quarterback is following instructions. He's following them alertly, yes. And what he's doing is not easy, just as it's not easy to read a defense and correlate his reading to the pass pattern his team is running, and determine which of his receivers will be open, and get the ball to the right one—all in less time than it takes to sneeze. But all the time, the quarterback is doing what the coaches programmed him to do. If all goes well, he is the hub of the circuitry that converts plans into action.

For every situation that requires an audible, there is a specific play the quarterback should call. And it isn't as though he has to pick the one specific play out of the whole playbook. A game plan has a limited list of possible audible calls. "If anyone tells you it's more than four or five, he's kidding you," says Washington quarterback Joe Theismann.

And those miserable fools on defense? The ones who got caught single-covering the tight end, leaving the middle of the field to greet him with wide-open arms? They knew what they were doing. They knew what the quarterback was doing, too. "When you're taking extra time at the line, shouting numbers in both directions, usually the defense is well aware of what you're doing," Theismann says. The defense can always call off a blitz. Sometimes, it chooses not to. Gambles don't always work.

X X X X X
O O O O

An audible can be either protective or aggressive. It can protect an offense from wasting a play when the defense has blocked off the running hole or pass route. It also can protect an offense from an unexpected blitz. Or it can take advantage of an unexpected weak area the defense is conceding.

But then, all audibles wind up being aggressive. If you're going to change out of a bad play, there's no sense replacing it with an ordinary play. In calling audibles, the rule is: Think big.

"Half of the big plays you see are from audibles," Paul Brown says.

Audibles aren't always what they used to be, though. More and more, they're getting to be inaudible. You can still hear an audible for a run play, and most plays are called at the line of scrimmage in a hurried, no-huddle offense at the end of a half, but for changing pass plays, there is something better. For changing pass plays, most teams prefer sight adjustments.

"We don't call as many audibles as we used to," Theismann says. "The trend is to have your quarterback read the defense on the move after the ball is snapped. It's more of a go-get-'em kind of offense, more run-and-gun. You run the play you called, and you know it's got something built into it that will work against anything.

"Really, what has happened is it's evolving to sort of a Vince Lombardi ethic. Let's do what we do well, even though they know what's coming. You say, 'Our best people can beat your best people.' If you do that, not only do you have a physical advantage, but you get a psychological advantage, too."

The problem with calling too many audibles, then, is that it puts the offense in the position of reacting to the defense. That's not where an offense wants to be. It wants to be telling the defense what to do.

Sight adjustments are sort of a second-generation improvement on audibles, as home computers are to video games. If a team wants to protect itself from an obviously ill-fated pass play, or to seize the chance for a big pass play, sight adjustments have several advantages:

1. They aren't limited to the few pass plays a team would have on its list of audibles. Any pass play can have sight adjustments built into it—without even changing the basic play.

2. A sight adjustment can be made without letting the defense know something is changing. An audible all but announces, across the line of scrimmage, *We're changing our play now, so you might want to change your defense.* It might make a psychological impact, too considering an audible also announces, *We called the wrong play. You guys sure had us pegged this time.*

3. Sight adjustments don't take any time. A team can line up with the 30-second clock well into single digits, and even if there isn't time to call an audible, it can still make a sight adjustment.

4. In fact, a sight adjustment can come *after* the snap. If a defense disguises its pass coverage before the snap, the quarterback may not realize his pass play is not well-chosen until it's too late to call an audible. But a receiver can still adjust his route after the ball is in play, when the defense has to commit its men to their proper stations for coverage.

Or suppose the defense was only faking a blitz. If the quarterback calls an audible to beat the blitz, and the defense isn't really blitzing, the quarterback could be worse off than if he had kept his mouth shut. As Theismann says, "You're in a blitz adjustment with two guys in the pass pattern, and they've got six guys covering." But an offense using sight adjustments can wait to make its change until someone actually blitzes.

5. With sight adjustments, there is less risk of garbled communication. True, the quarterback and the receiver have to make the same adjustment without saying anything to each other. That's a problem. But they've been taught to make that adjustment as a natural part of the play. And if the adjustment is obvious before the snap, they can reassure each other by making eye contact instead of just looking vaguely in each other's direction, as they ordinarily would do.

To call an audible, the quarterback has to make himself heard as far as 25 yards away. Stadiums get noisy enough, remember, that the 49ers abandoned the shotgun formation because the center couldn't hear the quarterback's signals *five* yards away.

A wide receiver should know when to listen for an audible. He sees the defense line up, just as the quarterback does. But his view isn't as good. And it's not a good idea just to *assume* the quarterback has called an audible. This can happen, too: the wide receiver might think he has heard an audible, so he runs the pass route for the appropriate audible play, but the quarterback was only pretending to call an audible. When the quarterback looks for the wide receiver, he can't find him.

Some teams have their quarterbacks make it sound as if they're calling an audible before every play. Even if a team doesn't run through the charade for every down, a quarterback is apt to pretend to call an audible more often than he actually calls one. The other players have to listen for what's called the hot color, or maybe a designated number, some verbal signal that *this is the real thing.* The hot color is what the wide receiver has to hear, 25 yards away. It's nice if he can hear the audible that follows it, too, but if he hears the hot color, he should know his game plan well enough to know which audible applied for the situation.

Defenses and offenses often play their own little game of Odds or Evens, varying only slightly from the children's game where each kid flashes one finger or two, one of them calls "odd" or "even" and the one who's right gets to punch the other one. In the football version, the defense flashes yes-blitz or no-blitz and the offense flashes yes-audible or no-audible, and the offense always has evens. If there is a blitz and no adjustment, or an adjustment and no blitz, the defense gets to beat up on the offense.

So there is a lot of faking of both blitzes and audibles. "That's where the actor in a quarterback comes out," Theismann says. "You really hope you convince them. Because if you're calling a dummy audible and they're not calling off their blitz, they're going to be coming and you're back there with no protection."

X X X X X
O O O O

Sight adjustments after the snap usually just follow common sense. The receiver goes where the defender isn't. Todd Christensen made many of his league-leading 92 catches in 1983 by simply running to the middle of the field and turning away from the nearest defender.

Other adjustments are more specific, like the one Charlie Joiner made in the playoff game against Miami, the time he went deep because the Dolphins covered his short route. That adjustment simply added on to Joiner's original route. Another type of adjustment can change the original route altogether, or even leave the route unspecified until the coverage becomes apparent.

In a 1983 game against Detroit, the Cleveland Browns wanted to pass the ball to wide receiver Dave Logan. They figured Detroit

Here are two sight adjustments a wide receiver might have to make after he has begun running his route. On the first one, he can run straight between two defenders double-covering him inside and outside, but if the players are covering him short and deep, he angles toward the end zone on a corner route. Another possible adjustment against short-and-deep coverage is a simple out, straight toward the sideline.

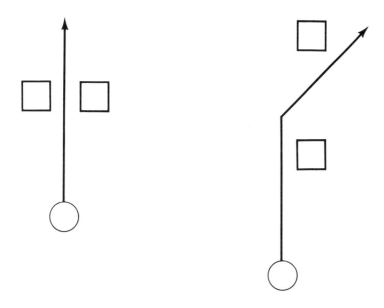

On the bottom adjustment, the receiver uses the area in front of a defender playing him loosely, but if the defender rolls up to meet him at the line of scrimmage, the receiver challenges him to a footrace.

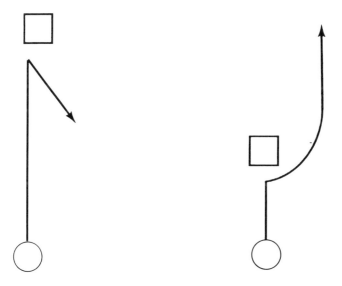

would assume as much, so they guessed Logan would be double-covered. Logan's route would depend on *how* he was double-covered.

The way to beat double-coverage is for the receiver to make his move when he's right between the defensive players, where the responsibilities might be a little fuzzy. So if the Lions covered Logan horizontally, inside and outside, he would run between them, straight downfield. That wouldn't work if they covered him vertically, short and deep, in which case Logan would get between them and veer toward the corner of the end zone. Logan's choices are the first two routes in the diagram on page 217.

The Lions covered Logan short and deep. He cut to the corner. Quarterback Brian Sipe pumped the ball toward a receiver running closer to the middle of the field than Logan, so the deep defender would have to edge inside and the short defender would have to chase Logan. That did the trick. Logan caught the 32-yard touchdown pass that was decisive in a five-point victory.

Those sight adjustments can't be made until the ball is in play, but many others are effectively just wordless audibles. They change a whole pass play, and they do it before the ball is snapped. These plays are common audibles that have become common sight adjustments:

★ Defense in a two-deep zone; offense sends its tight end deep between the zones. "That's one of the big calls in the game today," Sid Gillman says. For a team like San Diego, Tampa Bay, or Cleveland, with a very fast tight end, the call is almost automatic.

★ Cornerback lines up with a wide cushion between himself and the wide receiver; offense sends the wide receiver on a quick out. The cornerback is giving the receiver seven or eight free yards, so the receiver takes them. He makes his cut before he gets to the cornerback. He'll keep taking those yards all day, or he'll force the cornerback to play him tighter, making it possible for him to run a deeper route.

★ Cornerback rolls up to meet the wide receiver at the line; receiver runs a fade, or a quick bomb. The quarterback drops back just two steps and lets the ball fly to a spot 20 yards down the sideline. "You've got to challenge the cornerback if he crowds you like that," Gillman says. "The receiver says, 'Meet me at 20 yards.' That's where the ball's got to be. A good quarterback is taught, if it's zone coverage, to drill the ball so the defensive backs can't get to it. And if it's man coverage, to lay it up for the receiver to run under it, because the footrace is on."

The turning point in the Raiders' Super Bowl victory over Washington, even before a point was scored, may have been when Art Monk challenged cornerback Mike Haynes's tight coverage with three straight quick sideline passes the first time Washington had the ball. All three passes were incomplete. Haynes didn't have to relax his aggressive coverage, and the Redskin wide receivers were not factors in the game.

The fade is also a good route for beating the blitz. The ball is in the air before the blitzer can get to the quarterback. That's the idea for any sight adjustment against the blitz: don't bother blocking the blitzer, just don't give him anyone to tackle.

If the offense has a blocker assigned to each blitzer, it can go ahead with its original play. So sometimes, the sight adjustment (or audible) on a blitz is simply for a back to stay put and block instead of running a pass route. But in case the defense sends more players than the offense can block, the offense has designated its hot receiver, its emergency target. The hot receiver has to get open in a hurry, either along the sideline or in the area the blitzer has abandoned. So the short post (into the blitzing safety's area) is another popular adjustment against a blitz.

"But you can't pass every time you see a blitz," Theismann says. "Teams chart you. They'll know they can get you to pass just by showing a blitz."

There are two common run audibles for beating blitzes: the quick trap up the middle and a quick pitch toward the sideline. "The fade, the quick post, the quick out, the quick trap, and the quick pitch—those are about the only ways to take advantage of a blitz," Theismann says. "If you see one of them after a quarterback has been under the center a long time, he probably called an audible."

Another reason for changing a run play at the line of scrimmage is an overshifted (or undershifted) line. The quarterback cancels a run toward the side where the defense has shifted, and he replaces it with a run to the other side.

Football is always easier when the other team's players don't get in the way.

X X X X X
O O O O

Audibles haven't changed much since George Halas dreamed them up in the mid-forties, after the other teams had started figuring out how to stop his T-formation offense. Sid Luckman was Halas's quarterback, and he says his basic audibles were to run away from a shifted defense, to pass away from double coverage, and to throw a quick out or a quick post against a blitz.

"We used audibles 20 or 25 percent of the time after I got back from the service in 1946," Luckman says. "I'd look for some sort of tip-off, and if I saw what I was looking for, I'd shout, 'Red,' which would mean danger to the whole team. You couldn't audible every time you called 'Red,' so sometimes in the huddle I'd say 'Ignore red,' and that meant I was going to say 'Red' at the line, but it wouldn't mean anything."

Now, as in Luckman's day, the blitz is the most common reason for changing a play at the line of scrimmage. More than any other defensive tactic, the blitz requires an offense to protect itself at the same time it offers an opening to reach out and grab.

X X X X X
O O O O

Quarterbacks' audibles may get all the public attention, but before most plays, the center, middle linebacker, and strong safety do far more chattering. Next to them, the quarterback doesn't have much more to say than a gangster on trial, until it's time for him to chime in with a couple of numbers and a "Hut! Hut! Hut!" so the play can start.

"There are two areas in pro football where communication is critical," the Rams' Jack Faulkner says. "The offensive line and the defensive secondary. Obviously, if you have a missed assignment in the secondary, it can mean a big play. But if you screw up as an offensive lineman, too, you're in deep trouble. They have to be intelligent enough to know everything that goes on, to react to every shift of the defensive linemen."

For purely geographical reasons, all conversation on the line emanates from the center—as if he doesn't have enough to do with snapping the ball and bringing his arms back in time to keep some 270-pound nose tackle from using him to drill a hole in the ground. The center sizes up the defensive front before he stoops to grab the ball, and he gives the appropriate coded blocking assignment to the two guards, who pass it on to the tackles and tight ends. If the quarterback changes the play, the new blocking assignments go down the line the same way.

Nobody's breaking any big news here. The linemen should know their assignments before they hear them, even if the assignments keep changing because the defensive linemen are hopping around like wind-up toys. But it's comforting for a lineman to actually hear the same assignment he's thinking. An offensive lineman in a three-point stance doesn't exactly have a panoramic view, and the chatter up and down the line reinforces that he saw what he thought he saw.

Linemen make dummy calls, too, the same way a quarterback might fake an audible. They've even been known to make them

This is the kind of adjustment offensive linemen might make in their audible calls to each other. If the first blocking scheme doesn't work—with the center taking on the nose tackle and the guard pulling to cut off the linebacker—the guard and center can make a change.

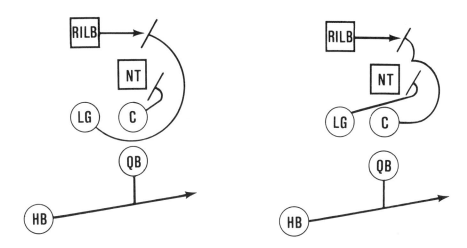

They still block the same two players in the second blocking scheme, but this time they double-team the nose tackle until the linebacker is close enough to the ball carrier that the center has to cut him off.

on the ribald side, on the off-chance that a call with enough drill-sergeant creativity to it might break a defensive lineman's concentration.

When the calls are for real, they're not instructing whom to block so much as how to make the blocks. The center doesn't stroll up to the line, glance both ways, and suddenly pound his forehead with his palm, thinking, *Ohmygosh, I've got to change these blocking assignments. We didn't expect them to line up like this.* When plays are drawn into a playbook, they stipulate blocking assignments for any way the defense is likely to line up. Those adjustments are part of the basic play.

But there are always alternative ways to block for a play. Suppose a play is a run to the right side. The center and the left guard are responsible for blocking the nose tackle and the right inside linebacker in a 3–4 defense. Now, the playbook designs a method for making those blocks that will work more often than not, but sometimes it won't. The important thing isn't following Method A in the playbook. The important thing is blocking the right inside linebacker and the nose tackle. If the best way to block the right inside linebacker and the nose tackle is to launch into them with somersaults, then that's fine with the coaches.

On this run to the right, Method A might have the center blocking the nose tackle and the guard pulling behind the center to cut off the linebacker as he heads toward the play. That's the blocking scheme in the first diagram on page 221. But maybe Method A didn't work the first time the team ran this play. Maybe the center couldn't handle the nose tackle by himself. That doesn't mean the center is a hapless oaf or that the play can't work again all game. It means the center and the left guard have to put their heads together the next time the offense goes to the bench, and they have to decide on a better way to block the play.

The second diagram on page 221 shows an alternative. Send both the center and the guard after the nose tackle. Double team him for a count or two. The linebacker isn't hurting anybody until he moves past the nose tackle, toward the play. When he does that, the center slips off the nose tackle and blocks the linebacker.

Another popular topic for pre-snap discussion is the possibility of stunts. In fact, stunts might be to offensive-line conversation what the weather is to elevator conversation. "If your guy stunts to me, do you follow him or do I take him?" Faulkner says. "If I'm going to take him regardless, do you have to take my guy or do you have the option to pull out and get the backer? That kind of thing."

X X X X X
O O O O

The offensive linemen may get pretty gabby, but they don't have to shriek. They're talking to the fellows next to them. The defense generally sounds like a playground at recess time.

"Basically, everybody's talking," says Tom Bass, San Diego's defensive coordinator. "But it isn't as chaotic as it sounds. Specific people are saying specific things to specific people."

Safeties are talking to cornerbacks and linebackers. Linebackers are talking to safeties and linemen. Linemen are talking to each other. They're talking about where to line up and who fills which lane if it's a run and who covers whom or where if it's a pass.

The defense called a play in the huddle, but it was just a starting point. The huddle call was just a frame for the picture that will take shape when the offensive players take and retake their positions. Defenses are based on offensive tendencies, remember, and tendencies are based on formations, so every time the formation changes—every time a man goes in motion—the defense changes, too. Like the offensive linemen's adjustments, the defensive adjustments shouldn't come as any big news flash to anyone. They've all been spelled out in the game plan. But it's more important for everyone to be in the *same* defense than for everyone to be in the *right* defense.

The players in the secondary are reinforcing each other. *Yes, that is the flanker going in motion across to the weak side. And that's right, our left cornerback is following him. And, just like we planned, the man-to-man coverage is still on with the safeties helping out deep against the wide outs. So the strong safety—there he goes now—is edging back a little so he can get over to the other side. Everything's under control.*

On the line, the chatter is informative. Defensive linemen are flying even more blindly than offensive linemen. They're in that same three-point stance, and their assignments might be changed by the motion of some back or wide receiver who might as well be under the stands, for all they can see of him.

Defensive linemen are reacting to what they're hearing behind them by calling their own audibles. Maybe a new stunt. Maybe they'll slant their initial charges in the opposite direction because the offense has changed strong sides. Maybe they have to move, shift from a basic 3–4 to an overshift. Sometimes a linebacker will give a lineman a pat on the hip to remind him. Audibles are important on the defensive line, as Dave Butz learned in his younger days on a Washington team that didn't cotton to younger players winning starting jobs. Butz has recalled how Diron Talbert would give him audibles that didn't exist so Butz would look bad enough to keep Talbert's pal, Bill Brundige, in the lineup.

Back in the secondary, here's what it sounds like:

The signal-calling linebacker breaks the ice by shouting out the formation. He uses the same terminology as the offense, but with the strong side reversed, as it looks to the defense. *Brown left! Brown left!* In a moment, all the linebackers and defensive backs are yelling "Brown left!" by way of saying, "Roger. We copy. Over."

"Then say they shift into a one-back set," says Buddy Curry, the outside linebacker who calls Atlanta's signals. "We've decided we'll play that with a Cover One, which is man coverage. So I start yelling, 'Silver! Silver!' calling out the adjustment.

"Now the one back goes in motion. I go with him, so I make a Gong call, which tells the defensive end on my side he has to contain because I'm following the back."

If the play is a pass, the talking continues after the snap. The linebackers and defensive backs have determined their basic coverage by now, but they still might not know which variation of that coverage they'll use. "Say you're in a coverage where the outside linebacker takes the farthest receiver out and the middle linebacker takes the second guy," says Gary Fencik, the Chicago safety who has called signals for defenses without a middle linebacker. "You don't know who to cover—even in man coverage—until they run the pattern."

Defensive signal callers are so important that when the New

York Giants traded signal-calling linebacker Brian Kelley before the 1984 season, it created rumblings of anxiety among their other linebackers. Kelley was the only Giant linebacker who hadn't been to a Pro Bowl, but he was *the defensive quarterback*, the man who conducts the defensive symphony of perpetual motion.

For Chicago, Fencik has been to Pro Bowls, but replacing a premier safety was the least of the Bears' worries when he was injured in 1983. They had other safeties, and enough defenses to hide the replacements' shortcomings. But even the most imaginative defensive coordinator can't use mirrors to produce a signal caller. In the game when Fencik went down, the Bears gave up a touchdown when they didn't respond to an obvious audible by calling off their blitz. It was a classic fade pattern. If the Bears hadn't blitzed, the fade might not have worked. As it turned out, though, the Bears lost in overtime.

When the defensive signals are wafting through the air, a sharp offensive player might be soaking in all those Silvers and Gongs for future reference. "I like a defense that talks a lot," Chicago wide receiver Brian Baschnagel says. "If they repeat their coverages enough, I might be able to pick them up. That way I know my own adjustments ahead of time."

That's the chance a defense has to take. If the linebackers and defensive backs aren't all playing the same coverage, the receivers won't have to worry about making sight adjustments. They'll get open just watching defensive players run into each other.

"One time we had the linebackers playing one coverage and the safeties playing a different one," Curry says. "When I watched it on film, I saw myself turn around and it almost looked like I got in an argument with a safety. We practically knocked each other over. Fortunately, nothing happened."

That kind of mix-up "doesn't happen as often as you might think," Tom Bass says. "Because with all your changes, you don't change the style of the defense you're playing. You wouldn't go from a blitz to a two-deep zone. If you changed, you'd go to another blitz."

The changes are simple not only to avoid confusion, but also to protect the defense from falling into dangerously predictable tendencies. If an offensive coordinator knew, for example, that a defense never played zone coverage when the flanker went in motion across the field, he would send the flanker in motion on every play and pepper the defense with his best pass plays for man-to-man coverage. "You don't want a situation where the offense can do something to dictate your alignment," Bass says. The offense is dictating enough to the defense as it is.

Win One for the Microchipper

. . . Halftime talks have all the emotional frenzy of a board meeting

People used to ask Bud Grant why he didn't move around much on the sideline. His answer was, he couldn't. He had to wear his telephone headset. He made it sound as if the first time he chased an official down the sideline, he'd get yanked back by the telephone cord like a barking dog that forgot it was chained to a pole.

The telephone lines to the coaches upstairs are more like umbilical cords than leashes. The NFL considers them so important, if one team loses its phone connection, the other team has to turn its phones off.

During a game, a team usually will have two or three offensive coaches and two defensive coaches upstairs on the press box level—nearly half the staff. The offensive coordinator is often among the upstairs coaches; the defensive coordinator, offensive-line coach, and special-teams coach are generally with the head coach downstairs. They need to be with the players to make adjustments and substitutions.

For the upstairs coaches, the game unfolds as though they're watching game film, only live. They have less noise, better comfort, and a better view than the sideline coaches. Many teams have their offensive plays called by an upstairs coach who can keep his game plan on a table for easy reference, out of the elements, except for spilled coffee. Even if the head coach calls the plays, he probably gets a recommendation from upstairs on most downs. "My guys up above would tell me what's the best run play and the best pass play," Paul Brown says. "Then we'd make a choice."

The upstairs coaches' job, in a nutshell, is to confirm that the opponent is following the same tendencies the computer printed out earlier in the week or to point out any deviations. Any surprises are likely to be subtle ones, difficult to pick out from the sideline.

If a normally reliable play barely reaches the line of scrimmage in the first quarter, it's an upstairs coach's job to explain why. He might say, "Forget that play today. They're overshifting to the

"There are certain things you're going to do, whatever happens. You've got pass plays where the quarterback puts the ball in the air and you don't care what kind of coverage they're in. Somebody's going to be open. And you've got certain runs you're going to use despite what the other side does. You're just going to block them by areas. That being true, what purpose does the guy upstairs serve?

"He's there because during the course of a ball game, things happen. You can have your game plan, and it can be a good game plan, and you can follow it down your card, but that card can only help you so far. Things always happen that you weren't expecting."—**Sid Gillman**

right. We ought to be using this one instead." Or he might report, "Yes, they're doing what we anticipated. The play's still good. The right guard just got beaten physically. We might want to change the blocking, but don't give up on the play."

Sid Gillman gives another example: "Say your offense uses a movement before the snap. You had a reasonable knowledge of how the other team would adjust to that movement, but suppose they do something else. Now you've got to take that into consideration before you use it again. You're not accomplishing what you wanted to accomplish with your motion.

"Or say their left corner is playing soft when we show motion to the strong side. We didn't expect it, but we ought to take advantage of it now by throwing in front of him."

The coaches aren't just looking for unpleasant surprises, then. They're looking for nice ones, too. As a matter of checklist routine, they're watching for the splits on the other team's line. They're seeing if the other defense is filling all the lanes on running plays. Maybe a running play went nowhere, but only because the defense overloaded to the side where the ball went. Now the offense might want to show the same formation and motion, hoping to get the same defensive response, and run the other way.

"The coaches upstairs are giving the coaches on the field all the information they need to say, 'Let's try this and see if it works,' " says Ted Plumb, an assistant coach who works upstairs for the Bears.

On each play, for offense or defense, the upstairs coaches are charting: (1) down and distance, (2) offensive formation, (3) offensive play, (4) defensive response, and (5) what happened. Someone is making the same charts on the sideline, but they can't lay their charts on a table. The coaches upstairs are not only making the charts, they're examining them to see what they mean. And they're watching specific areas: one takes the point of attack, another the linebackers, another the defensive backs.

They're taking pictures, too. (The NFL doesn't allow teams to use moving pictures during a game, but upstairs coaches use instant still cameras. The home team can't even put a television monitor in its own coaches' box unless it supplies the visitors with one, too.) The coach with the camera takes a shot of the linemen just before the ball is snapped and a later shot of the secondary. At halftime, a player or sideline coach might see something on the pictures that he missed during the game.

X X X X X
O O O O

The NFL standardized its game phone systems in 1983. There's a line for the defense, a line for the offense, and any number of extensions. The head coach can tap into either line.

"We used to use walkie talkies," says Jack Faulkner, who worked upstairs for Gillman with the Rams in the mid-fifties. "I'd be calling to the bench and some guy on the freeway with his car radio on would be going, 'Who's that?'

"After we went to phones, one time we went to Wrigley Field to play Halas. I went over on Saturday to hook up the telephone system. It plugged right in. I said, 'Fine,' plugged it in, and left.

"Well, we found out later, it plugged into the stadium switchboard. Bob Waterfield was our quarterback, and every time he called something, the Bears jumped right on it. After the game, we accused Halas of bugging our phone. Some reporters asked him about it. They said, 'Is that right?' and he said, 'Yup. So what?' "

Quarterbacks often go straight from the field to a headset, but they're not the only players who talk upstairs during the game. An offensive tackle might want to ask a coach if the pictures show any reason he's having so much trouble on a particular block. Or he might want to let the offensive coordinator know he had no trouble at all blocking his man toward the inside on those two runs around his end, and it might not be a bad idea to go that way more often. There's more time for that kind of information exchange at halftime, but a team can't always wait until halftime.

"An enormous amount of changes are made prior to halftime," says the Chargers' Tom Bass.

"You've got to make your adjustment when you need it," says Buddy Ryan, the Bears' defensive coordinator. "If something isn't working, I never could see telling the players to stay in there and do it harder. If people are kicking your brains out, you can't wait till next week to see the film. You've only got 16 chances."

X X X X X
O O O O

Halftime gives the coaches more time to compare their pre-game tendencies with the realities of the game. They might find something that had escaped them in the booth. They also have more time to adjust their plans to any discrepancies they've already found between tendency and reality.

But they don't make big changes.

"The idea of grandiose halftime adjustments is really over-rated," Fencik says. "There are always changes, but they're subtle. You've usually prepared for so much all week that nothing really completely surprises you. If you're having a problem, it's usually in executing. Or you might have to adjust because you've run up against a hot quarterback. But the biggest adjustment you're likely to make is if somebody gets injured."

So there are no mad halftime geniuses in the NFL coaching ranks. "It's not a time for screaming and haranguing," Brown says. Game plans are not fed to shredders. Remember, the game plan was not written on the backs of envelopes on the bus ride to the stadium.

"The halftime is designed for a fast inventory of what we have done or have not done, as against what you're doing," Gillman says. "That's when we decide: This is no good and this is no good, but this is going great. Let's use it more in the second half. We haven't done this; we can't forget it in the second half. And we need to run this a couple more times to set up that pass play. Then: What are they doing? It looks like they might be giving us this. We've got to be sure to try it."

Methodically, the game plan is being cleaned out like a messy closet. *These, we can throw out. There's a keeper. And say, that would look nice, too, with just this one alteration.* During the week, the game plan had to be crammed full for every possible occasion, from swimwear to parkas. But by the end of halftime, it's trimmed down to what's obviously useful, to what can help win the game in the second half.

Even if coaches were inclined to revamp their game plans, as opposed to editing them, they wouldn't have time for it. There are fifteen minutes between halves. It takes about a minute to get to the locker room from the field, and three more minutes to get back on the field and warm up. That leaves eleven minutes. "Your players can't absorb many changes in that time," Faulkner says. "You've got too many people involved."

Many of the eleven minutes in a halftime locker room are devoted to the pressing business of treating wounds, repairing equipment, replacing pads, and using the restroom. The coach for each position conducts a brief confab, drawing on a small blackboard while linebackers trip over receivers to squeeze within view of their coach's blackboard. Linemen, in particular, are interested in seeing the pictures from upstairs. People are grabbing some orange slices spread out on a table. For a player, that is halftime.

The head coach usually says a few words after an official tells him it's time to go back out. They're the obligatory Few Words people always are expected to say whenever protocol drops them into the center of attention, whether they're introducing a speaker, accepting an award, or coaching a football team. The words are rarely memorable. A coach might try throwing a chair or pounding a wall or raising his voice if the team went out and

"The main thing is to keep everybody calm," Faulkner says. "You want to reassure the players that everything is fine. There aren't any problems that can't be worked out."

played flat as a billiard table, but a coach who gets emotional at halftime is more likely to inspire laughter than fear or awe. *What's with this guy?*

"The main thing is to keep everybody calm," Faulkner says. "You want to reassure the players that everything is fine. There aren't any problems that can't be worked out."

That doesn't mean halftime changes aren't important. Bass recalls when San Diego trailed Cincinnati 24–17 at halftime of a 1982 Monday night game. He made a halftime adjustment and San Diego outscored the Bengals 33–10 in the second half. "We just moved some people over," Bass says. "We changed the alignment of some linebackers so they lined up on people the way we wanted them to."

Kansas City coach John Mackovic says the most significant halftime adjustment he remembers making came after he had left the dressing room. He already had studied the upstairs coaches' charts. Now he was just glancing at the regular statistics sheet. It showed his team had completed 8 of 19 passes. He thought about the game plan, which had called for long passes against the blitz. Hmmm. Didn't seem to be working. When he got to the bench, he looked for the quarterback. "Forget those long passes," Mackovic told the quarterback. "Let's try throwing underneath their coverage when they blitz."

Mackovic was coaching Wake Forest at the time. The Deacons were playing Maryland, with the country's top-ranked pass defense. Wake Forest had almost 300 yards passing in the second half and won the game.

"It's what you do with your information that counts," Mackovic says.

X X X X X
O O O O

One thing to remember at halftime is that the other team didn't just go to the locker room to get out of the sun. Those guys are making adjustments, too. That's why a coach will sometimes wait until halftime to make a change. He'll force the other team to react to his change on the fly, after the second half has begun.

"There's the beautiful thing about the one-back offense," Gillman says. Remember how a one-back team has enough formations to lump them together in packages? It can turn a dozen or so basic plays into a kaleidoscope of different-*looking* plays by using different packages weeks on end. And there's nothing to stop it from changing packages at halftime, either.

"You can have a first-half offense and a second-half offense," Gillman says. "The plays aren't changed. The pass patterns aren't changed. The kids don't have a lot of learning to do. But the sets are changed.

"So in the other dressing room, when the other coach is saying, 'When they line up this way, we'll do this,' you're over there telling your team, 'Go to Package Two.' "

All Teams Are Created Equal

... But the vaunted scheduling format has had little impact on NFL parity

The word parity has developed a bad connotation, so the NFL office has ashcanned it. The league prefers balance to describe how closely bunched its teams have become in the last several years. It's the same sort of word trickery, although less ambitious, that was at work when we were told missiles would henceforth be called peacekeepers. (Someday, the politicians and generals are bound to start calling their bombs 9 routes.)

By whatever name, the NFL has been undergoing a sort of Ice Age, a glacial leveling of the once-imposing peaks and valleys of its perennial dynasties and doormats. Gone are the days when a strong team can get away with playing a bad game, as Don Shula has said his Miami powerhouse was able to do in the early seventies. Gone, too, are the hopeless days that inspired Chicago tight end Fred Pagac, when asked what it would take for the Bears to win their division, to reply: "A few key plane crashes."

Parity comes in two flavors. They may not be separable, but they're distinct. There's Rags-to-Riches Parity, the proliferation of grimy-knuckled, stomach-growling teams crashing the annual playoff ball that used to be the haven of an exclusive aristocracy. And there's Bell-Curve Parity, the bulge in the middle of the standings where more than half the league has records of 7–9, 8–8, or 9–7.

The most prominent flavor in 1983 was Bell-Curve Parity. The belly of the NFL standings was its fattest since the 1970 merger, with 16 of the 28 teams finishing from 7–9 through 9–7. It even burped four 9–7 teams into the playoffs.

Rags-to-Riches Parity had its heyday in 1981, as the box on page 233 describes in more detail. That was the year the 49ers and the Bengals scrambled up from 6–10 records to meet in the Super Bowl, and the Jets and the Giants vaulted from fifth place to the playoffs. Rags-to-Riches Parity had to taper off sometime. After a certain point, the NFL runs out of candidates for surprising breakthroughs.

Still, the only team going to the playoffs as a matter of course was Dallas, which earned a record 10th straight post-season appearance but bolted from the playoffs as if from a burning building. San Diego had been the next most venerable playoff team, with four straight appearances, and San Diego didn't get any closer to the 1983 playoffs than it got to Bangor, Maine. That left Miami as Dallas' runner-up, with a breathtaking streak of three straight playoff seasons.

In 1980, 1981, and 1982 alone, 22 of the 28 teams had turns in the playoffs. After Denver and Seattle made it in 1983, the only teams that hadn't made the playoffs in the eighties were the Saints, the Colts, the Bears, and the Chiefs. (The Cardinals and the Patriots, however, had been playoff teams only because the field was enlarged to 16 teams in 1982.) Rags-to-Riches Parity may have passed its fad stage, but it's hardly off the market.

X X X X X
0 0 0 0

Of the two kinds of parity, Bell-Curve is clearly the hardest to swallow. People lead lives that are ordinary enough without having the word scream out at them from the NFL standings. After a week of 8–8 days, it's nice to sit down Sunday and watch a couple of teams with more than their chins above water. And the worst part of Bell-Curve Parity is when that vast, gray middle of the standings starts oozing into the playoffs—when we're expected to believe 9–7 is the mark of a championship team.

The American people will tolerate a lot of things. They're used to products falling apart before the label fades. They're used to being aggravated by service companies. They're used to waiting in lines to find out which line they should have been waiting in. But one place they'll draw the line is at 9–7 teams presuming to command respect just because they had better records against teams within the conference than some other 9–7 teams.

In the first eight years after the merger, through 1977, only one team won a division with a record just one full game above .500,

The creep toward Rags-to-Riches Parity in the NFL broke into a full gallop in 1981, when the two teams that went to the Super Bowl had been the league's worst over the previous two seasons. The other kind of parity, Bell-Curve Parity, kept surging through 1983.

In 1981

- 8 of the 15 teams that had not had winning seasons the previous year improved to winning records.
- 9 of the 13 teams that had had winning seasons the previous year fell to losing or .500 records.
- 6 of the 10 playoff teams had not been in the playoffs the previous year.
- 5 of the 6 division winners had not led their divisions the previous year.
- 4 teams improved their records by at least 5 games.
- 5 teams' records dropped by at least 5 games, 7 teams by at least 4 games.
- The New York Giants had their first winning season since 1972, their first playoff game since 1963. Kansas City had its first winning season since 1973 and first playoff game since 1971. Cincinnati had its first playoff game since 1975; San Francisco, its first since 1972.
- 12 teams finished with records from 7–9 through 9–7, and 4 were 8–8.
- 21 teams finished no worse than 7–9.
- Super Bowl teams San Francisco and Cincinnati lost a total of 7 games, including one Cincinnati lost to San Francisco. None of the other 6 defeats was against a team that finished with a winning record.
- 5 teams went into the eighth week with records of 1–6. 2 of them played each other. The other 3 all won against teams that eventually made the playoffs with at least 10 victories.

In 1983

- 5 of the 14 teams that had not had winning seasons the previous year improved to winning records.
- 8 of the 14 teams that had had winning seasons the previous year fell to losing or .500 records.
- 5 of the 10 playoff teams would not have qualified for a 10-team playoff field the previous year.
- 3 of the 6 division winners had not led their divisions the previous year.
- 4 teams improved their records by at least 3 games from a 9-game season.
- 2 teams' records dropped by at least 3 games from a 9-game season.
- The Detroit Lions won their division for the first time since 1957 and made the playoffs for the first time since 1970 (not counting their 1982 berth in a 16-team field with a 4–5 record). Seattle, a 1976 expansion team, made its first playoffs.
- 16 teams finished with records from 7–9 through 9–7, and 6 were 8–8.
- 22 teams finished no worse than 7–9.
- The Los Angeles Rams and Denver, after having 2 of the NFL's 4 worst records the previous year, each made the playoffs.
- The New York Jets and San Diego, co-favorites before the season to win the AFC championship, each finished tied for last place in their division.

or 8–6 in those 14-game seasons. But in the five full seasons from 1978 through 1983, there were four division winners at 9–7 and one (the nerve of them!) at 8–7–1.

In five seasons from 1973 through 1977, all the playoff teams, wild cards included, had just four representatives uppity enough to check in at two games over .500 (9–5) and *none* at anything worse than that. In the next five full seasons, eleven teams dared show up for the playoffs with 9–7 records, and eleven more trudged in at 10–6. The figures are inflated a little because the playoffs expanded from eight teams to ten in 1978, but they're not inflated all that much. Even if the playoffs had slammed the doors after eight teams, they would have let in seven 9–7 teams and seven 10–6 teams. That's the kind of riffraff giving parity a bad name.

Rags-to-Riches Parity, on the other hand, is not so bad. It's an acquired taste, certainly. Fans like to have teams they can count on, both patsies for the locals to beat up on and reliable winners they can either love or love to hate. They like their stars to have staying power. They enjoy watching a game and just *knowing* that, sooner or later, Terry Bradshaw or Roger Staubach is going to seize that game like a Frisbee and fling it out of reach of the poor saps trying to keep up with him. They like their Fearsome Foursomes and their Steel Curtains and their Purple People Eaters—all those ominous nicknames, as long as they have more spontaneity to them than a grandstand banner or a newspaper contest. It hasn't been easy getting used to the notion that defenses don't have ominous nicknames anymore because defenses aren't allowed to be ominous.

Bettors have the hardest problem with Rags-to-Riches Parity, and a fan is a bettor whenever he's trying to win a hundred bucks in an office pool, even if he doesn't know a single bookie's name. How does anyone figure those games, anyway? A Dallas zoo got the idea of letting a gorilla pick NFL games from a hat, and the ape went 33–22–1 in four weeks. This was in 1983, when some unfortunate experts who had to print their weekly picks in the newspaper barely broke even. Or *didn't* break even. And they didn't have to contend with point spreads.

The day of the Raiders-Redskins Super Bowl, a professional bookie said he took close to 20 calls before someone finally offered some money on the Redskins. He didn't move the line, though. The Redskins remained favorites. Hey, he could afford to spend some money on goodwill. He had a good season. And why not? Who was going to beat the point spread regularly in that crazy season? Now he was letting his clients wind up on a happy note. The Super Bowl was his loss leader, like the $1.49 gallon of milk at the corner drugstore.

But still. Is there anything all that horrible about having new champions now and then? As long as they're *really good*, and not 9–7 teams that found the back door unlocked? This is, after all, the Land of Opportunity. It's comforting to see there's still *some* arena where people can pull themselves up by their bootstraps, or even their regulation-length stockings.

"Who wants to go back to the days when four or five teams

dominated, and they'd come into your town and win easily, and the fans and media would laugh at the home team?" Bill Walsh says. "If all the cars at the Indianapolis 500 went 200 miles an hour, I guess everyone would think that was bad, too."

Sure it's unnerving to look up and realize you can only name three Seattle Seahawks in the AFC championship game, and one of them isn't playing. But the names aren't hard to learn. (They're right on the backs of the jerseys.) Besides, this is football. In all that plastic armor, the players all look pretty much alike. It's what they *do* that's exciting.

Even when the same teams are winning year after year, the names are changing. Football careers age faster than Lorne Greene's dogs. The Raiders were NFL champions in 1976, 1980, and 1983, and their lineups had 50 percent turnover from one champion to another.

When the 49ers barged in on the aristocracy in 1981, Walsh grew progressively sensitive to the uproar over parity, which tended not to discriminate between its two flavors. "They want to be able to stage the epic game," Walsh said of the football bluebloods who averted their eyes from his humble team's entrance into the elite. "They want it to be Army vs. Carlisle. That way they can sell more T-shirts."

After all, it wasn't as if San Francisco was 6–10 again and going to the Super Bowl by acclamation. The 49ers won 13 games that year. They set an NFC record. The conference still had a dominant team, it just wasn't the same old Rams, Vikings, and Cowboys. And yet, NFL purists looked at the 49ers as though they were mudtracks on the rug. The next year, the Redskins got the same treatment.

If anyone wanted to look hard enough, there was a new power structure beginning to congregate atop the NFL in 1983. Six teams won at least 10 games, and of those six, the two that had been out of the Super Bowl longest were Dallas and Pittsburgh. *Has it been that long?*

Not that the other four teams—the Raiders, Dolphins, Redskins, and 49ers—are shoo-ins for long playoff runs. When Washington returned to the Super Bowl after the 1983 season, it was the first time a defending champion had even made the playoffs in four years. In 1980, 1981, and 1983 (ignoring, for a moment, the strike-shortened 1982 season), the NFL had 15 different division winners in three seasons—the same number it had in the *eight* years from 1970 through 1977. (Fourteen different teams led divisions in 1980–82, and sixteen in 1980–83. In the four-year period, the NFC Central had four different winners and the AFC Central and NFC East each had three.)

One symptom of NFL parity is the squeezing of teams' records toward .500. Fewer teams have great records, fewer teams have terrible records, and more of them have mediocre records.

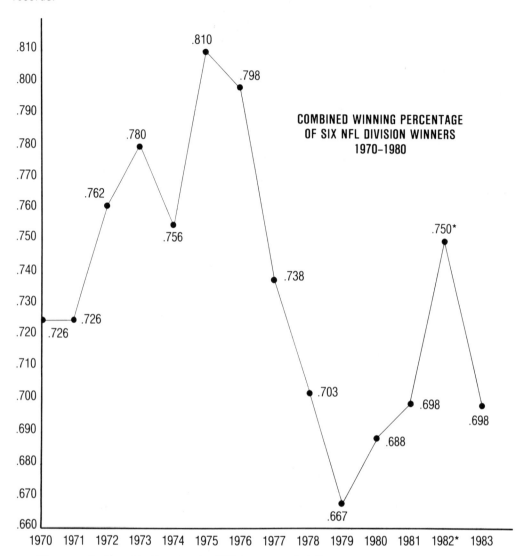

COMBINED WINNING PERCENTAGE
OF SIX NFL DIVISION WINNERS
1970–1980

*Season shortened to 9 games in 1982 because of strike.

In this first graph, notice how the combined winning percentage of the NFL's division winners has slipped since 1977. Aside from the strike-shortened 1982 season, when it was easier to inflate a winning percentage with a hot streak, none of the percentages in the other five years from 1978 through 1983 was as high as the lowest percentage in the first eight years after the NFL–AFL merger (1970–77).

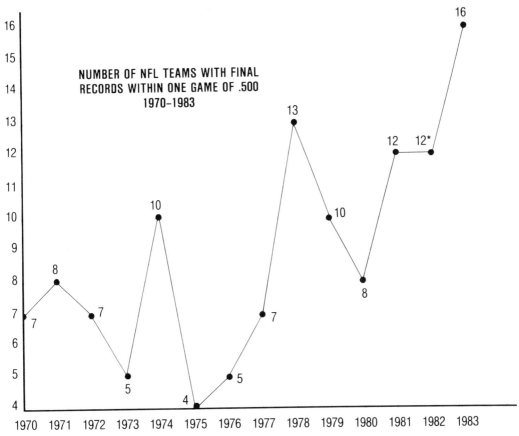

NUMBER OF NFL TEAMS WITH FINAL
RECORDS WITHIN ONE GAME OF .500
1970–1983

*Season shortened to 9 games in 1982 because of strike.

At the same time the best teams have been less impressive, there has been a marked
increase in ordinary teams, with records no more than a game away from .500 (6–8 through
8–6 for 1970–77, 3–5–1 through 5–3–1 for 1982, and 7–9 through 9–7 for the other seasons).

   The beginning of this parity Ice Age can pretty safely be
pinpointed in 1978, as the illustrations on pages 236–38 strongly
indicate. What touched it off then is a stickier question. A lot of
things changed in the NFL after 1977. The league adopted a
scheduling format that was friendly to fifth-place teams and
harsh to defending division champions. It added two weeks to the
schedule, and subtracted two from training camp. And, of course,
the playing rules changed, too. Let's look at how each of those
changes might have helped nudge parity along.

	1970–77 (8 years) (212 final records)	1978–83 (6 years) (168 final records)
Teams that finished more than 4 games above .500 (11–3, 12–4)	13 (6.1%)	3 (1.8%)
Teams that finished more than 4 games below .500 (3–11, 4–12)	15 (7.1%)	9 (5.4%)
Teams that finished within 1 game of .500	53 (25.0%)	71 (42.3%)

This table shows the drop in great or terrible records and the increase in ordinary records from the period of 1970–77 to 1978–83.

	1972–77 (6 years)	1978–83 (6 years)
Divison winners that had not won their division the previous year	13	21
Division winners that had not won their division in any of the previous three years	6	15
Teams that improved their records by at least four games*	13	18
Teams that had their records drop at least four games*	10	20

* Or 3½ games going to or from the shortened 1982 season.

Another symptom of NFL parity is the increase in rags-to-riches stories—teams coming from nowhere to win their divisions or dropping out of sight after winning their divisions. Or even doing each, in alternate years, as San Francisco did in 1981, 1982, and 1983.

One thing to get straight up front is that the so-called parity schedule has not been some magic elixir for nourishing parity. In fact, it has contributed very little to parity.

The schedule is supposed to work by giving a break to teams that finished in fifth place the previous year. While everybody else in a fifth-place team's division is playing the top four teams in another division, the fifth-place team is playing four games against other fifth-place teams. Meanwhile, first-place teams are playing three other teams that won their divisions the previous year.

But the factors truly responsible for parity, whatever they are, have made any scheduling gimmickry helpless to have much additional impact on parity. Think about it. For the schedule to have its desired effect, last year's first-place teams would have to be strong again and last year's fifth-place teams would have to still be creampuffs. If that were the case, there wouldn't be parity.

The problem with trying to handicap teams through scheduling is that a schedule can only be based on *last year's records*. If you accept that the scheduling format has helped bring about parity, you have to accept that there *is* parity, which means you have to accept that there is often a wide fluctuation in a team's record from year to year. Which means last year's record doesn't necessarily say anything useful about how strong a team will be *this* year. Which unravels the foundation of any scheduling format built on *last year's records.*

To put it one more way, the scheduling format can only help foster parity if parity doesn't exist. So it can help once. And it did, in 1979, for Tampa Bay. The Bucs went from fifth to first in their division, the only time an NFL team has done so. The next year, when they had to play a *real* schedule, they tied for fourth. The Bucs had taken advantage of the soft part of their fifth-place schedule, going 3–1 against the other fifth-place teams and 7–5 on the rest of their schedule.

Since then, three teams with fifth-place schedules have gone to the playoffs as wild cards (not counting 1982, when there were no full fifth-place schedules because there were no full schedules, period). Not one of them did as well against the other fifth-place teams (which were no longer in fifth place) as it did against the normal part of the schedule. The 1981 Jets were 2–2 on the creampuff portion and 8–3–1 against other teams. The 1981 Giants were *1–3* against the creampuffs, which they overcame by going 8–4 against the teams that were supposed to be stronger. The 1983 Broncos were 2–2 and 7–5.

The scheduling format has not been totally without impact, even if the impact has been mainly psychological. But if the hand-icapping were working the way it was designed, it would be hurting fourth-place teams. Now, fourth-place teams could stand a dose of Parity Elixir, too—especially those fourth-place teams that finished last in the four-team divisions. But fourth-place teams not only don't get the scheduling break provided fifth-place teams, they have to play the same schedules as first-place teams, only it's worse for them, because first-place teams don't have to play themselves. A fourth-place team has to play *five* games against teams that won their divisions the previous year.

So if the scheduling format is working, teams ought to be sprawling all over the league the year after they finish in fourth place. But according to the chart on page 240 fourth-place teams have been holding up remarkably well. San Francisco and Cincin-nati, parity's most dramatic success stories, managed to climb to the top from fourth place in four-team divisions.

As a group, teams that finished fourth the previous year have had a better rate of winning division championships, of making the playoffs, and of improving their records by at least three games than teams that finished fifth. Granted, fourth-place teams

Teams that finished the previous year in . . .	Fifth place	Fourth place in a 4-team division	Fourth place in all divisions
. . . and went on to:			
Win the division	1 (5%)	1 (10%)	5 (17%)
Make the playoffs	4 (20%)	2 (20%)	9 (30%)
Improve their records	16 (80%)	7 (70%)	22 (73%)
Improve their records by two or more games	12 (60%)	6 (60%)	18 (60%)
Improve their records by three or more games	8 (40%)	5 (50%)	13 (43%)
Improve their positions in the standings	14 (70%)	5 (50%)	17 (57%)
Improve their positions in the standings by at least two places	8 (40%)	2 (20%)	12 (40%)

The NFL's so-called parity schedule favors teams that finished in fifth place the previous year, letting them play four of their 16 games against each other. If the schedule actually were contributing to the league's rags-to-riches style of parity, then fifth-place teams would have tended to improve much more than fourth-place teams in the five years the scheduling format has been in effect (1978–83 except 1982, when full schedules weren't played). That has not been the case. By some measurements on the chart below, fifth-place teams have fared less well even than fourth-place teams in four-team divisions, which also had to climb from last place but did not have the benefit of a fifth-place schedule.

were better to start with, but that's not necessarily the case with fourth-place/*last*-place teams, and they've done all right, too. The above chart still looks just about as it would be expected to look if schedules were passed out randomly.

But let's suppose, just for a moment, that the schedule is the elixir it's made out to be, that it really does help prod hapless teams back into the competitive mainstream. In that case, a far more serious question pops up. In that case, *Where does a professional sports league get off rigging its schedule in favor of some teams at the expense of others?* The NFL spends millions of dollars protecting its image of Fairness and Integrity from the demons of drug abuse, legalized gambling, greedy agents, and whatnot, and at the same time, it goes on unabashedly cranking out gerrymandered schedules.

It's not as if the worst teams are floundering around without any other life rings. They already get first crack at draft choices and players cut by other teams. They already get equal shares of the televison bounty, even if the networks do all they can to spare us the sight of them.

At its best, the parity schedule is helpless, and the only effect it has is to siphon off some of the credit due to coaches like Walsh, Joe Gibbs, Forrest Gregg, and Chuck Knox, their players, and their coaching and management staffs. And at its worst, it pokes holes in the Fairness and Integrity that the NFL claims to be all about.

The scheduling format does have one good element. It guarantees a minimum of common opponents among division rivals. A team that finishes first through fourth will have all 16 opponents in common with one team in its division, 12 with two others, and 10 with the fifth-place team (counting games between two teams among their common opponents). That's such a noble scheduling concept, it's amazing that it took the NFL until 1978 to give it a whirl.

But a schedule that guarantees common opponents within each division does not have to be based on the previous year's standings. Before the NFL went to its current format, it used a rotating schedule that guaranteed every team would visit every other team in a seven-year period. That's another good idea.

Without a rotating schedule, here's what happens: Walter Payton and Franco Harris went into their tenth season in the NFL together in 1984, when they appeared likely to become the league's two most prolific rushers of all time. In those ten years, Payton's and Harris's teams played each other twice, both times in Pittsburgh. The Steelers hadn't been to Chicago since 1972, and unless both teams finish in fifth place, they won't make that trip before 1986, if then.

There is no reason the NFL can't have a rotating schedule *and* guaranteed minimums of common opponents among division rivals. It took me about one working day, without a computer, to make sure it was possible. The result was an eight-year schedule that guaranteed twelve common opponents a year for every pair of division teams, and more than half the pairs had fifteen or sixteen opponents in common. No team went more than eight years without visits from every other team. With all its manpower, the NFL office no doubt could do even better.

Another overrated factor in parity is the longer schedule. Somehow, the notion has spread that adding two games to the schedule has touched off a rash of injuries. It probably has increased injuries by two-fourteenths, or even less because people used to get injured in the two exhibition games that were subtracted from the schedule. The fact is, teams often are healthier for their last two games than they are for, say, their ninth and tenth.

This much is true: San Francisco, Cincinnati, and Washington were practically injury-free in the years of their surges. But avoiding injuries has always been an important element in winning football championships. If avoiding injuries helps more now than ten years ago, that's because teams are closer in abilities for other reasons. Every edge is magnified.

"You have to emphasize conditioning," says Dan Henning, who was Washington's offensive coordinator when it won the Super Bowl. "That's why off-season programs are so important. Well-conditioned teams have a better chance of staying healthy."

If anything, an evenly distributed increase in injuries would help the stronger teams stay stronger. They have more depth. They can afford more injuries.

It also is true that longer schedules tend to compress a team's record toward .500. But that doesn't explain why division winners averaged 11–3 records in 1970–1977 and 11–5 in 1978–83.

X X X X X
O O O O

The major rule changes have contributed to parity. The way it used to be, a team with a great defense was a dominant team. Miami and Pittsburgh had defenses in their glory years that Walsh says, "were impossible to deal with. Now you can deal with them."

Now the imposing NFL units are offenses. But a great offense is not as reliable as a great defense. Never has been. Many more things can go wrong with an offense. Its timing is more intricate. Its fortunes are bound more tightly to one player, and quarterbacks do have bad days. Because of the elusive technique involved in throwing a football, they're more likely to have subpar days than defensive ends or linebackers. They get hurt, too. It's harder to replace a quarterback or a key receiver or runner than it is to replace a defensive player, because on the best defenses, the whole usually is greater than the sum of the parts.

So an offense that sputters in the eighties doesn't have that great defense to fall back on. It was always there for the Steelers. Their 1976 team struggled to a 1–4 start, so the defense allowed just 28 points in the last nine games, all victories. That defense was upset-proof. From 1972 through 1979, the Steelers were 50–1 against teams with losing records. But when the Steelers' offense fell apart in 1983, they lost four of their last five games, all against teams that finished 9–7 or worse.

By making the pass easier, the NFL has made it easier to catch up in a game. The teams that scored first in 1977 games won 69.4 percent of the time, compared to 64.5 percent for teams that scored first in 1983. Those percentages applied to a 16-game record, are almost a full game apart.

And by making it easier to catch up in a game, the NFL made it easier to catch up in the standings. For one thing, a new quarterback or receiver can make a bigger difference than he could in the seventies. For another, those caught-up games add up. And when the ball is flying every which way, an inferior team has a better chance of coming away with an upset. A fluke is parity's best friend.

The Falcons weren't as good as the 49ers in 1983. But they beat the 49ers. They scored a touchdown nine seconds before half-time, on a 64-yard fumble return. And they scored the game-winning touchdown on the game's last play with a 47-yard touchdown pass that was the ultimate fluke: a batted ball. White Shoes Johnson, who caught the pass, had even fallen down on the play or he wouldn't have been in position to win the game.

"It's just so tragic," Walsh said the next day, still stunned. "You can put hundreds of hours of work into football and all the science and nuances of the game and the skill—and it can come down to something like this. I guess that's one of the reasons the game's so popular. That's not very popular with coaches, though. I'd hate to think of it happening to anybody."

X X X X X
0 0 0 0

Of all the NFL's changes in 1978, the one with the most impact on parity is probably the one least often noticed: training camp became two weeks shorter.

Unless a team plays in the Hall of Fame game, it has five weeks of training camp before the preparation week for the season opener. That's less than three-quarters of the seven weeks it used to have. There is no longer enough time to drill a very good team into an indomitable machine like the Lombardi Packers or the 17–0 Dolphins or the 50–1, four-out-of-six-Super Bowl Steelers.

That machine has to be put together, tuned up, and polished in training camp. Only in training camp does a coaching staff have almost unlimited time to work with individual players on their techniques. Only in training camp is there time to run whole units through the mind-numbing repetition that makes a perfectly run play as instinctive as picking up a ringing phone.

Once the regular season begins, the emphasis shifts from teaching players how to play their positions. Regular-season prac-tices barely have time for implementing game plans. Instead of coaching fundamentals, teams have to coach the ways to apply those fundamentals toward beating the next opponent. If training camp is too short for mastering those fundamentals, little mis-takes pop up more often in regular-season games. And the best teams aren't quite so good anymore.

X X X X X
0 0 0 0

A change in 1977 may have done more for parity than any change the NFL made the next year. In 1977, the draft moved to May 1 or thereabouts.

It had been three months earlier. So now teams have three more months to double-check their scouting reports. Three more months to keep from making mistakes. "You know so much more about a player when you draft him," Walsh says. Teams still make mistakes. Scouting never will be a perfect science. But those extra three months have trimmed the list of mistakes.

If there are fewer mistakes in drafting, that has to help the teams that were making the most mistakes in the first place. The teams most in need of a Parity Elixir.

For the stronger teams, those good players the bad teams used to miss are no longer sneaking through to the end of a round. Dallas, for example, used to stay on top by outscouting the other teams. But the Cowboys haven't had a particularly good draft since 1977, and they've flat-out blown two first-round picks. The draft is playing Robin Hood.

"I don't think there's as great a difference in talent between one team and another as there used to be," Giants general manager George Young says. That is the crux of parity. As Young says, "That makes it easier for a team to have an opportunity to win. But not necessarily to establish a dynasty."

From Playgrounds to Playbooks

... NFL talent is spread so evenly,
rookies make more impact all the time

The bonus for teams drafting wisely now is the increased quality in rookies. "It seems like we're getting better athletes every year," Atlanta general manager Tom Braatz says. That's not necessarily to the colleges' credit. As Bill Walsh says, "Often what it means is the colleges have circumvented the entrance requirements. But they are better athletes coming in."

They can play right away. And coaches are more willing to *let* them play right away. As evenly as the talent is spread, one or two rookies can make the difference between 8–8 and 10–6, between the great gray middle and the playoffs.

So rookies have not only contributed to parity by playing well, the best ones often for the worst teams. They've been beneficiaries, too. Ice Age thrivers. The closer teams are in talent, the more incentive coaches have to get talented rookies into the game.

There's a psychology involved in parity. It helps perpetuate itself by offering hope. Not long ago, even the best rookie couldn't do much for an ordinary team but help it creep a little higher among the also-rans. The playoff teams were so far out of sight, using a rookie wasn't worth the risk. He would only make mistakes. Rookies simply didn't play. It wasn't written down anywhere, but it might as well have been.

Then along came San Francisco in 1981 with the dizzy notion of drafting almost a whole defensive backfield. The 49ers played four rookies in their five-back defense. And they won the Super Bowl with them.

Of course, Walsh was the first to admit he hadn't done anything especially daring or far-sighted. What was he going to do? Trot out those same stumblebums who had let opponents complete two-thirds of their passes the year before? As George Young says, "The great decisions in this league are usually made by divine providence. Something happens. You have to make a move. It works out. People say, 'Gee, they were smart. They used a guy a little early and it paid off.' People forget about the guy who got hurt, or whatever it was that made you make the move in the first place."

After that 1981 season—with Ronnie Lott and the other 49er defensive backs, Lawrence Taylor and Hugh Green revitalizing their teams' defenses, George Rogers and Joe Delaney running for 1,000 yards, Neil Lomax and David Woodley winning games at quarterback, Cris Collinsworth catching passes for 1,000 yards, Everson Walls leading the league in interceptions, Stump Mitchell setting a record for combined net yards, and a fuzzy-cheeked offensive line helping Washington win eight of its last eleven games—Dallas personnel chief Gil Brandt said, "I don't think there's been a year in my 22 years in the league when so many

---

"The great decisions in this league are usually made by divine providence," as George Young says, "Something happens. You have to make a move. It works out. People say, 'Gee, they were smart. They used a guy a little early and it paid off.' People forget about the guy who got hurt, or whatever it was that made you make the move in the first place."

---

rookies have made so much of an impact." That's the key word. Impact. There are coaches and personnel directors who aren't willing to say rookies play football better than they did five or ten years ago, but there's no getting around the impact they've had.

The changing nature of the game has helped them make that impact, as we've seen. Rookies are especially well-suited to specialized part-time roles, and they always have been able to play sooner at the high-profile positions, aside from quarterback (positions many people insist on calling skill positions as though the offensive line is no more than football's loading dock or assembly line). As the game gives players more opportunities to overcome their mistakes with big plays, rookies look more and more attractive at wide receiver and cornerback, not to mention blitzing linebacker and receiving back.

Rookie running backs, especially, have had little use for the idea of easing into the fray. In the five full seasons from 1978 through 1983, 12 rookies rushed for more than 1,000 yards. In 1981–83, four of the six conference rushing championships went to rookies.

When Lawrence Taylor went to the Giants, Young says, "Our major concern was, How soon are we going to be able to line him up with the first unit at linebacker? We felt he had the ability to play with the first unit. But you can't put a rookie in right away. Players will resent that. From an internal matter, a rookie has to pass that stage where he earns the job.

"As it turned out, there was no problem. The veterans could see where Lawrence belonged from the day he came in."

After 1981, coaches may not consciously have said, "I've got to get some rookies in *my* lineup, too." The way coaches look at it, they always use the best players they have. But knowing what Lott, Taylor, and the rest have done can change any coach's point of view. Rookies might just start looking better.

"Going into the year, you're looking for young players who can help immediately," Walsh says. "Some time ago, it was: In a few years, he'll really be good. Now people expect them to play right away."

They still expect mistakes from rookies. But the other guys' rookies are going to make mistakes, too. Rookies don't lead coaches so far out on a limb anymore.

X X X X X
O O O O

Teams playing catch-up aren't the only ones using rookies. The ones at the top, naturally, had no reason to subject their machines to youthful indiscretions when they could roll along between 11–3 and 12–2 and the only question each year was how far they would advance in the playoffs. When they needed to replace someone, they dipped into the bench and found a high draft choice who hadn't played as a rookie—or as a second- or third-year man, either—but had learned enough by now to chip in on the caretaking of the machine.

Now, of course, the replacement process isn't so orderly, even on good teams. There isn't a team in the NFL that can afford to keep drafting players for the purpose of letting them watch.

"We play that annual game of best athlete available," Young says. "I hate to use the word, subterfuge, but we draft for need more than we'll ever admit. If anyone's looking to trade with a team and he wants to know what their needs are, all he has to do is look at how they drafted in the first five rounds."

New Orleans coach Bum Phillips is even more frank about the best-athlete song and dance. "I think it's a cop-out we all use," he says. "We say we'll draft the best athlete available. But deep down, what we do is draft the best athlete available at a position we need. You look up on the board and see 20 or 30 or 40 players who could come in and start for you, so obviously you're going to pick in an area where you need him.

The thing coaches tend not to do is say, 'We would like a wide receiver or a running back' or whatever. The players you've got, they'll hear that and think, Well he must not like me."

More teams are sending their coaches out to meet rookies before the draft, too. By the time the rookies go through minicamps and conditioning programs, maybe living in town two months before training camp, the coaches have gotten to know them.

"When he comes to camp, he's not just one of 90 guys doing a 20-minute drill," Marv Levy says. "And by the time the veterans come to camp, the rookies have been there a week. You're not allowed to bring veterans into training camp until two weeks before the first game. So you have more time to work with rookies alone than used to be the case."

When the veterans do report, a rookie might not be so polite about stepping aside and saying, *Here's your position back. Thanks for letting me use it while you were gone.* "What I'm seeing," says Joe Gibbs, "is more players coming out of college ready to fight for a starting job. They're not so awed."

This attitude isn't peculiar to football players. Other businesses, too, have noticed the tail end of the Baby Boom producing aggressive entry-level employees with their eyes riveted on specific goals. They've grown up competing in a demographic bulge and living in a worldwide community of live television. Of course they're more sophisticated.

Everson Walls asked around about how to make the proper Cowboy impression. He was just an undrafted free agent, but he lived near Dallas, and he went through most of the team's offseason drill of workouts and skull sessions. "You want to get them to notice you," Walls says. "Stay in their face and keep your name on their mind."

That doesn't mean breaking ranks in a disciplined defense to go for the spectacular play. Being spectacular helps, but only if it comes naturally. "On the field," Walls says, "you just have to be coachable. If they want you to play man-to-man coverage with the receiver on your inside shoulder, they're going to film the practice and critique it, so you better be playing man-to-man on your inside shoulder."

None of this means Walls checked his awe at the door. He may not have flashed it around like some rube, but he didn't forget those guys a few yards away were the same ones he had watched and admired on television.

"I always looked at it like that," Walls says. "I think that's extra motivation. It's not intimidating. It tells you, You're good enough to play with these guys now."

X X X X X
O O O O

It could just be, then, that the teams themselves have more to do with parity than any grand league-wide changes. Especially where the Rags-to-Riches brand is concerned. The penthouse has settled within reach, and the players and managements on the teams below aren't so willing to accept that their lot is merely to gaze at it yearningly. They *go for it.*

At the same time rookies were bursting on the scene in 1981, teams were trading more aggressively than usual to improve themselves. The 49ers got Fred Dean. The Giants got Rob Carpenter, who carried their ground attack. The Redskins got Joe Washington. The Packers got John Jefferson. The Chargers got Wes Chandler. Even Pittsburgh, which hadn't traded for a regular player since 1973, broke down in 1984 and dealt for Woodley. A quarterback, no less.

Once a team enjoys a little success, parity's psychological impact really kicks in. In 1983, when the Lions were driving toward their first division championship in 26 years, quarterback Eric Hipple said, "Last year I'd go into a game or a play thinking, I hope this happens. Well, I've quit hoping. I've gotten rid of self-doubts."

"I think you're looking at much more efficient managements," Walsh says. "Teams are willing to replace players when it's necessary, and the ones that haven't been, haven't been as successful. Maybe managements are less socially familiar with the players. The old-line teams had their players and coaches and management in kind of a family atmosphere. I think it's a little more structured business now."

You still have Robert Irsay getting the names of his coach and general manager wrong at a major press conference. At New Orleans and Houston, the owners surface periodically with egg on their faces. Minnesota and Cincinnati maintain their reputations as tightwads. But overall, when the owners defer to the football managers, NFL teams aren't making nearly as many foolish moves as they once did.

Remember when good teams always seemed to have high draft

choices because the bad teams weren't smart enough to keep their draft choices? That doesn't happen so much anymore. Dallas had one of the first two choices in the 1974, 1975, and 1977 drafts but hasn't been able to pick anyone's pocket since then. In 1970, Chicago traded the second choice in the draft for three Green Bay players who wound up playing a total of two seasons for the Bears. The Packers used the choice to draft Mike McCoy, whom they traded seven years later for another first-round choice. They spent that choice on Ezra Johnson, who was still playing well enough in 1983 to lead the team in sacks. These days, when teams trade early first-round choices, they trade them for extra choices later in the first round, not for washed-up players.

Teams also are more open-minded toward medical advances, conditioning gadgets, protective equipment, and even such mental toys as sensory deprivation rooms—many things that would have been unheard of 10 years ago. The Cowboys used to have the market pretty well cornered in such peripheral innovations. No more.

There's still a long way to go before football people shed their superstitions entirely in the area of body and mind improvement. It's still widely believed, for example, that the size of a thigh muscle is the best measurement for a player's progress after conventional knee surgery, even though the smaller muscles

"The NFL has done nothing to achieve parity. Yet they act as if they are some ordained group that has directed there be parity. There have not been any extra draft choices given to certain teams. Not one concession has been made to any team to create parity. It's a culmination of hard work by individual organizations."—**Bill Walsh**

associated with balance and agility are equally important. And the industry is only beginning to tap the resources of vitamin therapy, vision training, and posture alignment, among other frontiers that would seem of interest in a physical activity.

"You'd think they'd make more effort," says Alan Page, "to find out how various types of conditioning correlate with performance. And how to develop the things that make you a better football player, so they're not wasting players' time with useless drills." Track and field, to name one sport, is kilometers ahead of football in that regard. Track and field has a pioneer ethic of individual athletes who respect no artificial barrier. There are indications, on some teams anyway, the same ethic is seeping into pro football.

Kicking and Scratching

... Special teams are the best place to get a leg up on the balanced NFL

If teams are closer in talent, if every slight edge cuts more sharply than ever on a path to the playoffs, then the most sensible edge for any team to hone would be its kicking teams.

Kicking plays decide a lot of NFL games. A reasonable guess would be at least two a week, since they account for one of every seven plays and involve considerably more yardage per play than scrimmage plays. Over a season, the gains and losses on punts and kickoffs can vary more than 1,000 yards from one team to another. So good coverage and return teams can be as valuable as a 1,000-yard running back.

In 1983, six NFL teams ranked among the NFL's top 10 in both kickoff return differential and punt return differential—those figures being the difference between our returns and their returns. The six were Detroit, Denver, Seattle, Miami, and both Los Angeles teams. All six made the playoffs.

It isn't that hard to get an edge in return and coverage teams. The start-up ingredients are speed and exuberant youth, both of which NFL teams are collecting anyway for reasons that have nothing to do with returns and kick coverage. Yet on an amazing number of teams, kicking plays are little more than an afterthought at best, drudgery or purgatory at worst. Even the kicking-teams coach is often the new guy on the staff or someone whose other duties leave him with a little more slack time than the other assistants.

251

Kicking plays are given relatively little practice time. Aside from most of the short Saturday practice, the time they get is usually at the beginning or end of a workout, where it has the effect on players of a picture. *Let's get this over with*—so we can go on to the real part of practice, or go home.

And kicking units are generally stocked with leftovers. Few teams are willing to wear down their starters on return and coverage plays, even as principal return men. Only recently have more than a few teams seen the benefit of drafting someone to do nothing but return kicks, even when the alternative is someone with less than a chance in 10 of making the squad. The kicking teams have little continuity because their personnel keeps changing, as they lose players promoted to the starting 22. So they're composed of a few veterans who can't quite crack the lineup and, mostly, players in their first or second year. That's where most rookies have a chance to make the roster. But those rookies were probably stars on their college teams, immune from the indignity of having to sweat on mere kicking plays, and so they're less experienced on kicking teams than they are at their regular positions (which they aren't ready to play yet because they're too inexperienced).

Covering kicks and blocking for returns require specific techniques, just like playing offensive tackle or outside linebacker. The jobs are not easy. Players are so spread out, and they're able to pick up so much speed, that their eyeballs aren't necessarily pointing in the same direction after they collide.

X X X X X
O O O O

Still, pro football has undergone improvements in its kicking games. One of the more significant ones can be traced to the NFL's addition of some punting statistics to its official releases. They were:

★ Touchbacks, or punts into the end zone.
★ Punts landed between the goal line and the 20.
★ Net punting average, or how far the punting play advanced the line of scrimmage (punt yardage minus return or touchback yardage).

Coaches always had stressed these things, to whatever extent they stressed anything in the punting game, but now their exhortations had the official backing of statistics.

One of the statistics still is widely misinterpreted, though. Punters are given undue credit for sheer volume of punts inside the 20. It stands to reason that teams with better offenses won't give their punters as many chances to kick (San Diego's Maury Buford didn't even punt often enough in 1982 to qualify for the league lead in punting average), and teams with better defenses will give their punters more opportunities within range of the 20. The meaningful statistics are the *percentage* of a punter's kicks that go inside the 20 and, better still, the *ratio* of kicks inside the 20 to touchbacks. Jeff Hayes's 29 punts inside the 20 with just two touchbacks, for Washington in 1983, was a remarkable (and little noticed) stat.

Coaches are applying more creative gimmickry to kicking plays, too. Washington tried a cross-field pass on a punt return in the 1983 NFC championship game. The touchdown it scored was called back because the pass didn't go backward, but the thought was there.

Seattle helped nail down a 1982 victory against Chicago when fullback Don Doornink punted on third down. *A quick kick.* And why not? Especially on third-and-very-long from deep in your own territory, where the ball has plenty of room to bounce with nobody back to return it. Bear coach Mike Ditka groused that it was a playground stunt, but you could see the wheels turning. What seemed to upset him most was he hadn't thought of it first. The Bears' quarterback, Jim McMahon, was a punter in college. He was perfect for a quick kick, and he made one later that season and another in 1983. It's almost a no-lose play, because as Ditka has said, "I don't know of anybody who has a special play for third-and-18."

When Jack Pardee was coaching in the NFL (where he won two Coach of the Year awards from 1975 through 1980), he said, "If you just had guts enough to do it, probably the highest percentage play in football is the fake punt. Run or pass. You just have to give the punter the prerogative to make the decision and you don't second-guess him." You just set certain guidelines, such as making sure he's beyond his own 40-yard line, and you give him keys that will assure the play a clear path before he tries it.

In 1983, punters ran eight times for a 19.5-yard average and never lost yardage. They threw seven passes and completed four, a figure that could be improved with practice. Chicago's Bob Parsons once completed six in a row in two years playing for Pardee, and the Giants' Dave Jennings was 3 for 3 before throwing an incompletion in 1983. For a punter who has trouble with blocked kicks, even an incomplete pass here and there would slow down the rush.

Fake field goals might even be better, except they risk blowing three points. But when a team's in an all-out rush, it's awfully vulnerable to a short pass upfield, and most holders can throw. That's why it's smart, in overtime, to try for the winning field goal on third down instead of waiting for fourth. The opponent has to be wary of a fake. If the kicking team throws an incomplete pass (or even recovers a blocked kick), it still has another chance to kick.

X X X X X
0 0 0 0

The most conspicuous players on kicking teams are the ones who usually lead their teams in scoring. Placekickers' rate of improvement has been the headiest in pro football. As a group, their 71.7 percent accuracy in 1983 cleared the previous NFL record by more than four percent.

Three of them were better than 85 percent. Ten were better than 80 percent. Fourteen—representing half the teams in the league—made more than three of every four field goal attempts.

Lou Groza's old record of 88.5 percent field-goal accuracy (23 for 26) stood for 28 years before Jan Stenerud broke it in 1981. Stenerud was 22 for 24, for 91.7 percent, and his record stood one year. In 1982, Mike Moseley went 20 for 21, making 95.2 percent, and was named the NFL's Most Valuable Player. The top two career percentages through 1983 also belonged to active players: Rolf Benirschke and Rafael Septien.

These guys aren't just making chip shots, either. Matt Bahr, the NFL leader at 87.5 percent in 1983, was 6 for 8 beyond 40 yards. Baltimore's Raul Allegre, who scored the winning points in five of his team's seven victories, was 4 for 5 from beyond 50 yards.

In a 1983 overtime game against Kansas City, Seattle coach Chuck Knox sent his field goal unit into the game on third-and-three from Kansas City's 25-yard line. That's a 42-yard field goal, remember. Three yards is not an insurmountable distance to pick up on third down, especially considering the score was already 48–48, and another first down would move the decisive field goal to a more comfortable distance.

But Knox had decided 42 yards was close enough. Which it was. Norm Johnson's kick was good. The state of the NFL's placekicking art has risen to the point where a 42-yard field goal can be taken for granted.

X X X X X
0 0 0 0

A number of important players on kicking teams are easy to overlook. The snapper, for one. How many people even know who he is unless he sails the ball over the head of a punter or placement holder? With at least two defensive players poised to clobber him, he has to pass the ball between his legs to an upside-down target with more accuracy than a quarterback.

A good snapper is hard to find. The Rams' regular snapper was injured in the last regular season game of 1983, and they were in the playoffs. They needed a new snapper, a reliable one. Coach John Robinson remembered one he had coached at Southern Cal, so he gave the kid a call. Mike McDonald was still around town, selling insurance and preparing to test for a job with a suburban fire department. He reported for duty and made $16,000 for two weeks' work.

The holder is just as important. When the rest of the team can run off the practice field, the holder and the snapper have to stay out with the kicker and help him practice. The holder has to catch the ball, spin the laces away from the kicker, place the ball on a precise spot, and take his hands out of the way in half a second. Any kick taking more than 1.2 to 1.4 seconds is considered easy pickings for blocking, and the rest of the time is budgeted for the snap. Placements don't have to be quite so precise for soccer kickers, but on a bitter day with turf that's squishy or ice-hard, when the holder's frozen fingertips have been mere rumors since halftime, the proposition can still get a little dicey.

A good holder is irreplaceable, as Denver kicker Fred Steinfort found out when the Broncos cut back-up quarterback Matt Robinson in 1981. Robinson had been Steinfort's holder, acknowledged as one of the league's best, when Steinfort went 26 for 34 (76.5 percent) on his field goal attempts in 1980. Without Robinson, Steinfort was 17 for 30 (56.7 percent) in 1981, which turned out to be his last year with the Broncos. Another excellent holder is the Bears' Brian Baschnagel, who has been versatile in catching passes, blocking, carrying the ball, returning kicks, and covering kicks in his pro and college career. Those other things, lots of people can do. When Baschnagel's college coach, Woody Hayes, talked about Baschnagel's value at Ohio State, the first thing he said was, "Best holder I ever saw."

Coaches are getting away from having their number one quarterbacks hold for kicks, although Joe Theismann does it well for Moseley. Bud Grant and Tom Landry, two coaches who have not underrated the importance of kicking teams, believe the first-string quarterback is absolutely wrong for the job. His offense just failed to score a touchdown, or the team wouldn't be trying a field goal in the first place. He's probably not in the highest spirits. Why use a holder whose mind might be somewhere else?

In fact, why a quarterback? Of all the players who handle the ball, the quarterback (on a team that doesn't use the shotgun) is the least experienced in catching it. He even has a receiver next to him, catching return tosses, when he warms up on the sideline. A punter would be the most logical choice for handling a snap, and that is the direction some teams are going.

Then there's the kickoff man. He isn't always the field goal kicker. In fact, Moseley attributed his sensational 1982 season to the rest he got because Jeff Hayes relieved him of his kickoff chores. More and more emphasis is being put on height and direction of kickoffs, as with punts, instead of sheer distance. Keeping the ball away from the return man for an extra 1½ seconds lets the coverage men get another 15 to 20 yards downfield and delays the timing of the return team's blocking. Ray Wersching's crazily bouncing kickoff in San Francisco's Super Bowl victory caused a fumble that set up a demoralizing field goal at the end of the first half.

The punt chasers, the outside men on the coverage team, make some of the most athletic plays in football. They're the only offensive players allowed to cross the line of scrimmage before the kick, so they're almost always greeted by two blockers. Still, they often arrive at the return man just after the ball, and they're expected to perform the acrobatics that keep the ball from going for a touchback.

The punt returner is conspicuous, but he's still underappreciated. He's making the hardest catch in the game. It's not some lazy fly ball to centerfield. And his ability to make quick decisions is more important than his speed. Fair catch? Return it? Let it land? Almost always, he's not supposed to catch the ball inside the

---

"Anybody can play on special teams, but to be good, I think you have to be kind of sick, where you really don't care about your body. Actually, getting your bell rung doesn't feel too bad. It feels kind of good."—**Hank Bauer**, San Diego's three-time winner of Pro's Pro Award as Special Teams Player of the Year.

"My father taught me how to snap the ball when I was in eighth or ninth grade. He told me football teams always need a guy who can make the deep snap. He also taught Jim, my older brother; and Joel, my younger brother. I think we're the only family that goes out and plays catch not facing each other."—**Jay Hilgenberg**, Chicago Bears center.

---

10. But there may be nobody back there telling him where he is, and he sure can't look down at the yard markers.

Where quickness, shifty moves, and good hands are essential in punt returning, a kickoff returner is more apt to be a pure sprinter. Preferably a big one with long strides. He should take no sidesteps. He's racing the kickoff coverage men. But he also must hit the wedge of three blockers in front of him at just the right time. Too soon, and he runs into them. Too late, and the coverage men can come around the blockers.

In kickoff coverage, the star is the player who can make two or three different blockers take cracks at him, even if he has to keep picking himself up. The rule is: don't give yourself up one-for-one. A kickoff chaser won't get noticed for that, though. The way to attract attention is to leave his lane. Each man on kickoff coverage has a specific lane, sort of a vertical zone of responsibility. If one man wanders into the wrong lane, he leaves the return man an open lane that rolls out a green carpet to the end zone.

X X X X X
0 0 0 0

The extra-point play is the only time a team can actually take a point away from its opponent. That's how people think of it. A touchdown is worth seven points, and if the team somehow blows the kick, it loses a point. Only one in twenty are missed.

Many teams, for some reason, offer only token rushes to block the kick. How can that be? It's not as though they're afraid the kicking team might fake it. All it takes to block any kick are "hard work and not believing the kick is a foregone conclusion," says Alan Page, who ranks with Ted Hendricks as the NFL's best kick blockers ever.

There are three ways to block a place kick. From the side, from the middle, or from the top, with someone jumping behind the middle of the line. The rushing team has the manpower advantage, 11-on-9 since the kicker and holder can't block. But time is on the side of the kicking team, since the ball is beyond the line of scrimmage in less than 1½ seconds.

The placement is 7½ yards behind the line of scrimmage, give or take a few inches on uneven ground. Any deeper placement would give the outside rush man an inviting angle. Any closer, and the kick might not clear the inside men.

Whoever blocks the kick, it's usually made possible by the inside rush men numbered 5, 6, and 7 on the diagram on page 258. Those players can either slip through the line to block the ball themselves, back the offensive line up far enough for the leaper behind them, number 11, to block it, or force the offensive linemen to narrow their splits and let the outside man, number 1, start from closer to the ball.

The kicking team doesn't want to narrow its splits. The outside is where it's most vulnerable. That wingback on the side of the rush, the defense's left (in the diagram) has to block the players. He wants to concentrate on number 2 and brush number 1 just enough to slow him down.

On the defense's right side, number 9 and number 10 aren't trying to block the ball. They're called retrievers, and they're responsible for keeping the ball in safe hands if someone else blocks it. If they don't, the kicking team can pick it up and make a first down. Against Chicago in 1980, Green Bay's Chester Marcol

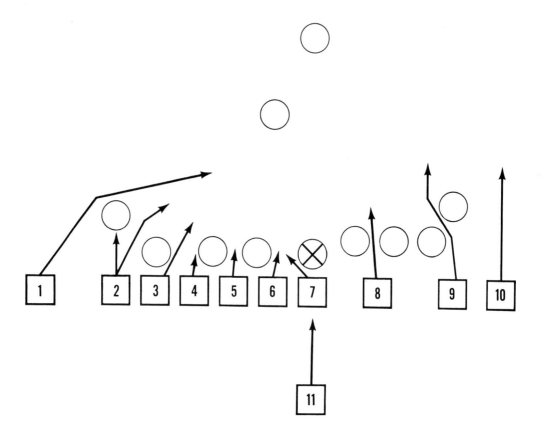

An attempted extra point or field goal can be blocked from any of three places. In this diagram, the defensive players numbered 5, 6, and 7 gang up on two offensive players to cave in the offense's center wall of protection. If they move in far enough, one of those three interior linemen can block the kick. Or they can enable number 11, the leaper behind them, to jump from close enough to the ball to block it. Or they can force the offensive line to narrow its splits, which protects against the inside rush but gives number 1 a shorter outside path to the ball. Numbers 9 and 10 are not trying to block the kick. Their job is to be in position to pick the ball up if it is blocked.

kicked a ball that Page blocked so cleanly, it bounced right back to Marcol, as if he had thrown it off a wall. Marcol had a clear shot for a touchdown. "He looked like the guy in the New York Life commercials," Chicago kicker Bob Thomas said. But the touchdown counted.

Most blocked kicks bounce off an inside rush man. From the outside, a rush man must not only get in position fast enough, but he also has to aim his dive so it will intersect the flight of the ball. For an inside man, it's just a matter of seeing the ball and raising his arms. Or knowing *when* to raise his arms, if he can't see the ball.

Page liked to be right on the center, position number 7, although many teams consider that a sacrificial position for tying up an offensive lineman—for effectively *blocking* the center to open a hole for the next man over. As Page saw it, "I'm the closest one to the ball. Where I'm lined up should be the easiest place to block it. Ideally, I can even get my whole body in front of it."

The Vikings are the most dangerous kick-blockers now, as they often have been, and a disproportionate number of their blocks come from the leaper, Matt Blair. They sometimes even use two leapers. Few teams have people with Blair's 6–5 height, basketball-trained jumping ability, and timing. But that's no reason to just watch the other team kick and hope it goes wide. "It doesn't really matter who gets it," Page says. "What matters is that the job gets done."

Black and Silver and Dreaded All Over

... The Raiders only seem to be behind the times because they're so far ahead

Much was made of how the Los Angeles Raiders, in winning the 1983 NFL championship, thumbed their noses at the fancy-schmancy, state-of-the-art football trends bubbling to the surface. They used relatively few formations, almost never with one back and two tight ends. They let their quarterback call the plays. They used the same terminology they had used in the sixties. Even coach Tom Flores said, obviously not the least ashamed, "We're kind of old-fashioned."

Well, kind of. On the other hand, Flores likes to characterize the Raiders' style as attack football. Aggressive, head-first, take-no-prisoners football, risking mistakes but forcing the other team to make more. Which is precisely the way many NFL teams have begun playing in the early eighties. It's just that the Raiders have been doing it that way for 20 years. In 1983, they ranked next-to-last in penalties and fourth-from-the-bottom in turnovers lost, and they made enough big plays to make up for it.

"We leave a lot of openings for big plays," tight end Todd Christensen says of the Raider defense. "But it also creates big plays for us."

Attack football on defense is tight, man-to-man coverage, bumping a lot of receivers at the line or attaching to their hips and trailing them. Which is what many NFL defenses are doing more often. It means rushing the passer all-out, even at the expense of depleting the coverage. Which is another thing many NFL defenses are doing more often.

The Raiders didn't frustrate the Redskins' one-back attack, the turbocharged front-wheel drive of modern offenses, by using some horse-and-buggy contraption. They beat the Redskins with a defense that was even more innovative, essentially a five-man line using inside linebackers on the line instead of outside linebackers. They didn't win the Super Bowl by leaning back, closing their eyes and listening to the times pass them by like cars on a highway. They've been paying attention. And in a league where any team can move the ball, great defense is more valuable than ever.

On offense, the Raiders are known for passing deep. Never mind that dump-off ball-control game. But look who caught their passes in 1983. Christensen and Marcus Allen had more than half the Raiders' receptions between them. A tight end and a running back. They sure weren't running fly patterns all the time. Christensen even made a considerable number of those new-fangled sight adjustments.

The Raiders didn't use three wide receivers terribly often, either. That bucked another trend. But why should they bring in a third wide receiver? To take out Christensen? Allen? The idea of

"A lot of teams are concerned with peripheral things like image and dress code and silly things that have nothing to do with football. This organization isn't concerned with that. It just wants to know if you can play.

"At Dallas, my level of subservience wasn't quite what they wanted. I don't fashion myself as an iconoclast, but it just didn't work there. It's more comfortable here."—**Todd Christensen**, Los Angeles Raiders tight end

situation substitution is to get your best players into the game. The Raiders' best receivers were already in there.

Mainly, the Raiders' offense is notorious for going where it wants to go. None of this finessing around, like more fainthearted teams. *We don't take what the defense gives us. We take what we want.* True enough, and the Raiders also are uncommonly skillful at coaxing a defense into giving them what they want.

They don't bang their heads against a wall until one of them, the heads or the wall, caves in. One of those old-fashioned formations—the Raiders call it their "East" formation—sends both wide receivers to the right side and the tight end to the left side. It creates the matchups the Raiders are looking for. It lets them run against defenders better suited for stopping the pass, and pass against defenders better suited for stopping the run. They still use the old throwback because it still works.

The Raiders are more aggressive than most NFL teams. They've always been at the extreme among man-to-man defenses, and many of their pass patterns are the deepest and most time-consuming in the league. That's one of the reasons they make big plays. But another reason is so many of their players have the knack for making good plays.

Ah, yes, *the players*. The ultimate edge for staying out of the NFL's gloomy, great gray mass in the middle. The Raiders have cornerbacks who can cover man-to-man, and pass rushers who can see to it their coverage won't go on forever. They have the offensive linemen and the unflappable quarterback who make it possible to run six-second pass patterns. The Raiders have those players for two reasons. They know how to spot them, and they know how to keep them happy.

X X X X X
0 0 0 0

One thing that continually amazes people about the Raiders is their ability to win with other teams' rejects. Christensen, quarterback Jim Plunkett, and defensive end Lyle Alzado are the best examples from the 1983 team—all acquired free or nearly free. Even Marcus Allen was far from a highly touted blue-chipper when the Raiders drafted him in the middle of the first round. Christensen, Plunkett, and Alzado all had been considered promising—even productive—players at one time. That wasn't the reason they were turned loose. But that is the only reason the Raiders consider. Look around the league, and you won't find many ex-Raiders playing for other teams.

Al Davis, who owns and runs the team, still may be the league's best talent scout. He has no peer at taking square pegs out of round holes and putting them where they'll excel. Christensen, like Billy Cannon before him, moved to tight end from running back. The Raiders' career leader in 100-yard rushing games, Clem Daniels, had been a defensive back at Kansas City. Most Raider guards, including both starters on the 1983 team, have been moved inside from tackle.

The Raiders will redefine positions, too. Ted Hendricks was a free-lancing linebacker long before Miami's A. J. Duhe. Dan Birdwell did some things in the sixties that Duhe is doing now. When the Raiders' fourth linebacker was better than their fourth lineman in 1976, they went to a 3–4 defense and became the first 3–4 Super Bowl team. Rod Martin was blitzing from weak-side linebacker when Lawrence Taylor was still in college.

Other rejects who land in the Raider lineup are simply examples of other teams' stubbornness. "Renegades and bad guys," Tom Flores says, parroting what the rest of the league says about his players. It was hard, before the 1983 season, for any NFL player with a 1984 USFL contract to find a job. Dave Stalls found one with the Raiders.

Where others see a player's failure, the Raiders see how he can be improved. Where others see malcontents, the Raiders see men of conviction.

"A lot of guys have come to the Raiders who had contract problems or were given up on or went against the grain," Alzado says. "To me, it's guys just standing up for what they believe in. Look at Mike Haynes. God decided to create a cornerback when he made him. But other people wouldn't pay him what he was worth. Al Davis would. Other teams are stupid enough to let players like him go, and Al Davis gets them."

"We're here because we weren't allowed to be individuals elsewhere," said Cedrick Hardman, a retread on the Raiders' 1980 champions.

"I don't want 49 clones," Flores says. "We allow players to be themselves."

"What's more American than that?" says Gene Upshaw, the former Raider all-pro guard now directing the players' union.

Indeed. The Raiders aren't a bunch of marauding vagabonds in a halfway house, after all. They are the very embodiment of Life, Liberty, and the Pursuit of Happiness. American settlers did not flee across an ocean for the inalienable right to wear sports coats on airplanes and keep their helmets on in practice. The Statue of Liberty does not say, "Give me your huddled masses yearning for bed checks."

"When players from other teams come here, they can't believe how well the management treats us here," says Derrick Jensen.

Davis pays his players well, for openers. When was the last time you heard a Raider screaming to renegotiate? Before any discontent gets that far, Davis pulls him aside and gives him a raise.

But it's more than that. It's wide-bodied airplanes. It's replacing equipment, no questions asked. It's nice team parties. It's respect.

The Raiders used Tampa Bay's locker room when they practiced for the Super Bowl. They couldn't believe it. Signs all over the place. An actual printed *code of behavior.* Rules having nothing to do with football. Warnings appropriate for children. *Wear shorts in the weight room. Put your uniform here. Don't unplug the whirlpool when someone's using it.*

"Do this. Don't do that," Howie Long said. "If those signs were in our locker room, they'd be torn down in a day."

"We fine players," Flores says. "If you're fined, you're fined. It's not a major catastrophe. If you're five minutes late the next time, I add a zero to the fine."

"The only thing the Raiders demand is that you be on the practice field, pay attention in meetings, and play on Sunday," Bob Chandler said when he was with the 1980 Super Bowl winners. "We don't have so many rules. The burden is on us to police ourselves. If you have any sense, you want to prove Tom Flores is right and get the job done on your own rather than prove him wrong and have him set down restrictions and rules. This team works harder than any team I've ever been with."

And it shows up after the two-minute warning. A coach can't hang signs in the huddle. "That's when you've got to bring it up from inside you," Upshaw says. "That's when the Raiders show how they're different."

That's when a team has to rely on its players to win the game. It's not hard to lose sight of the players, among the forest of computer printouts and the mishmash of formations. But without good players, the best-designed plays might as well be drawn in the sand at low tide.

"You can have all the trick plays you want, and they're not going to matter," Jack Faulkner says. "If I've got better players than you've got, I'm going to win. You can be scrambling around at halftime, making all sorts of great changes. But the guy with the best team, he can go in at halftime, have a Coca-Cola, smoke a cigarette, and say, 'How long 'til we go out?' "

Distraction or Attraction?

... In the USFL, the most important strategy is marketing

Some rich people who liked football, apparently even more than they liked money, decided not long ago to form their own football league and stage games in the spring and summer. Not some cards-and-dice league for a table game, mind you. Real football, with real football players, some of whom even had worn real NFL uniforms. And because this was *football* they were talking about, the public reaction was not some distant, nodding, "That's nice"—the sort children elicit when they tell a story to a parent who is trying to read the paper. The public reaction was to sit bold upright and talk about this darned idea of playing football in the wrong season.

The most amazing thing about the reaction, though, was what people most wanted to know. *Is that new league going to make it?* Not: Will they play good football? Or: I thought spring was the baseball season. But right to the bottom line, as if this were a new clothing style, or a new television station.

That's what purveyors of the new league, the United States Football League, wanted. This was going to be different from all those other new sports leagues that periodically light up the sky like fireworks and fizzle almost as fast. This was going to be a made-for-TV production, just like *Winds of War*—which proved shortly before the USFL began play in early 1983 that made-for-TV productions don't have to be critically acclaimed to be economic successes. That was another thing the USFL had counted on.

Since then, the new league has gotten sidetracked a bit from its original concept. It was aiming for low overhead and high profile. The idea was to dole out two or three big-number contracts per team to headline players who would lure fans to their TV sets, and parcel out the leftover change to the others. It was the same star system that has prevailed forever in the entertainment world, where a million-dollar singer's back-up musicians are likely to make scale, but had never been able to penetrate the sporting world's more heightened sense of fair play. The important thing wasn't stiffing the spear carriers, though. It was keeping all the teams in the same financial ballpark to ensure competitive balance, better known as parity.

That was the formula. Take box-office stars, add nail-biting suspense, and filter it through the country's biggest television markets. The league has tried to stock itself with top TV markets and Sun Belt cities on the come.

The formula was unraveling before the 1984 season's halfway mark. Boston's franchise had been chased out of town by yawning indifference. The league office was operating ownerless (and virtually fanless) teams in Washington and Chicago. The burghers of Los Angeles had neglected to participate in the buzzing excitement over their team's new quarterback, Steve Young, whose contract was reported to be anywhere from $36 million to $43 million and by the time the annuity ran out and Social Security kicked in. And that was another problem. Some renegade owners were playing havoc with the spirit of competitive balance by stuffing chunks of their personal fortunes into the pockets of whichever talented, young players they could cajole into endorsing six-figure checks.

But still, in spite of all that, the national TV ratings were holding up. They weren't poking holes in the roof, but they were better than ABC and ESPN had been getting without spring football. The USFL had a long way to go before proving it would outlast Steve Young's annuity, but it was winning on the most important front.

Over the short haul, the USFL wasn't so much interested in television's bottomless dollar pit as it was in its endorsement. This is showbiz, sweetheart. Brent Musburger is listed in the World Almanac under "Noted Personalities—Entertainers," right there in front of Bob Newhart, Olivia Newton-John, and Jack Nicholson. The TV deals, up front before the first game, certified the new league as something worth watching.

The USFL was able to change the rules for survival of new

leagues. In the past, it always had been accepted that a league had to bring its quality of play to a certain standard before it could count on any sort of television backing—either its money or its seal of approval. By starting out as television software, the USFL was in a position to let television generate the interest and revenue necessary to upgrade its quality of play. The cart was going to pull the horse, because the cart was powered by satellite.

The new league had bypassed square one, that all too elusive *quality of play*, which had run so many previous new leagues aground. It could go straight to marketing strategies, a luxury normally reserved for those children's toys that have their coming-out parties on half-hour television specials.

There is a different problem only the USFL has had to deal with, namely changing the people's minds about considering football an autumn game. But in television, it picked the perfect ally. Television's very survival has depended on selling people products they didn't know they needed, from breath spray and light beer to digital clocks and Pac-Man.

X X X X X
0 0 0 0

The problem developing for the USFL is it's not sure what it's selling. It's not sure it still wants to be a Triple-A pro football league, adding enough good rookies each year to pull even with the NFL far down the road. It's making rumblings about taking on the NFL monster now. Early in 1984, even the conservative league office talked of switching to a fall schedule in 1987. Which would lead naturally to the new American dream among emerging businesses: being swallowed whole by the giant in the field and making a bundle. In the USFL's case: merging with the NFL.

The USFL's spring schedule isn't the only stumbling block on that path. The NFL is so afraid of antitrust suits, it won't even stop its own owners from literally auctioning off their teams' fans, shopping around from city to city in search of a happier home. In that case, the NFL certainly isn't likely to merge with its only competitor unless it has Congressional approval. Which it isn't likely to get without approval of the players' union. And how likely is that? The USFL has driven up NFL players' salaries beyond their wildest imaginations.

Besides, if the USFL is successful enough to make the jump from spring to fall, it will have been successful enough to encourage twelve or sixteen or eighteen more rich football fans to start up another new springtime league.

But who knows? Congressmen and the two leagues might already be making quiet plans for a merger.

Meanwhile, it will not be easy to compete financially with the NFL from the foundation of spring television revenue. People watch more television from September through December than they watch from March through July. That's why the networks show reruns in the spring and summer. Ratings that would be considered very good in the USFL's time slot amount to half the NFL's normal ratings, and the USFL's ratings were not yet very good in its second season.

So far, the financial machinations of some USFL teams have taken on the nature of a high-stakes chain letter. Four of the original twelve owners sold out within a year. They hadn't realized what they were getting into until they actually saw $3–4 million swirl down the drain in one year, but that was OK because they were able to sell the franchises for as much as $7 million. Chain letters ultimately burst, and a chain letter of this magnitude would squirt red ink all over.

That would be fine in the cases where owners are willing to dip into their personal fortunes. In the old American Football League's first year, Lamar Hunt lost $1 million operating his new team. That was a lot of money in those days. Someone asked Hunt's father, H. L. Hunt, how long Junior could go on losing money like that, and H.L.'s answer was 100 years.

The USFL attracted some latter-day Lamar Hunts willing to make that kind of commitment, but they only created another problem. It also had a team sending press releases out at bulk mail rates, so they weren't delivered until after the game they were promoting, and it has had other teams operating just as frugally. The wide financial disparity has shown up on the field as a far cry from parity, recalling the fate of the old All-America Conference after World War II. With the Cleveland Browns dominating it year after year, people lost interest, and the league soon folded.

Even as it has designs on catching up and merging with the NFL, the USFL's talent pool is going to consist largely of NFL rejects. But that isn't all bad, especially if it continues judiciously hiring head coaches from among such bright but untapped former NFL assistants as New Orleans' Dick Coury, Birmingham's Rollie Dotsch, Jacksonville's Lindy Infante, and Philadelphia's Jim Mora, among others. It's not uncommon, even within the NFL, for a player to struggle a year or two with his first team, learning all the while but perhaps too gradually to make an impression on his coaches, and then turn up on a new team looking like a new player.

"When I was on the Eagles' staff," says Chicago Blitz coach Marv Levy, "Bob Kuechenberg was a fourth-round draft choice and we cut him in training camp. At that time in his career, we made the right decision. But of course, he came back and made all-pro all these years. How many people like Kuechenberg are there who haven't had the second chance? They went off into other pursuits and their latent abilities remained latent."

If the USFL can coach its less heralded players well enough for a lot of Bob Kuechenbergs to sprout up, it still isn't home free. That might be what NFL teams are waiting for. When the new league was born, there was sentiment around the NFL that it could even be helpful. The NFL had been in some need of a Triple-A league for years. Now it had one.

X X X X X
0 0 0 0

To the NFL, the USFL has generally been regarded as another of those infernal nuisances it lumps under the umbrella heading of Distractions. The USFL siphoned off some good players, but most NFL owners feel pretty comfortable that they answered the players' *We Are The Game* contention once and for all during the 1982 strike. It also forced NFL owners to share with the players some of the money they had managed to withhold through the strike, which is a matter they have taken less lightly. But even that could be a mixed blessing, as NFL people see it. The party line, anyway, is the more the USFL throws dollars around like confetti, the sooner the NFL can close the book on that particular nuisance.

Besides, even if worse comes to worst, the NFL owners can hold out until they can invite Pay TV to enrich them in 1987. By then, the other pro sports leagues not only will have worked the bugs out of subscription television, they'll have desensitized American fans' outrage over paying for televised sports. The NFL does seem to land on its feet.

The irony, looking back on the 1982 strike, is that the NFL Players Association had gone into collective bargaining with a strategy based on the NFL's monopoly status. The USFL came alive during those negotiations, but the NFLPA was already in too deep with its pitch for a fixed percentage of the owners' gross revenues to turn back. And the owners weren't smart (or flexible) enough to push for guaranteed but reasonably capped salary levels, with special provisions for matching USFL bids on players they really wanted to keep.

So the owners bought themselves a new problem. It wasn't just that salaries rose dramatically. Even the NFL owners had to realize they had been holding salaries at a ridiculously low level, given the revenue the league was generating. Almost worse than the money was the *inconvenience* of having to kowtow to these young studs every couple of years because they might up and leave, punching holes in the lineup on their way out the door. At the Super Bowl, after the 1983 season, Joe Gibbs said one of the key elements in maintaining a winning team had become *keeping your players signed.* That is Priority One for any general manager now, along with avoiding the public relations embarrassment of losing a first-round draft choice. A team has to identify the 12 or 15 players it can't live without, and make sure they're under contract at least through the next season.

In 1983, the NFLPA said 50 percent of the league's veterans signed new contracts, an unusually high figure, suggesting a lot of current contracts were torn up and sweetened. It also said the average raise for those contracts was 70 percent. Going into the 1984 season, reasonable people were estimating an average 1984 salary of $200,000. So the few spendthrift owners in the USFL have probably made NFL players richer than the ones in their own league.

Another new problem for NFL owners—one the union created on purpose—is that agents representing NFL veterans now have to abide by NFLPA regulations. One of those regulations is that agents must keep the union abreast of all player negotiations as they progress, a rule one agent says, "gives the union a microphone in the office of every NFL team." Salaries are no longer secrets, which alone tends to make them more inflatable. And another regulation established maximum fees for agents. The USFL has no such maximums, which can give an agent the incentive to place his client in the USFL—particularly when he is finding work for a released player, which can be one of an agent's most time-consuming jobs and, now, one of his least rewarding financially.

Then there is the matter of underclassmen becoming eligible for the draft. The legal ruling in early 1984 did not specifically bar the NFL from turning players away until their college classes have graduated. It applied only to the USFL. But it became clear that the NFL, too, would have to accept underclassmen as soon as somebody went to the bother of writing its name on the top of a lawsuit.

That was nothing to go home and kick the dog over. But image is so important to the NFL, and it didn't want the colleges taking potshots at its Fairness and Integrity, even if the colleges' outrage over letting underclassmen turn pro is so much balderdash. College coaches howl that this deprives their student athletes of a full education, as if they had been ushering them into classrooms in the first place. Fewer than one-third of NFL players have college diplomas as it is. USFL teams, if only for public relations, provide money for players to finish their schooling, even for players who don't make a team.

X X X X X
O O O O

Whatever storm clouds the USFL has hung over the NFL's parade, they haven't prodded the enormous beast into significant counteraction. The most noticeable unified stance the owners took at their 1984 Honolulu meeting was against celebratory dances after touchdowns and sacks. If there was any NFL policy toward the USFL, it was to wait patiently for this particular nuisance to bounce out of sight on its own rubber checks.

The NFL draft remained four months after the USFL's draft. The league's predraft courting of college seniors increased only slightly from 1983, when it consisted essentially of waiting for the phone to ring. Some individual teams waved the banner of NFL Glory in front of prized draft prospects, but one of those teams was not Cincinnati, which had the first choice. So the other teams watched helplessly as two likely first picks went over the wall before Cincinnati traded its choice.

Keeping the draft late does have merit for the NFL, although the merit began to wear thin by the time the USFL had filched four of the 1984 class's top six players, by most independent scouting evaluations, and as many as 30 percent consistently through the top 100. Still, it was the NFL as a league that lost those players. Not specific teams, which are less able to absorb the loss of a first-round choice. And to some owners, it was a small price to pay for not having to bid on rookies head-to-head with the other league.

The USFL, and the money it was costing NFL owners, was just another entry on the league's growing list of distractions.

The disturbing march of players through courtrooms seemed to rank first. Outdated as the notion may seem, and irrational as it is, children still look up to pro football players. Since when did rationality have anything to do with children's heroes? It might not be fair to expect thoroughly pampered athletes in their early 20s to set examples for anyone, but that's the way it is. It comes with the paycheck, which doesn't necessarily mesh with Average America's notion of fairness, either.

Drug busts are especially disturbing to the NFL because of the danger a heavy cocaine user might be asked to clear his drug debt by fixing a game for a gambler. But it's still curious that the NFL has turned its back on so many drunk-driving episodes— which are just as illegal and more pervasive in society—even as it preaches the importance of setting good examples for young people.

League executives, too, have spent more than their share of time in courtrooms, generally either defending antitrust suits or trying to regain some control over the location of their teams. More distractions.

X X X X X
0 0 0 0

Television ratings dropped for the second year in a row, as did attendance, after rising steadily from 1978 through 1981. A number of explanations were offered, although the best might be simply that both New York teams made the playoffs in the peak television year, 1981. Others blamed the dullness of games within parity's great gray mass, which encompassed most games. Also cited was general disgust among fans, stemming from either the strike or those image-mussing distractions.

More than any particular distraction, the NFL's biggest problem might be that the whole group of distractions are overshadowing the game itself. Part of that is because daily newspapers have not kept up with the realities of nonsports news seeping onto the sports pages. What they need is a separate section within the sports section, produced by separate reporters.

As it is, a reporter assigned to cover any professional sports team is responsible for any arrests, contract negotiations, free-agent movement, legal action, and hints thereof when they pertain to the team he's covering. Since newspapers are in the business of reporting breaking news first, and these peripheral sports stories usually take the form of breaking news, they get into the papers at the expense of stories that shed light on athletes and their performances. Papers don't have the space and report-ers don't have the energy to cover the distraction beat and still explain the new defensive scheme that cut opponents' passing yards in half or describe how that tough rookie lineman cried when he was promoted to the lineup two days after learning his father had cancer.

Covering the NFL these days just doesn't leave a lot of time to write about football.

INDEX